W9-AOM-849

DISCARD
WITHDRAWAL

THE WORLD BOOK OF AMERICA'S
PRESIDENTS

Portraits of the Presidents

World Book, Inc.
a Scott Fetzer company

Chicago

Staff

President
Robert C. Martin

**Vice President
and Publisher**
Michael Ross

Editorial

Managing editor
Maureen Mostyn Liebenson

Senior editor
Jeanne Johnson

Permissions editor
Janet T. Peterson

Indexers
David Pofelski
Tina Trettin

Writers
Susan Blum
Marlene Targ Brill
James I. Clark
Theresa Kryst Fertig
Kathleen L. Florio
Hortense Leon
Anne V. McGravie
Katie Sharp

**Executive director of
research and product
development**
Paul A. Kobasa

Researcher
Loranne Shields

Art

Executive director
Roberta Dimmer

Art director
Wilma Stevens

Photography manager
Sandra Dyrlund

Designer
John Horvath

Production assistants
John Whitney
Laurie Schuh

Product production

**Senior manager, pre-press
and manufacturing**
Carma Fazio

Senior production manager
Madelyn Underwood

Production manager
Jared Svoboda

**Manufacturing production
assistant**
Valerie Piarowski

Text processing
Curley Hunter
Gwendolyn Johnson

Proofreaders
Anne Dillon
Chad Rubel

Advisers

Robert V. Remini, Ph.D.
Professor of American History
Research Professor of Humanities
University of Illinois

Mark A. Lause, M.A.
Roosevelt University
Chicago, Illinois

William F. Vandercook, M.A.
University of Illinois at Chicago
Chicago, Illinois

For information on other World Book products, call 1-800-WORLDBK (967-5325), or visit our Web site at **http://www.worldbook.com.**

The publishers wish to acknowledge permission for use of materials from the following resource: Betty Glad, *Jimmy Carter, In Search of the Great White House* (New York, 1980), W.W. Norton & Company, Inc.

© 2001 World Book, Inc. All rights reserved. This volume may not be reproduced in whole or in any part in any form without prior written permission from the publisher.

World Book, Inc.
233 N. Michigan Ave.
Chicago, IL 60601

ISBN 0-7166-3696-4
Library of Congress Catalog Card No. 00-107127
© 1999, 1994, 1989 World Book, Inc., 1982 World Book Encyclopedia, Inc. All rights reserved.

Printed in the United States of America

9 10 11 12 13 14 15 10 09 08 07 06 05 04 03 02 01

Contents

Alphabetical Listing of Presidents

Introduction

The Presidents of the United States have come from all walks of life. Some, like Franklin D. Roosevelt and John F. Kennedy, enjoyed wealth. Others, like Millard Fillmore, knew poverty. They grew up both on the frontier, like Andrew Jackson, and in refined society, like Theodore Roosevelt. Their education also varied. Woodrow Wilson was a scholar and university professor, while Andrew Johnson was a tailor with no formal schooling at all.

The major section of the volume, "All Americans Native Born: The Lives of the Presidents," opens by placing the Presidents in the context of U.S. history. They are listed with brief descriptions of the era in which they served. A table follows, organizing the Presidents chronologically. Details of their lives and administrations can be found and compared easily by using this table.

Biographies that bring the Presidents to life come next. Each one has a full-page illustration of the President, and more illustrations show the first lady and important events in the President's private life and administration. A fact box gives details about the President, including birthplace, occupation, and the votes that gained the nation's highest office. The biographies also contain boxed "events" from the President's administration. These show the economic, social, and scientific scene in America and the world during the term of office, as well as the nation's population and growth in statehood. Then, "Treasured Words from the Presidents" shows what they had to say about the America of their times.

The appendixes that follow are full of useful information, all having to do with the presidency. Look there for how the executive branch of the government is organized, plus Article II of the Constitution, which outlines the responsibilities of the President. Capsule descriptions of all the Vice-Presidents and a vice-presidential chart are also in this section.

A special feature of the appendixes includes the presidential oath of office. A topical index ends the volume, an aid to quickly locate the information you seek about the lives of America's Presidents.

All Americans Native Born:
THE LIVES OF THE PRESIDENTS

The Presidents
in United States History

George Washington, 1789-1797
John Adams, 1797-1801
Thomas Jefferson, 1801-1809
James Madison, 1809-1817

A New Nation, 1784-1819

During this period, the United States became welded into a solid political unit under the U.S. Constitution. The nation faced severe financial problems and threats from powerful European nations. The War of 1812 with Great Britain was fought to a standstill. After the war, the United States focused attention on internal development, entering a period of bustling economic growth.

James Monroe, 1817-1825
John Quincy Adams, 1825-1829
Andrew Jackson, 1829-1837
Martin Van Buren, 1837-1841
William Henry Harrison, 1841
John Tyler, 1841-1845
James K. Polk, 1845-1849
Zachary Taylor, 1849-1850

A Growing Nation, 1820-1849

In the early 1800's, settlers by the thousands moved west. Western areas gained admittance to the Union as states, and Westerners began a struggle for more political power, which Easterners still largely held. Americans worked for reforms in areas such as women's rights, improvements in education, and the abolition of slavery. The era was a relatively peaceful one, although the Monroe Doctrine was issued.

Millard Fillmore, 1850-1853
Franklin Pierce, 1853-1857
James Buchanan, 1857-1861
Abraham Lincoln, 1861-1865
Andrew Johnson, 1865-1869

War Within the Nation, 1850-1869

After the Mexican War, the long dispute between the North and the South over slavery came to a head. Debate and compromise failed to settle the issue. The Civil War began in 1861. It took more American lives than any other military conflict. When it ended in 1865, the Union was preserved, and slavery was soon outlawed in the United States. Large parts of the South lay in ruins, and there was long-lasting bitterness and division between the North and South.

Ulysses S. Grant, 1869-1877
Rutherford B. Hayes, 1877-1881
James A. Garfield, 1881
Chester A. Arthur, 1881-1885
Grover Cleveland, 1885-1889
Benjamin Harrison, 1889-1893
Grover Cleveland, 1893-1897
William McKinley, 1897-1901
Theodore Roosevelt, 1901-1909
William H. Taft, 1909-1913

Industry and National Reform, 1870-1916

After the Civil War, U.S. industry, centered in the Northeast, changed. Machines increased production capacity tremendously. A new nationwide network of railroads enabled business to distribute goods far and wide. Inventors developed new products, produced in large quantities. Investment in business was heavy, and "big business" grew. Large cities developed. Business fortunes existed side by side with extreme poverty. Widespread discontent brought new reform movements. Frontier life in the West and Reconstruction in the South came to a close, while in foreign affairs, the nation became a world power.

Woodrow Wilson, 1913-1921
Warren G. Harding, 1921-1923
Calvin Coolidge, 1923-1929

The Nation as a World Power, 1917-1929

For the first time in its history, the United States entered a full-scale war on foreign territory, playing an important role in the World War I Allied victory. The next decade, called the "Roaring Twenties," saw a booming economy and fast-paced lifestyle. In 1929, a stock market crash triggered the Great Depression.

Herbert Hoover, 1929-1933
Franklin Delano Roosevelt, 1933-1945
Harry S. Truman, 1945-1953
Dwight D. Eisenhower, 1953-1961

Depression and World War II, 1930-1959

The Great Depression lasted more than 10 years. Its effects were felt worldwide. The poverty it caused in the United States had never before been experienced on such a scale. During this period, dictators came to power in foreign nations. They began conquering neighboring countries, leading to World War II: the most destructive conflict in history. An Allied victory in the war brought the United States great relief and joy. The economy prospered and a huge, well-to-do middle class emerged. Problems included the new threat of nuclear war, the growth of Communism, and discontent among Americans who were not prospering.

John F. Kennedy, 1961-1963
Lyndon B. Johnson, 1963-1969
Richard M. Nixon, 1969-1974
Gerald R. Ford, 1974-1977
Jimmy Carter, 1977-1981
Ronald Reagan, 1981-1989
George H. W. Bush, 1989-1993
Bill Clinton, 1993-2001
George W. Bush, 2001-

The Nation Since 1960

For much of this period, the nation's foreign policy focused on containing Communism and on combating terrorism abroad. The economy expanded despite recurring inflation and recession. Crime and violence in the nation increased greatly. More Americans lived in suburbs than cities for the first time. Many groups intensified demands for greater civil rights. Americans began challenging the government's foreign-policy decisions, particularly in Vietnam. The country continued to be a leader in science and technology, with great advances made in medicine and space exploration.

Presidents of the United States

	Born	Birthplace	College or University	Religion	Occupation or Profession
1. George Washington	Feb. 22, 1732	Westmoreland County, Va.		Episcopalian	Planter
2. John Adams	Oct. 30, 1735	Braintree (now Quincy), Mass.	Harvard	Unitarian	Lawyer
3. Thomas Jefferson	Apr. 13, 1743	Goochland (now Albemarle) County, Va.	William and Mary	Unitarian*	Planter, lawyer
4. James Madison	Mar. 16, 1751	Port Conway, Va.	Princeton	Episcopalian	Lawyer
5. James Monroe	Apr. 28, 1758	Westmoreland County, Va.	William and Mary	Episcopalian	Lawyer
6. John Quincy Adams	July 11, 1767	Braintree (now Quincy), Mass.	Harvard	Unitarian	Lawyer
7. Andrew Jackson	Mar. 15, 1767	Waxhaw settlement, S.C.(?)		Presbyterian	Lawyer
8. Martin Van Buren	Dec. 5, 1782	Kinderhook, N.Y.		Dutch Reformed	Lawyer
9. William H. Harrison	Feb. 9, 1773	Berkeley, 0Va.	Hampden-Sydney	Episcopalian	Soldier
10. John Tyler	Mar. 29, 1790	Greenway, Va.	William and Mary	Episcopalian	Lawyer
11. James K. Polk	Nov. 2, 1795	Near Pineville, N.C.	U. of N. Carolina	Methodist	Lawyer
12. Zachary Taylor	Nov. 24, 1784	Orange County, Va.		Episcopalian	Soldier
13. Millard Fillmore	Jan. 7, 1800	Locke, N.Y.		Unitarian	Lawyer
14. Franklin Pierce	Nov. 23, 1804	Hillsboro, N.H.	Bowdoin	Episcopalian	Lawyer
15. James Buchanan	Apr. 23, 1791	near Mercersburg, Pa.	Dickinson	Presbyterian	Lawyer
16. Abraham Lincoln	Feb. 12, 1809	near Hodgerville, Ky.		Presbyterian*	Lawyer
17. Andrew Johnson	Dec. 29, 1808	Raleigh, N.C.		Methodist*	Tailor
18. Ulysses S. Grant	Apr. 27, 1822	Point Pleasant, O.	U.S. Mil. Academy	Methodist	Soldier
19. Rutherford B. Hayes	Oct. 4, 1822	Delaware, O.	Kenyon	Methodist*	Lawyer
20. James A. Garfield	Nov. 19, 1831	Orange, O.	Williams	Disciples of Christ	Lawyer
21. Chester A. Arthur	Oct. 5, 1829	Fairfield, Vt.	Union	Episcopalian	Lawyer
22. Grover Cleveland	Mar. 18, 1837	Caldwell, N.J.		Presbyterian	Lawyer
23. Benjamin Harrison	Aug. 20, 1833	North Bend, O.	Miami	Presbyterian	Lawyer
24. Grover Cleveland	Mar. 18, 1837	Caldwell, N.J.		Presbyterian	Lawyer
25. William McKinley	Jan. 29, 1843	Niles, O.	Allegheny College	Methodist	Lawyer
26. Theodore Roosevelt	Oct. 27, 1858	New York City, N.Y.	Harvard	Dutch Reformed	Author, rancher
27. William Howard Taft	Sept. 15, 1857	Cincinnati, O.	Yale	Unitarian	Lawyer
28. Woodrow Wilson	Dec. 29, 1856	Staunton, Va.	Princeton	Presbyterian	Educator
29. Warren G. Harding	Nov. 2, 1865	near Blooming Grove, O.		Baptist	Publisher
30. Calvin Coolidge	July 4, 1872	Plymouth Notch, Vt.	Amherst	Congregationalist	Lawyer
31. Herbert Hoover	Aug. 10, 1874	West Branch, Ia.	Stanford	Friend (Quaker)	Engineer
32. Franklin D. Roosevelt	Jan. 30, 1882	Hyde Park, N.Y.	Harvard	Episcopalian	Lawyer
33. Harry S. Truman	May 8, 1884	Lamar, Mo.		Baptist	Businessperson
34. Dwight D. Eisenhower	Oct. 14, 1890	Denison, Tex.	U.S. Mil. Academy	Presbyterian	Soldier
35. John F. Kennedy	May 29, 1917	Brookline, Mass.	Harvard	Roman Catholic	Author
36. Lyndon B. Johnson	Aug. 27, 1908	near Stonewall, Tex.	S.W. Texas State	Disciples of Christ	Teacher
37. Richard M. Nixon	Jan. 9, 1913	Yorba Linda, Calif.	Whittier	Friend (Quaker)	Lawyer
38. Gerald R. Ford††	July 14, 1913	Omaha, Nebr.	Michigan	Episcopalian	Lawyer
39. Jimmy Carter	Oct. 1, 1924	Plains, Ga.	U.S. Naval Academy	Baptist	Businessperson
40. Ronald W. Reagan	Feb. 6, 1911	Tampico, Ill.	Eureka	Disciples of Christ	Actor
41. George H. W. Bush	June 12, 1924	Milton, Mass.	Yale	Episcopalian	Businessperson
42. Bill Clinton	Aug. 19, 1946	Hope, Ark.	Georgetown	Baptist	Lawyer
43. George W. Bush	July 6, 1946	New Haven, Conn.	Yale	Methodist	Businessperson

Note: Each President has an illustrated biography in this section. *Church preference; never joined any church. **The National Union Party consisted of Republicans and War Democrats. Johnson was a Democrat. †Inaugurated Dec. 6, 1973, to replace Agnew, who resigned Oct. 10, 1973. ††Inaugurated Aug. 9, 1974, to replace Nixon, who resigned the same day. ‡Inaugurated Dec. 19, 1974, to replace Ford, who became President Aug. 9, 1974.

	Political Party	Age at Inauguration	Served	Died		Age at Death	Runner-Up		Vice-President	
1.	None	57	1789-1797	Dec.	14, 1799	67	John Adams	(1789, 1792)	John Adams	(1789-1797)
2.	Federalist	61	1797-1801	July	4, 1826	90	Thomas Jefferson	(1796)	Thomas Jefferson	(1797-1801)
3.	Democratic-Republican	57	1801-1809	July	4, 1826	83	Aaron Burr	(1800)	Aaron Burr	(1801-1805)
							Charles C. Pinckney	(1804)	George Clinton	(1805-1809)
4.	Democratic-Republican	57	1809-1817	June	28, 1836	85	Charles C. Pinckney	(1808)	George Clinton	(1809-1812)
							De Witt Clinton	(1812)	Elbridge Gerry	(1813-1814)
5.	Democratic-Republican	58	1817-1825	July	4, 1831	73	Rufus King	(1816)	Daniel D. Tompkins	(1817-1825)
							No opposition			
6.	Democratic-Republican	57	1825-1829	Feb.	23, 1848	80	Andrew Jackson	(1824)	John C. Calhoun	(1825-1829)
7.	Democratic	61	1829-1837	June	8, 1845	78	John Quincy Adams	(1828)	John C. Calhoun	(1829-1832)
							Henry Clay	(1832)	Martin Van Buren	(1833-1837)
8.	Democratic	54	1837-1841	July	24, 1862	79	William H. Harrison	(1836)	Richard M. Johnson	(1837-1841)
9.	Whig	68	1841	Apr.	4, 1841	68	Martin Van Buren	(1840)	John Tyler	(1841)
10.	Whig	51	1841-1845	Jan.	18, 1862	71			None	
11.	Democratic	49	1845-1849	June	15, 1849	53	Henry Clay	(1844)	George M. Dallas	(1845-1849)
12.	Whig	64	1849-1850	July	9, 1850	65	Lewis Cass	(1848)	Millard Fillmore	(1849-1850)
13.	Whig	50	1850-1853	Mar.	8, 1874	74			None	
14.	Democratic	48	1853-1857	Oct.	8, 1869	64	Winfield Scott	(1852)	William R. King	(1853)
15.	Democratic	65	1857-1861	June	1, 1868	77	John C. Frémont	(1856)	John C. Breckinridge	(1857-1861)
16.	Republican, Nat'l Union**	52	1861-1865	Apr.	15, 1865	56	Stephen A. Douglas	(1860)	Hannibal Hamlin	(1861-1865)
							Geo. B. McClellan	(1864)	Andrew Johnson	(1865)
17.	Nat'l. Union**	56	1865-1869	July	31, 1875	66			None	
18.	Republican	46	1869-1877	July	23, 1885	63	Horatio Seymour	(1868)	Schuyler Colfax	(1869-1873)
							Horace Greeley	(1872)	Henry Wilson	(1873-1875)
19.	Republican	54	1877-1881	Jan.	17, 1893	70	Samuel J. Tilden	(1876)	William A. Wheeler	(1877-1881)
20.	Republican	49	1881	Sept.	19, 1881	49	Winfield S. Hancock	(1880)	Chester A. Arthur	(1881)
21.	Republican	51	1881-1885	Nov.	18, 1886	57			None	
22.	Democratic	47	1885-1889	June	24, 1908	71	James G. Blaine	(1884)	Thomas A. Hendricks	(1885)
23.	Republican	55	1889-1893	Mar.	13, 1901	67	Grover Cleveland	(1888)	Levi P. Morton	(1889-1893)
24.	Democratic	55	1893-1897	June	24, 1908	71	Benjamin Harrison	(1892)	Adlai E. Stevenson	(1893-1897)
25.	Republican	54	1897-1901	Sept.	14, 1901	58	William J. Bryan	(1896, 1900)	Garret A. Hobart	(1897-1899)
									Theodore Roosevelt	(1901)
26.	Republican	42	1901-1909	Jan.	6, 1919	60	Alton B. Parker	(1904)	Charles W. Fairbanks	(1905-1909)
27.	Republican	51	1909-1913	Mar.	8, 1930	72	William J. Bryan	(1908)	James S. Sherman	(1909-1912)
28.	Democratic	56	1913-1921	Feb.	3, 1924	67	Theodore Roosevelt	(1912)	Thomas R. Marshall	(1913-1921)
							Charles E. Hughes	(1916)		
29.	Republican	55	1921-1923	Aug.	2, 1923	57	James M. Cox	(1920)	Calvin Coolidge	(1921-1923)
30.	Republican	51	1923-1929	Jan.	5, 1933	60	John W. Davis	(1924)	Charles G. Dawes	(1925-1929)
31.	Republican	54	1929-1933	Oct.	20, 1964	90	Alfred E. Smith	(1928)	Charles Curtis	(1929-1933)
32.	Democratic	51	1933-1945	Apr.	12, 1945	63	Herbert Hoover	(1932)	John N. Garner	(1933-1941)
							Alfred M. Landon	(1936)		
							Wendell L. Willkie	(1940)	Henry A. Wallace	(1941-1945)
							Thomas E. Dewey	(1944)	Harry S. Truman	(1945)
33.	Democratic	60	1945-1953	Dec.	26, 1972	88	Thomas E. Dewey	(1948)	Alben W. Barkley	(1949-1953)
34.	Republican	62	1953-1961	Mar.	28, 1969	78	Adlai E. Stevenson	(1952, 1956)	Richard M. Nixon	(1953-1961)
35.	Democratic	43	1961-1963	Nov.	22, 1963	46	Richard M. Nixon	(1960)	Lyndon B. Johnson	(1961-1963)
36.	Democratic	55	1963-1969	Jan.	22, 1973	64	Barry M. Goldwater	(1964)	Hubert H. Humphrey	(1965-1969)
37.	Republican	56	1969-1974	Apr.	22, 1994	81	Hubert H. Humphrey	(1968)	Spiro T. Agnew	(1969-1973)
							George S. McGovern	(1972)	Gerald R. Ford†	(1973-1974)
38.	Republican	61	1974-1977						Nelson A. Rockefeller‡	(1974-1977)
39.	Democratic	52	1977-1981				Gerald R. Ford	(1976)	Walter F. Mondale	(1977-1981)
40.	Republican	69	1981-1989				Jimmy Carter	(1980)	George H. W. Bush	(1981-1989)
							Walter F. Mondale	(1984)		
41.	Republican	64	1989-1993				Michael S. Dukakis	(1988)	J. Danforth Quayle	(1989-1993)
42.	Democratic	46	1993-2001				George H. W. Bush;	(1992)	Al Gore	(1993-2001)
							H. Ross Perot			
							Robert J. Dole;	(1996)		
							H. Ross Perot			
43.	Republican	54	2001-				Al Gore	(2000)	Richard B. Cheney	(2001-)

GEORGE WASHINGTON

1st President of the United States
1789–1797

When the Continental Congress chose George Washington to lead American forces in the War for Independence, he had strong doubts. Speaking to his fellow Virginian, Patrick Henry, Washington said: "Remember, Mr. Henry, what I now tell you. From the day I enter upon the command of the American armies, I date my fall and the ruin of my reputation."

Washington may have been thinking of his bad experiences leading troops against French and Indian forces on the western frontier 20 years earlier. In any case, he proved a poor prophet. His reputation as a leader grew during the Revolution. And when a new government went into operation under the Constitution, no one but Washington would do as the country's first President.

The first Washington in America, John, came to Virginia from England in the mid-1650's. George, of the fourth generation, was born on Feb. 22, 1732, in the family plantation home known eventually as Wakefield, in Westmoreland County. The plantation was near where Pope's Creek flows into the Potomac River. George was the first son of six children Augustine Washington had with his second wife, Mary Ball.

When George was about seven, the family moved with its 20 slaves to a new home across the Rappahannock River from Fredericksburg, Va. Little is known about Washington's schooling. He learned to read and write, and he mastered enough mathematics to qualify as a surveyor. George kept numerous copybooks, entering in them items such as "Rules of Civility and Decent Behavior in Company and Conversation." In one he expressed in verse his own ideas on "True Happiness":

Martha Custis, land-rich Virginia widow, chose George Washington from among the numerous competitors for her hand, marrying him in January 1759.

These are the things which once possessed
Will make a life that's truly blessed:
A good estate on healthy soil
Not got by vice, nor yet by toil:
Round a warm fire, a pleasant joke,
With chimney ever free from smoke;
A strength entire, a sparkling bowl,
A quiet wife, a quiet soul . . .

Washington might have gone to school in England, as his half brothers Lawrence and Augustine had. But his father died in April 1743, and at age 11 George became the head of the house. The elder Washington had left at least 49 slaves and more than 10,000 acres (4,047 hectares) of land. The plantation, to be called Mount Vernon, went to Lawrence. Washington was to inherit Ferry Farm.

Mary Ball Washington held all of her children—especially George—on a short leash. In one instance, at least, that may have proved fateful for America's future. When Washington was 14, he might have joined the British navy, had his mother not interfered. Had he become a midshipman on a British frigate, one can only guess the course American history might have followed.

Washington described himself as "6 feet high" at age 16. Dark hair topped his well-shaped head, and his complexion appeared light, with a suggestion of slight sunburn. By age 20, Washington may have been as tall as 6 feet 3½ inches (192 centimeters), and he weighed close to 200 pounds (91 kilograms). He moved with surprising grace for someone so large. His friend Thomas Jefferson later called him the best rider of his age, and "the most graceful figure that could be seen on horseback."

Through his brother Lawrence's wife, Anne, Washington became acquainted with her father, William Fairfax. Fairfax treated Washington as a son, and he introduced him to high planter society. Lord Fairfax, Anne's cousin and a wealthy plantation owner, was also to help Washington.

William Fairfax gave the 16-year-old Washington an assignment. He was to journey to Fairfax land in the Shenandoah Valley, west of the Blue Ridge Mountains, as part of a surveying team. And on the first night out, camped at a crude cabin, George learned what frontier life was like. He described the incident in his journal:

We got our supper and [were] lighted into a room
and I, not being as good a woodsman as the rest
of my company, stripped myself very orderly and
went in to the bed, as they called it, when, to my
surprise, I found it to be nothing but a little straw
matted together, without sheets or anything else,
but one threadbare blanket, with double its
weight of vermin, such as lice, fleas, etc., and I
was glad to get up. . . . I put on my clothes, and
lay as my companions [on the floor].

Washington next worked as a surveyor for the Virginia government and for individual landowners. In the spring of 1750 he began acquiring land, obtaining nearly 1,500 acres (607 hectares)

Full name: George Washington

Born: Feb. 22, 1732

Birthplace: Westmoreland County, Va.

Died: Dec. 14, 1799

Burial site: Mount Vernon, Va.

Spouse: Martha Dandridge Custis

Occupation: Planter

Terms: 1789–1797

Vice-President: John Adams

Runner-up: No opposition

Electoral votes: 69; 132

Runner-up: 34; 77 (for John Adams)

in the Shenandoah Valley. He hoped to sell the land at a profit to pioneers crossing the Blue Ridge.

Early Military Career

In 1753, commissioned as a major in the militia by Acting Governor Robert Dinwiddie, Washington led a force of Virginians north to the Ohio River Valley in the area that is now Pennsylvania. His mission was to deliver the governor's demand that French forces operating out of Canada call off their plans to fortify the Ohio River Valley. Britain and France claimed that land, and Virginians considered it a part of their colony. The French commander at Fort Le Boeuf, near Lake Erie, in effect laughed at the young Virginian and the governor's message.

Dinwiddie sent Washington back the following year, and this time armed conflict resulted. Washington and his soldiers won a skirmish with the French. However, French forces smothered the small garrison that the Virginians had hastily thrown up at Fort Necessity in southwestern Pennsylvania.

The 22-year-old officer limped home in defeat. He had blundered in the wilderness and he felt disgraced. But he learned

George Washington, shown here with the tools of his trade, worked as a surveyor for William Fairfax and the colony of Virginia.

from the experience. Experience, rather than schooling, accounted for most of Washington's education.

Washington tasted defeat again in 1755. He was a member of a British-colonial expedition under General Edward Braddock, moving against the French Fort Duquesne, where Pittsburgh now stands. Braddock lost his life in a surprise French-Indian attack. Washington had two horses shot out from under him, and he said that four bullets went through his coat. But he escaped injury and helped organize a retreat to Virginia.

Washington returned to civilian life looking forward to good years in the 1760's. Lawrence Washington had died in 1752, and Mount Vernon eventually passed to George. Now a large landowner, he was also married.

George probably met Martha Dandridge Custis at White House, her plantation home near Williamsburg, or at a neighbor's home in the spring of 1758. She had married Daniel Custis at age 17 and he died in 1757, leaving her with two young children and about 17,000 acres (6,880 hectares) of land. Martha Custis' landholdings made her one of the richest widows in Virginia.

Now 26, Martha was a petite and plump 5 feet (152 centimeters) tall. Her hands were small, her features dainty, and she had brown hair and hazel eyes. Martha proved the person Washington had written of in his youthful poem. She was "a quiet wife, a quiet soul." The marriage produced no children, but for both it was a happy one.

His new wife by his side at Mount Vernon, Washington ran the plantation like a business. Unlike many other planters, he did not tie his entire fortune to tobacco. That crop sold on an uncertain English market. Washington raised other crops as well, such as corn and wheat. Mount Vernon became nearly self-sufficient, supporting a white population and an ever-growing number of slaves.

Slavery was an integral part of the Southern way of life. Washington accepted it. He refused to break up families or friendships by selling slaves off Mount Vernon, however. And his will provided for their freedom upon Martha's death.

Growing troubles with England in the 1760's and 1770's, especially over taxation, cast an ever longer shadow over the Washingtons' contented days at Mount Vernon. Colonial resistance led finally to armed conflict at Lexington and Concord in April 1775 and at Bunker Hill in Massachusetts on June 17, 1775—two days after Washington became commander-in-chief of the Continental Army.

Revolutionary Commander

Washington, with command of an army faced by war, begged Martha not to add her worries to his own, saying he would enjoy more real happiness in one month with her at home. "But as it has been a kind of destiny that had thrown me upon this service," he added, "I shall hope that my undertaking it is de-

The Colonial Gazette *displayed Washington's message on the British surrender in 1781 and discussed the value of French aid.*

THE COLONIAL GAZETTE

Num. 39.]   SUPPLEMENT.   Price 2 Pence

Oct.   1781

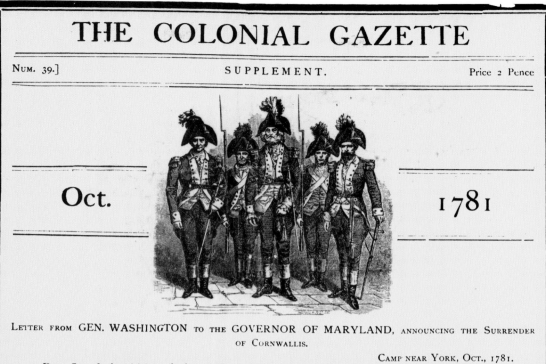

LETTER FROM GEN. WASHINGTON TO THE GOVERNOR OF MARYLAND, ANNOUNCING THE SURRENDER
OF CORNWALLIS.

CAMP NEAR YORK, OCT., 1781.

DEAR SIR : Inclosed I have the honor of transmitting to your Excellency the terms upon which Lord Cornwallis has surrendered the Garrisons of York and Gloucester.

We have not been able yet to get an account of prisoners, ordnance or stores in the different departments ; but from the best general report there will be (officers included) upwards of seven thousand men, besides seamen, more than 70 pieces of brass ordnance and a hundred of iron, their stores and other valuable articles.

My present engagements will not allow me to add more than my congratulations on this happy event, and to express the high sense I have of the powerful aid which i have derived from the State of Maryland in complying with my every request to the execution of it.   The prisoners will be divided between Winchester, in Virginia, and Fort Frederick, in Maryland.   With every sentiment of the most perfect esteem and regard, I have the honor to be

Your Excellency's most obedient and humble servant,   G. WASHINGTON.

The French at Yorktown.

Few things, indeed, suggested by the history of the war are more instructive than a parallel between the fate of Burgoyne and the fate of Cornwallis.   The defeat of Washington on Long Island and the loss of New York had been attributed to the fact that his troops were raw militia.   Yet it was mainly with just such men, and not with Continentals (as the regular soldiers of the united colonies were called), that the American commanders in northern New York overcame, in two successive battles, the well-disciplined and admirably appointed army of Burgoyne.   This was the one brilliant military triumph achieved by either party in the whole course of the struggle; yet, strange to say, its most substantial fruit was its favorable effect on the negotiations which for two years Franklin had been pushing at the court of Versailles.   It was not, however, until the beginning of the ensuing year that the French Ministry would even promise assistance to the colonies; and although their advances of money may from that time forward be said to have kept the continental army on its feet, they did not render effective military aid until the arrival of Count De Grasse in the Chesapeake, about the beginning of September, 1781.

The surrender of Cornwallis was the direct result of the advantage gained by De Grasse over Admiral Graves in the naval battle which took place off the mouth of Chesapeake Bay on September 5, 1781. For the first time during the war, the English failed to have a preponderance of naval strength in American waters, and for almost the first time an English Admiral, commanding a force not greatly inferior to his opponents, sailed pusillanimously away after an indecisive action, in which the French loss in killed and wounded was actually the greater.   After this unexpected and inexcusable behaviour on the part of an English naval officer, the surrender of Cornwallis was clearly an obvious necessity.   On one side there was the French fleet, comprising twenty four ships of the line

carrying 1,700 guns, and 19,000 seamen.   On the land side was Rochambeau with French troops, aggregating 8,400 men, and 5,500 Continental troops under Washington, together with 3,000 militia, who were of less account.   Against this military and naval force, Cornwallis had 7,500 men within the works of Yorktown, exclusive of 800 marines, disembarked from some English frigate which had lain in the river.   Under these circumstances the surrender of the English force was plainly a mere question of time.   It may be said, however, that the presence of the land force at a place where it could so happily co operate with the French fleet, bears witness to great strategical ability, and it has been usual to give the credit of the combination to Washington.   It is clear, however, that throughout the summer of 1781, the American commander had not seriously contemplated anything but a concerted attack on Sir Henry Clinton in New York.   From the day, however, that De Grasse arrived in the Chesapeake, and notified the American and French commanders that he would take his ships no further northward, it required no great strategist to perceive that the land forces must operate in Virginia, if at all.   In that moment the objective point of Washington and Rochambeau was palpably the force which Cornwallis, in obedience to Clinton's orders, had collected at Yorktown.   Cornwallis, on his part, justified in remaining on the peninsula, because he counted English fleet, and neither then, nor before, nor afterward, any Englishman have supposed it possible that an Admiral possessing the armament which Graves controlled would have acknowledged himself beaten on the sea by Frenchmen till half of his ships were sunk.

In view of these facts, it behooves us in this great celebration at Yorktown, to render our French visitors the honors they deserve, for the event commemorated is more truly and emphatically a French than an American achievement.

signed to answer some good purpose." He then left to take personal command of troops around Boston.

The Revolutionary War years brought Washington much disappointment and frustration. He had to coax and flatter Congress, sometimes sarcastically, for money to feed, supply, and pay soldiers. Desertions distressed him. An officers' plot to replace Washington shocked him. Benedict Arnold's treason grieved him. Lost battles sometimes left him close to despair. Probably no other person had the strength of character and personality to keep the army together and in the field. And Washington's soldiers loved him.

Washington would see Mount Vernon only one more time in the next eight years. Martha often joined him, though, when the army was encamped. Her presence was especially comforting to both Washington and his troops during the terrible winter of cold and sickness at Valley Forge in 1777–1778. One person there recalled:

> Every fair day, she might be seen, with basket in hand, and with a single attendant, going among the huts seeking the keenest and most needy sufferer, and giving all the comforts to him in her power.

The fighting ended at Yorktown in Virginia in 1781. There, with French help, Washington forced the British General Cornwallis to surrender. Two years later, a treaty making America independent ended the war.

Washington's time of rest and retirement after the war proved short, however. He was soon caught up in discussions about how to strengthen the national government. This led to the Constitutional Convention at Philadelphia in 1787. Washington attended as a delegate from Virginia and he served as the convention's president.

With the Constitution in effect in 1789, no one else was considered as the first President of the United States. Members of the Electoral College gave Washington 69 votes, the largest possible total. John Adams, with 34 votes, became the first Vice-President.

The First President

New York City was the nation's first capital under the Constitution. Washington took the oath of office as President there in Federal Hall on April 30, 1789. Martha joined him later. The government rented a three-story house for them on Cherry Street, a location now in the shadow of the Brooklyn Bridge.

Washington found the presidency crowded with ceremonial activities. He finally placed a notice in a New York newspaper: the President would receive "visits of compliment" only between 2 and 3 P.M. two days a week.

The Washingtons held receptions, both formal and informal. Informal evening receptions were more relaxed than others. But even at those, Martha saw to it that there was a definite beginning and end. After introductions and tea and cakes, the guests conversed quietly, with Martha seated on the sofa. Finally, not-

George Washington visits his troops at Valley Forge in the winter of 1777, accompanied by Lafayette, a French noble.

ing the time, she arose. "The general retires at 9 o'clock," Martha announced, "and I usually precede him. Good night." With a bow to all, the President and his wife left the room.

George Washington lent the presidency dignity, and numerous patterns were established during his first term. Congress passed the Bill of Rights, the first 10 amendments to the Constitution. It established a system of federal courts. It fixed the President's salary at $25,000 a year and the Vice-President's at $5,000. At Washington's suggestion, Congress established the Cabinet. Washington chose Cabinet officers he knew and trusted, including Alexander Hamilton as secretary of the treasury. Washington relied heavily on Hamilton and James Madison, then a member of Congress from Virginia, for advice. In the beginning, he asked Cabinet members individually for opinions. Only toward the end of his first administration did he begin calling the group together for meetings.

To Washington, a distressing part of his presidency was the rise of political parties. He condemned what he called "factions." Parties developed, however, as farmers, business persons, and other interest groups tried to bring influence to bear. Leaders of budding political parties sat in Washington's first Cabinet. Hamilton headed the Federalist Party. Jefferson and Madison formed the Democratic-Republican Party.

The two groups split on many issues, including foreign affairs. Britain and France were at war in the 1790's. Federalists

The inauguration of Washington as first President at Federal Hall,
New York City, April 30, 1789.

wanted the United States to support Britain, while Democratic-Republicans favored France. Washington decided that America's best course lay in remaining neutral, and he made that policy stick. But Washington did not escape criticism—some of it bitter—from both sides within his Cabinet and from the public at large.

After two terms, at age 64, Washington would not consider a third. Issuing his farewell address in 1796, he left for Mount Vernon with Martha. He departed with great public gratitude. In eight years he had set the new nation firmly on its course. He had, indeed, been the Father of His Country.

Martha's delight at being home was boundless. Washington himself could not have been more pleased at being just with family again. There was much work to do, for Mount Vernon had been neglected. Washington labored every day, but he was feeling sorely the aches, pains, and complaints of old age. He was also becoming forgetful at times.

On Dec. 12, 1799, Washington wrote in his journal: "Morning cloudy. Wind to northeast and mercury 33. . . . At about 10 o'clock it began to snow, soon after to hail, and then to a settled cold rain." Washington was out in that weather from 10 in the morning until 3 in the afternoon.

Washington later complained of a sore throat. His doctors decided that he had quincy, a severe form of tonsillitis. They could do nothing for him as the membranes in his throat gradually closed. On Dec. 14, 1799, as servants stood anxiously outside the bedroom door, and as Martha sat near the foot of the bed, George Washington died.

Martha remained at Mount Vernon until she died on May 22, 1802, only a few days shy of her 71st birthday.

President Washington's Times
1789–1797

The U.S. Flag had 13 stars when Washington took office. Five states joined the Union: North Carolina in 1789, Rhode Island in 1790, Vermont in 1791, Kentucky in 1792, and Tennessee in 1796. No new territories were organized. The U.S. population was about 4,900,000 in 1797.

1789–1799	The French Revolution ended absolute monarchy in France.
1789	On June 1, Washington signed the first act of Congress, concerning the administration of oaths.
1789	Congress established the Department of Foreign Affairs (now the Department of State).
1790	On February 1, the Supreme Court held its first session.
1790	On July 16, Washington signed plans Congress had approved for a U.S. capital on the Potomac.
1790	The first national census began. It showed 3,929,214 persons in the United States.
1791	Congress chartered the Bank of the United States.
1791	Congress established the District of Columbia.
1791	The Cabinet held its first recorded meeting.
1791	On December 15, the Bill of Rights became law. The first 10 amendments to the Constitution, they guarantee basic liberties to Americans.
1792	Rival national political parties began developing in the United States.
1792	Congress established a national mint.
1793	Eli Whitney's cotton gin led to mass production of cotton and the increased use of slave labor.
1793	On April 22, Washington issued the Neutrality Proclamation to keep the United States out of the war between France and Great Britain.
1793	On September 18, Washington laid the cornerstone of the U.S. Capitol in Washington, D.C.
1794	The Whiskey Rebellion brought the first test of federal power when Washington sent troops to crush an uprising by Pennsylvania farmers.
1795	Washington signed the unpopular Jay Treaty to maintain trade with Great Britain.
1795	The first hard-surfaced toll road was completed. It extended 62 miles (100 kilometers) from Philadelphia to Lancaster, Pa.

JOHN ADAMS

2nd President of the United States
1797–1801

John Adams was the first President to live in the White House.
And neither he nor his wife Abigail liked it much. They moved
in November 1800 after Washington, D.C., had become the nation's capital. John arrived first.

The entire area of the infant federal city then held about
8,000 persons, and the community was raw and far from finished. So was the President's home. "As I expected to find it a
new country, with houses scattered over a space of ten miles,
and trees and stumps in plenty with a castle of a house—so I
found it," Abigail wrote her sister.

The White House lay in the middle of nowhere. A narrow
dirt road called Pennsylvania Avenue cut through the brush,
connecting the house with the unfinished Capitol 1½ miles (2.4
kilometers) away. Tree stumps dotted the mansion's front yard.
The grounds were muddy. Inside, wet plaster glistened in the
few rooms that were completed, and staircases had not yet been
installed. There was no water supply. And for a place "sur-
rounded with forests," Abigail exclaimed, "can you believe that
wood is not to be had"—and in chilly fall weather. Candles had
to be placed here and there for light because there were not
enough lamps.

John and Abigail gradually settled in as construction continued. They held their first White House reception on Jan. 1, 1801.

The first White House couple had family histories that
reached back to the original Puritans of the 1600's. John Adams'
first male ancestor in America was Henry Adams, who arrived in
Massachusetts about 1640. The future second President was born
in Braintree, later Quincy, a village about 10 miles (16 kilome-

John Adams

Abigail Smith Adams' education, brilliance, and Puritan background matched her husband's, making them a "perfect" couple.

ters) south of Boston, on Oct. 30, 1735. He was the eldest of three sons, and his parents, John and Susanna, expected much of him. Years later, in an autobiography, Adams recalled:

> As my parents were both fond of reading, and my father had destined his first born, long before his birth, to an education I was very early taught to read at home and at a school of Mrs. Belcher . . . who lived in the next house on the opposite side of the road. . . . I was [later] sent to the public school close by the Stone Church.

He found the boarding school kept by Mr. Marsh more to his liking. And, he said in his autobiography, "I began to study in earnest." For entrance to Harvard College, Marsh prepared John in Greek, Latin, and mathematics.

The youth appeared all fear and trembling for entrance examinations at Harvard at age 15. But he passed, and afterward declared in relief: "I was as light when I came home as I had been heavy when I went."

Colonial Lawyer

Susanna and John Adams hoped their son would become a minister. John aimed for the law. After graduating from Harvard in 1755, he taught elementary school in Worcester, Mass. After about a year, Adams began his law studies under James Putnam of Worcester. He was ready for practice in 1758, and he gradually built up a good business in and around Boston.

A leading lawyer, Jeremiah Gridley, advised Adams "not to marry early. For an early marriage will obstruct your improvement and . . . involve you in expense." Adams had only one serious romance before he met Abigail Smith, when he came close to proposing to a young woman named Hannah Quincy.

Abigail Smith, born in 1744, was John Adams' equal intellectually. Frail as a child, she was not allowed to attend school. She was a minister's daughter, and her parents probably taught her to read and write. Abigail then educated herself in her father's and grandfather's libraries. She was no beauty, but her brilliance attracted John when he met Abigail in the early 1760's. And, although Adams seemed egotistical, haughty, and overbearing at times, his intellect and great warmth toward family attracted his future bride. Both were Puritans with a strong sense of duty. Both were interested in books and conversation. Abigail Smith and John Adams could have been considered a perfect match.

During their 54 years of marriage, Abigail smoothed Adams' rough edges. She was his friend and adviser, as well as his wife. John and Abigail had five children who lived—Abigail, John Quincy, Susanna, Charles, and Thomas.

John Adams became associated with colonial opposition to British tax and other policies in the 1760's. Like others, he expressed outrage at the Stamp Act of 1765. He endorsed the colonists' refusal to pay a tax in the form of a stamp placed on legal papers, playing cards, and a host of other items.

When the Continental Congress met in Philadelphia in Sep-

Full name: John Adams

Born: Oct. 30, 1735

Birthplace: Braintree (now Quincy), Mass.

Died: July 4, 1826

Burial site: Quincy, Mass.

Spouse: Abigail Smith

Occupation: Lawyer

Political party: Federalist

Term: 1797–1801

Vice-President: Thomas Jefferson

Runner-up: Thomas Jefferson

Electoral vote: 71

Runner-up: 68

A drawing of about 1725 shows Harvard College, which produced five Presidents: both Adamses, both Roosevelts, and Kennedy.

tember 1774, John Adams was a delegate from Massachusetts. In June 1776 he joined Thomas Jefferson, Benjamin Franklin, Robert R. Livingston, and Roger Sherman on a committee to draw up the Declaration of Independence.

Two years later, Congress sent Adams to France, where he joined Franklin and Arthur Lee. There they sought aid for the Revolutionary cause. Later, Congress gave Adams a post in The Netherlands. After the Revolutionary War, he became the first American minister to Great Britain. Abigail and the younger Abigail went with John to London. There the former rebels were presented to King George III and his queen, who received them with royal courtesy.

By the time the Adamses returned home in 1788, the Constitution had been written and a new government was forming. As he believed he should be, John Adams was chosen first Vice-President. In New York City, the nation's capital at the time, the Adamses lived at Richmond Hill, about 1½ miles (2.4 kilometers) from the city.

As Vice-President, John Adams soon learned that he did not hold an exalted position. He called it "the most insignificant office that ever the invention of man contrived or his imagination conceived." Under the Constitution, the Vice-President's only duties were to preside over the Senate and cast a vote in case of a tie.

John Adams served two terms as Vice-President. As political parties developed during George Washington's administration, he joined the Federalist Party. In 1796, Adams and Thomas Jefferson, leader of the Democratic-Republican Party, became candidates for the presidency.

The Constitution then stipulated that the person receiving

United States Commissioners at the Preliminary Peace Conference with British negotiators, Paris, 1782. The commissioners are (from left to right) John Jay, John Adams, Benjamin Franklin, Henry Laurens, and the Secretary of the Commission, William Temple Franklin. The artist, Benjamin West, intended to include the British negotiator, Richard Oswald, and his secretary. Oswald, however, would not pose, and there was no portrait from which West could take his likeness, so the picture was never finished.

the most electoral votes would become President, provided the votes constituted a majority of the number of electors appointed. The one with the next highest number would be Vice-President. When the Electoral College vote in 1796 left Adams and Jefferson ranked as one and two, the President and Vice-President belonged to different political parties. The 12th Amendment to the Constitution, adopted in 1804, changed the voting method. It requires that electors cast separate ballots for President and Vice-President.

Foreign affairs caused John Adams considerable grief as President. The war between Great Britain and France that had begun during Washington's presidency continued. Adams, like Washington, struggled to keep the United States neutral. This caused him trouble with Democratic-Republicans, who supported France, and Federalists, who favored Britain. At the same time, Adams refused to grant government jobs to party members just because they were Federalists. He insisted on selecting those who were most qualified, and this got him into deeper trouble with his party.

One-Term President

The New Year's reception in 1801 belied Adams' difficulties. It was the first and only one the Adamses held in the White

House. They received in the Oval Room, which had been furnished with crimson damask upholstery and with the family's own piano and harp. Enough logs had been found to feed crackling fires in the fireplaces. Abigail, dressed in velvet and brocade, greeted guests while seated in a chair. The President, in black velvet jacket and knee breeches, and silk stockings and silver knee and shoe buckles, stood beside her. Guests enjoyed tea, coffee, punch, wine, and cakes and tarts. The Marine band, making its first official appearance, entertained.

By now, John Adams was a lame-duck President. Thomas Jefferson and Aaron Burr had defeated him in his bid for reelection in 1800, and the House of Representatives had chosen Jefferson as President.

Abigail left for Quincy in February. Adams slipped quietly out of town on March 4 before Jefferson's inauguration.

Quincy remained the center of a quiet retirement life for the Adamses. Abigail died in 1818. John lived to see their son, John Quincy, elected President in 1825. On July 4, 1826, as part of the Independence Day celebration in Washington, D.C., President John Quincy Adams attended a reading of the Declaration of Independence before a throng of people. And in Quincy, on that 50th anniversary of the nation he had helped to found and guide, John Adams died. He had lived nearly 91 years.

President Adams' Times
1797–1801

The U.S. Flag had 15 stars when Adams took office. No new states joined the Union. Two territories were organized: Mississippi in 1798 and Indiana in 1800. The U.S. population was about 4,900,000 in 1797.

1798	Amendment 11 to the Constitution was proclaimed, limiting the powers of the federal courts.
1798	In the XYZ Affair, angry Americans spurned French demands for tribute and called for war.
1798	Congress organized the Department of the Navy.
1798	The Alien and Sedition Acts, aimed at defeating Jefferson for the presidency, passed.
1798, 1799	Kentucky and Virginia resolutions declared the Alien and Sedition Acts unconstitutional.
1799	Napoleon became dictator of France.
1800	Congress established the Library of Congress.
1800	The capital became Washington, D.C. The White House became the President's official home.

THOMAS JEFFERSON

3rd President of the United States
1801–1809

Nearly a century and a half after Thomas Jefferson's death, a group of Nobel prizewinners gathered in Washington, D.C., for a presidential reception. And there John F. Kennedy, the 35th President, paid tribute to the third: "I think this is the most extraordinary collection of talent, of human knowledge, that has ever been gathered together at the White House, with the possible exception of when Thomas Jefferson dined alone."

Jefferson's was a giant intellect. He was many persons rolled into one: architect, inventor, diplomat, politician, leader of state, scientist, scientific farmer—and master writer. Yet he wanted to be remembered for just three things, inscribed on his tombstone: "author of the Declaration of American Independence, of the Statute of Virginia for religious freedom, and father of the University of Virginia."

Thomas Jefferson was born to Peter and Jane Randolph Jefferson at Shadwell, the family plantation in Goochland (now Albemarle) County, Va., on April 13, 1743. He was the third child in a family of six sisters and four brothers.

Tom Jefferson enjoyed a carefree youth—hunting, fishing, canoeing, and horseback riding. When he was nine years old, he began Latin, Greek, and French studies with William Douglas, an Anglican minister who ran a nearby boarding school.

When Jefferson was 14, his father died. This left him, the oldest son, as head of the family. Thomas also inherited Shadwell, which covered 2,500 acres (1,012 hectares) and held 30 slaves. His father's friend, John Harvie, became Jefferson's guardian, managing Shadwell while Tom obtained more schooling. Until 1760, Jefferson attended the boarding school of James

Martha Jefferson, born in 1772 and known as "Patsy," often served in the White House as hostess during the presidency of her widowed father.

Full name:
Thomas Jefferson

Born: April 13, 1743

Birthplace: Goochland (now Albermarle) County, Va.

Died: July 4, 1826

Burial site: Monticello, Va.

Spouse:
Martha Wayles Skelton

Occupation:
Planter, lawyer

Political party:
Democratic-Republican

Terms: 1801-1809

Vice-Presidents:
Aaron Burr;
George Clinton

Runners-up:
Aaron Burr;
Charles C. Pinckney

Electoral vote: 73; 162

Runners-up: 73; 14. In first election, Jefferson and Burr tied in electoral votes and election was thrown into the House of Representatives, where Jefferson won. Burr became Vice-President.

Maury, an Anglican clergyman, near Charlottesville.

Harvie hired a dancing master, Alexander Ingles, to instruct the Jefferson brood at Shadwell. Ingles may also have taught Jefferson to play the violin. That instrument became for many years a favorite form of relaxation for him.

Jefferson entered the College of William and Mary at Williamsburg when he was 16. After two years at William and Mary, Jefferson remained in Williamsburg to study law under George Wythe, a most learned and scholarly lawyer. Jefferson later spoke of Wythe as "my second father," "my ancient master, my earliest and best friend."

His law studies completed in 1767, Jefferson divided his time between court cases in Williamsburg and managing Shadwell. In 1769, he began the construction of his own house, Monticello, which he designed, and the house was livable when Shadwell burned to the ground the following year. Jefferson lost his library and many notes and papers on law cases. A few books were salvaged and servants saved his violin.

Sometime in 1770, the tall, slender, sandy-haired Jefferson met a young widow, Martha Wayles Skelton, in Williamsburg. She was the daughter of John Wayles, a lawyer and master of The Forest, a plantation in Charles City County.

Jefferson frequently visited Martha in 1770 and 1771, and he found himself competing for the affections of the pretty woman with auburn-tinged hair and hazel eyes. A mutual love of music may have helped him win Martha. The story goes that two suitors came to call on her. They heard her and Jefferson playing a duet and departed without a word, regarding their chances as hopeless.

Thomas Jefferson and Martha Skelton were married at The Forest on New Year's Day 1772. They had one son and five daughters. Only two children reached adulthood—Martha, called Patsy, and Mary, known as Polly. Some scholars say that Jefferson was also the father of one or more children with Sally Hemings, one of his slaves at Monticello, several years after his wife's death.

In Williamsburg, the capital of Virginia, Jefferson had often stopped by the statehouse in the 1760's to observe Virginia's lawmaking body, the House of Burgesses, in action. And there one day in 1765, he heard Patrick Henry deliver his famous and impassioned speech against the Stamp Act. Amid cries of "Treason!" Henry warned King George III against trying to tax the colonists by forcing them to pay for a stamp placed on legal papers and other items. "I attended the debate...at the door of the lobby of the House of Burgesses," Jefferson recalled, "and heard the splendid display of Mr. Henry's talents as a popular orator. They were indeed great; such as I never heard from any other...." Henry and Jefferson became good friends.

Eloquent Writer

Four years later, Thomas Jefferson himself was a member of the House of Burgesses, and caught up in revolutionary ferment. Jefferson lent his pen to arguments against British taxation and other policies, and in the spring of 1775 he was a Virginia delegate to the Continental Congress in Philadelphia.

The Declaration of Independence Committee are (from left to right) Thomas Jefferson, Roger Sherman, Benjamin Franklin, Robert R. Livingston, and John Adams.

Jefferson's handwritten copy of the Declaration of Independence, which faced further editing and heated debate in the Congress.

In June 1776, Congress moved for independence from Great Britain. It appointed a committee that included Jefferson, John Adams, and Benjamin Franklin to draw up a declaration. The writing task fell to Jefferson, then 33. On July 2, Congress began to debate what he had produced.

Thomas Jefferson suffered during that debate, much of it heated. From his point of view, the delegates tore his work apart. As Jefferson squirmed and groaned inwardly, they argued, sometimes haggling for an hour over a single word.

At last, on July 4, Congress accepted the Declaration of Independence. The one part that escaped any major change was pure Jefferson, containing some of the most moving and eloquent expressions ever set to paper. As he had hoped, he would be remembered for his words:

> When in the course of human events, it becomes necessary for one people to dissolve the political bands which have connected them with another, and to assume among the powers of the earth, the separate and equal station to which the laws of nature and of nature's God entitled them, a decent respect to the opinions of mankind requires that they should declare the causes which impel them to the separation.
> We hold these truths to be self-evident, that all men are created equal, that they are endowed by their creator with certain unalienable rights, that among these are life, liberty and the pursuit of happiness.

Thomas Jefferson had no taste or ability for the military. He served during the Revolutionary War in what for him was a better capacity—as a Virginia legislator and, from 1779 to 1781, as that state's governor. During his time in the legislature, Jefferson worked to insure religious liberty in Virginia.

Governor of Virginia

The Anglican Church had been the established denomination in Virginia. It received money from the government to maintain buildings and pay ministers. Although the church lost that support in 1776, nothing in the Virginia law said that this religious group or some other church might not receive special treatment in the future. Jefferson wanted Virginia to declare religious toleration and freedom of religion for everyone and for all time. In 1786, Virginia passed a law Jefferson had written earlier, and in which he took special pride—the Statute of Religious Freedom. This is the second accomplishment for which Jefferson wished to be remembered.

Jefferson's two years as governor marked a low point in his career. Virginia was nearly stripped of defenses as it supplied food, equipment, and soldiers to George Washington's army and other forces fighting the British. Then, a British force under

At New Orleans on Dec. 20, 1803, a French detachment fires a salute as the U.S. flag replaces the French tricolor over Louisiana.

General Lord Cornwallis invaded Virginia in 1781. The state government—and Jefferson—fled west from Richmond, which had become the capital, to Charlottesville. The British occupied Richmond for a time. Early in June 1781, British cavalry under Lieutenant Colonel Banastre Tarleton struck out for Charlottesville, aiming to take Jefferson and the legislators as prisoners. They almost did.

The governor had left Charlottesville for Monticello, not far away. When Jefferson heard that the British were coming, he hastily bundled Martha and the children into a carriage and sent them to safety on a neighboring plantation. He left Monticello just in time to avoid capture.

Fighting ended with Cornwallis' surrender at Yorktown, Va., in October 1781. However, Jefferson, his good name under a cloud, was bitter. He was blamed for Virginia's lack of defense in the face of the British invasion. And stories of his flight to avoid capture, along with hints of cowardice, made for much snickering in Virginia taverns. He was glad to put his governorship behind him.

But much deeper distress lay ahead. Lucy Elizabeth Jefferson was born on May 8, 1782, after a difficult delivery. Martha had been in ill health, and she did not recover. Late that summer Jefferson wrote in his diary: "Sept. 6—my dear wife died this day at 11:45 A.M." The younger Martha Jefferson remembered her father's sorrow:

> A moment before the closing scene, he was led from the room in a state of insensibility . . . he fainted, and remained so long insensible that they feared he would never revive. . . . He kept his room for three weeks and walked almost incessantly, night and day. . . . When, at last he left his room, he was incessantly on horseback. . . . In those melancholy rambles I was his constant companion.

Jefferson never remarried. Lucy Elizabeth died of whooping cough in October 1784.

Diplomat and President

At that time Jefferson was a member of Congress. He became minister to France in 1785, returning in November 1789 to serve as President George Washington's first secretary of state.

With James Madison, Jefferson formed the Democratic-Republican Party in the 1790's to oppose the Federalist Party, among whose leaders were Alexander Hamilton, secretary of the treasury, and Vice-President John Adams. Adams and Jefferson had been friends. They had worked together in the Continental Congress and on the Declaration of Independence. Now they became political enemies.

Thomas Jefferson ran for the presidency against Adams in 1796 and became Vice-President when he received the second highest number of electoral votes. He opposed Adams again in 1800. This time Jefferson tied with Aaron Burr, each receiving 73 electoral votes. The House of Representatives awarded the presidency to Jefferson.

*In September 1804, American warships bombard the Harbor of
Tripoli, the notorious pirate base in Africa.*

The new Chief Executive believed that the presidency under
Washington and Adams had been too aristocratic and distant
from the people. To emphasize his belief in democracy and
equality, Jefferson walked to his inauguration on March 4, 1801.
He also discontinued the formal receptions Washington and
Adams had held. He eliminated much ceremony in the White
House, and he was always available to visitors. But Jefferson
also entertained elegantly at state dinners and private gatherings.
The meals were usually French or Italian, prepared by an excel-
lent chef.

Presidential orders for food at the Washington market and
elsewhere often ran to $50 a day. Jefferson was said to have
spent $10,000 on wines during his administration. He popular-
ized ice cream as a dessert and also liked to serve persimmon
beer, brewed in the White House from his own recipe. He preferred beer and ale as table beverages.

Crusty John Adams protested that Jefferson spent too much
time entertaining. He remembered that as President he had held
levees, or receptions, once a week, "so that all my time might
not be wasted by idle visit. [Jefferson's] whole eight years were
a levee."

Since Jefferson was a widower, his daughters Martha and
Mary often filled in as White House hostess. Martha, who had
married Thomas Mann Randolph, brought her children with her.
Her seventh, James Madison Randolph, was the first child born
in the White House, in 1806. Dolley Madison also served as
hostess. The wife of Jefferson's secretary of state, she was one of
Washington society's bright lights.

Jefferson's first term as President is best remembered for the
purchase of Louisiana from France in 1803. At a cost of about
$15 million, less than 3 cents per acre (1.2 cents per hectare),
the United States obtained vast territory west of the Mississippi

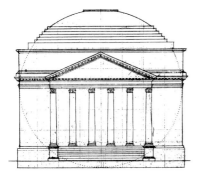

Jefferson's drawing for the rotunda at the University of Virginia, which he helped found. It opened to 40 students in March 1825.

River that doubled the nation's size. Jefferson sent Meriwether Lewis and William Clark to head an expedition to explore that land.

Continued war between Great Britain and France troubled Jefferson's second term. Both nations interfered with American trade, and Jefferson finally persuaded Congress to pass the Embargo Act, cutting off trade with both nations. This harmed New Englanders mainly because it forbade the export of any American produce and the sailing of any American ship to a foreign port. New England consisted of maritime states, where much income came from shipping and sailing. Thousands of persons in that region were affected by the Embargo Act.

Jefferson turned over the presidency to James Madison in March 1809. The new President rode to his inauguration in a carriage, but Jefferson, ever the democrat, joined the crowd behind him on horseback.

Elder Leader of State

Jefferson's retirement did not end his interest in national affairs. As the Sage of Monticello, he kept in touch with President Madison and Madison's successor, James Monroe. After the War of 1812, when the British burned several government buildings in Washington, D.C., including the congressional library, Jefferson sold his library to the government. One of the finest collections in the country, these books became the basis for today's Library of Congress.

At Monticello Jefferson experimented with new crops and with herbs and flowers. He read widely, wrote, and made architectural sketches. In the 1820's, he worked to establish the University of Virginia at Charlottesville, the third and last item for which he wished to be remembered. He designed the buildings there, and the school opened in March 1825 with 40 students.

Jefferson also carried on an extensive correspondence. To have exact records of his letters, he used a polygraph, a device he improved. It held two pens that worked in unison. As a person wrote with one pen, the other automatically made a copy.

John Adams was a favorite Jefferson correspondent. The two had put aside their political differences and once more were fast friends. In letters they discussed history, government, science, and philosophy.

Jefferson died at Monticello the afternoon of July 4, 1826, at the age of 83. That afternoon John Adams also lay on his deathbed, and his final thought was of his old friend. "Thomas Jefferson still survives," Adams murmured just before he died, not knowing of Jefferson's death. It was fitting that those two elder leaders of state should depart on the 50th anniversary of the nation they had served so well.

President Jefferson's Times
1801–1809

The U.S. Flag had 15 stars when Jefferson took office, even though there were 16 states. Ohio became a state in 1803. Four territories were organized: Orleans in 1804, Louisiana in 1805, Michigan in 1805, and Illinois in 1809. The U.S. population was about 7,040,000 in 1809.

1801–1809	The Napoleonic Wars raged in Europe for all but a brief period during Jefferson's administration.
1802	Congress established the U.S. Military Academy at West Point, N.Y.
1803	Chief Justice John Marshall established the Supreme Court's power of judicial review.
1803	The United States purchased the Louisiana Territory from France for about $15,000,000.
1803	John Dalton proposed his atomic theory of matter.
1804	Richard Trevithick of Great Britain invented the steam locomotive.
1804	Amendment 12 to the Constitution provided that the President and Vice-President be elected separately.
1804	Napoleon crowned himself Emperor of the French.
1805	The War with Tripoli ended with the Barbary pirates agreeing to respect the U.S. Flag.
1805	Lewis and Clark reached the Pacific coast. Their expedition strengthened U.S. claims to the Oregon country.
1806	Zebulon M. Pike explored the Rocky Mountains and sighted Pikes Peak.
1807	Aaron Burr, who served as Vice-President during Jefferson's first term, was tried for treason and acquitted.
1807	Great Britain abolished the slave trade throughout the colonies.
1807	Fulton's *Clermont,* the first commercially successful steamboat, puffed up the Hudson on its first trip.
1807	Congress passed the Embargo Act, forbidding U.S. ships to carry goods to other nations.
1808	Congress prohibited the importation of African slaves into the United States.

JAMES MADISON

4th President of the United States
1809–1817

James Madison was one American President whose wife attracted more favorable attention than he did. Author Washington Irving described Dolley Madison as fine and portly, with "a smile and a pleasant word for everybody." Then Irving added: "as to Jemmy Madison—ah! poor Jemmy!—he is but a withered little apple-John."

That was unkind, and inaccurate. Madison was not known for his sense of humor, but his was no soured and shriveled personality, either. It is true, though, that Madison earned a greater reputation as the Father of the Constitution than as President.

Madison was born on March 16, 1751. He grew up at Montpelier, the family plantation. Little is known about him until age 11, when he enrolled in a boarding school 70 miles (113 kilometers) from home, or about a three-day horseback ride away. Madison began his mastery of Greek, Latin, mathematics, geography, and English literature at this time.

After more preparation in the classics under a tutor, Madison left Montpelier at age 18 for the College of New Jersey, later to become Princeton University. Entrance exams there were tough, but Madison had no trouble. He completed the Princeton curriculum in two years instead of three and received his B.A. degree in September 1771.

The 20-year-old youth stood 5 feet, 6 inches (168 centimeters) tall. He wore his hay-colored hair in bangs. His pale complexion made his blue eyes seem especially intense. One eye was near-sighted, the other far-sighted.

Madison was widely read, not only in Greek and Latin but possibly in other languages besides English. The ideas on gov-

James Madison

Dolley Payne Madison served as official White House hostess for 16 years, assuming the duties of first lady for the widowed Thomas Jefferson and continuing during the 8 years her husband was in office.

Full name: James Madison

Born: March 16, 1751

Birthplace: Port Conway, Va.

Died: June 28, 1836

Burial site: Near Montpelier, Va., at Montpelier Station

Spouse: Dolley Payne Todd

Occupation: Lawyer

Political party: Democratic-Republican

Terms: 1809-1817

Vice-Presidents: George Clinton; Elbridge Gerry

Runners-up: Charles C. Pinckney; De Witt Clinton

Electoral votes: 122; 128

Runners-up: 47; 89

ernment he developed equipped him well for his leading role at the Constitutional Convention in 1787. He authored about one-third of the *Federalist* papers, urging ratification of the Constitution. Most of these appeared in 1787 and 1788. He also closely wove the system of checks and balances into the Constitution following debate and compromise. He was elected to the House of Representatives from Virginia in 1789. Originally opposed to the Bill of Rights as a part of the Constitution, Madison later introduced it and shepherded those first 10 amendments to the Constitution through Congress.

Still a bachelor at age 43, Madison's life changed after Senator Aaron Burr of New York introduced him to Dolley Payne Todd one day in 1794. The two may possibly have met before. Now 26, Dolley had lost her husband and an infant son to the yellow fever epidemic that swept through Philadelphia in 1793. The plague brought death to about 5,000 persons there. Philadelphia's total population at the time was about 28,500.

When Madison proposed in the spring of 1794, Dolley hesitated. She doubted whether it was proper to remarry less than a year after her husband's death. Besides, Madison was 17 years her senior, and he was an intellectual. She had enjoyed only a meager education in North Carolina and Virginia, where she was from. Dolley Todd and James Madison seemed to have only one characteristic in common—their height.

Martha Washington was related to Dolley's sister Lucy by marriage. Martha may have tipped the balance. She said to Dolley one day: "Are you engaged to James Madison?"

"No," Dolley replied, "I think not."

Responded Martha: "Well, if you are, don't be ashamed, be proud. He'll make a husband all the better for those 17 extra years. Between him and [General Washington] there's great esteem and friendship." Dolley and the future fourth President were married on Sept. 15, 1794, at Harewood, a Washington family estate in Virginia.

In Philadelphia Dolley quickly established herself as a social leader, aiding her husband's career. Dolley's plain Quaker background had done little to prepare her for proper fashions in dress and entertaining. She learned from books and manuals. And she learned quickly and well. The Washingtons often came to dinner. So did Thomas Jefferson, who considered Madison his protégé.

Social life accelerated after Madison became secretary of state under Jefferson in 1801. Since Jefferson was a widower, Dolley often served as hostess in the White House. Not every guest was enchanted with the state dinners of a round of beef, soup richly flavored with basil and garlic, boiled cabbage, ham, and apple pie. The wife of Anthony Merry, British minister to the United States, remarked that the fare was "more like a harvest home supper than the entertainment of a secretary of state." However, the painter William Dunlap called Dolley "the leader of everything fashionable in Washington"—a trendsetter.

Society ladies followed Dolley's lead especially in turbans, a headdress for which Dolley became well known. They struggled to keep up with her collection of shoes. When Dolley bought a macaw—a kind of parrot—other fashionable ladies soon did so.

Madison was elected President in 1808. With the White House

Montpelier, the Virginia estate of James Madison, still attracts
many visitors. Madison and his wife retired there after he left the presidency.

now her home, Dolley Madison redecorated it. The congressional appropriation for furnishings and decoration was $14,000. Dolley's initial purchases were around $5,000. Among other things, she bought a piano, china, silver, and draperies.

Madison in the White House

Most of James Madison's troubles as President lay in foreign affairs. He inherited from Jefferson the problem of how to protect American shipping from harassment and loss at the hands of Great Britain and France, then fighting the Napoleonic Wars. In addition, the British in Canada encouraged Indian raids on the western frontier. Finally, backed by many members of Congress from the West and South, Madison chose war with England in 1812.

Save for a few victories at sea and in the West, the War of 1812 went badly for the United States. In 1814, a British invasion force chased an American army from the battlefield at Bladensburg, Md., as President Madison watched from a nearby hilltop. The British then swept on toward the capital. Many Washingtonians and government officials—including the President—left for safer quarters. Dolley got out just in time, with British troops scarcely 3 miles (5 kilometers) away. She took what silver and other White House possessions she could hastily load in a carriage, including Gilbert Stuart's portrait of George Washington. One observer reported seeing "Mrs. Madison in her carriage flying full speed through Georgetown, accompanied by an officer carrying a drawn sword."

The British stayed in Washington only long enough to set fires, and the Madisons and others returned to find the Capitol and other government buildings in ruins. "The poor Capitol! nothing but its blackened walls remained!" Margaret Smith wrote to a friend. "Those beautiful pillars in that Representatives Hall were cracked and broken, the roof, that noble dome,

British invaders take Washington, D.C., on Aug. 24, 1814,
burning ships along the Potomac and public buildings in the city.

painted and carved with such beauty and skill, lay in ashes in
the cellars beneath the smouldering ruins." Fire had also gutted
the White House. For the remainder of Madison's term, he and
Dolley lived first in what was called the Octagon House in
Washington and later, in 1815, in a house on the corner of
Pennsylvania Avenue and 19th Street.

"Mr. Madison's War" added nothing to his reputation. But
it served to wean Americans from their British heritage, making
them more nationalistic, and it stimulated the development of
American industry. The war also produced the words of "The
Star-Spangled Banner." The lawyer Francis Scott Key wrote
them down as he stood on a prisoner-exchange boat watching
the unsuccessful British bombardment of Fort McHenry, which
guarded Baltimore.

After attending James Monroe's inauguration in March
1817, the Madisons retired to Montpelier. Madison kept in touch
with other elder leaders of state such as Jefferson and John
Adams. He helped Jefferson found the University of Virginia
and participated in writing a new constitution for Virginia in
1829.

James Madison died at 85 on June 28, 1836. Dolley returned
to Washington, once again to associate with Presidents and other
high officials at dinners and receptions. She died at 81, on July
12, 1849.

President Madison's Times
1809–1817

The U.S. Flag had 15 stars when Madison took office, even though there were 17 states. Two states joined the Union: Louisiana in 1812 and Indiana in 1816. Two territories were organized: Missouri in 1812 and Alabama in 1817. The U.S. population was about 8,900,000 in 1817.

1811	The Cumberland Road was started as part of the federal program to improve canals, roads, and bridges.
1811	William H. Harrison shattered the Indian forces in the Battle of Tippecanoe.
1812	The United States went to war with Great Britain for several reasons, among them to protect freedom of the seas and the American shipping trade.
1812	Napoleon invaded Russia but had to retreat.
1814	The White House was burned by the British during the War of 1812. Madison had to flee the capital to avoid capture.
1814	"The Star-Spangled Banner" was written by Francis Scott Key during the British attack on Baltimore.
1814	Denmark gave Norway to Sweden.
1814	New England Federalists held a secret meeting called the Hartford Convention. Rumors sprang up afterward that the members planned the secession of the New England states.
1814	The Treaty of Ghent, signed by Great Britain and the United States, ended the indecisive War of 1812.
1815	To many historians, this year saw the beginning of the Era of Good Feeling, a time of relative peace, unity, and optimism in the United States.
1815	Andrew Jackson won a stunning battle at New Orleans.
1815	Belgium united with The Netherlands to form a single country.
1815	Napoleon was defeated at Waterloo.
1816	The first savings banks in the country were founded at Philadelphia, Pa., and Boston, Mass.

JAMES MONROE

5th President of the United States
1817–1825

They called James Monroe "the last of the cocked hats," referring to the three-cornered headgear worn by soldiers during the Revolutionary War. This description was appropriate. Monroe had served in the war as an officer. He was also old-fashioned. Long trousers had begun to replace knee breeches as male attire in the 1790's, but Monroe ignored the change. He wore knee breeches throughout his presidency.

On April 28, 1758, James Monroe was born in Westmoreland County, Va., in a roughly built, two-story frame house. At age 12, he began to attend a private school run by Parson Archibald Campbell. Parson Campbell's school prepared Monroe well for the College of William and Mary in Williamsburg. He entered there in 1774 at 16. He did not complete college, however. On Sept. 28, 1775, Monroe became a second lieutenant in the Third Virginia Regiment. He was with George Washington at Valley Forge in 1777–1778, and he fought in the battles of Germantown and Monmouth. Monroe became a colonel at 22, a rank he held until the end of the war.

James Monroe studied law under Thomas Jefferson for a few months in 1779–1780, and won election to the Virginia legislature soon after he had left the army. In 1783, he was elected to the Congress of Confederation.

In 1786, Monroe decided to practice law in Fredericksburg, Va., and to make the meeting of Congress in New York his last. He also fell in love.

News of the romance astonished New York society, for the object of Monroe's attention was Elizabeth Kortright, a beauty known for her exclusiveness. New Yorkers could hardly believe

James Monroe

Her friends could not understand why Elizabeth Kortright, belle of New York society, should want to marry the tall, raw-boned Virginian, James Monroe.

that she had consented to marry Monroe, the "not particularly attractive" Virginia member of Congress.

This was not an accurate description. Monroe was attractive enough. He stood nearly 6 feet (183 centimeters) tall, and his raw-boned physique was well proportioned. He certainly was, as one observer noted, "respectable looking."

Early in March 1786, Monroe wrote to his uncle, Judge Joseph Jones, that "on the Thursday ensuing I was united to the young lady I mentioned. To avoid the idle ceremonies of the place [New York City] we withdrew into the country for a few days. We have been several days since returned to her father's house since which I have as usual attended Congress."

Monroe left Congress and began to practice law in Fredericksburg, but he was soon back in the Virginia legislature. In July 1787 he wrote to Jefferson: "Mrs. Monroe . . . added a daughter to our society who though noisy, contributes greatly to its amusement." She was named Eliza. A son, born in 1799, lived only two years. Another daughter, Maria Hester, was born in 1803.

Between 1790 and 1802 Monroe served in the Senate, as a diplomat, and as governor of Virginia. Then Thomas Jefferson appointed him to assist the U.S. minister in France who negotiated the Louisiana Purchase of 1803. Monroe remained in the diplomatic service for four years, as minister to Great Britain and as an envoy on a special diplomatic mission to Spain. Under President James Madison he was secretary of state and, for a time, secretary of war.

Madison supported Monroe for the presidency in 1816 against the Federalist candidate, Rufus King. Monroe won 183 out of the total 217 electoral votes cast. Four years later, after the Federalists had disappeared as a party, the "last of the cocked hats" was unopposed and received all but one of the electoral votes for re-election.

After the inauguration in 1817, the Monroes lived for nine months at 2017 I Street in Washington before moving into the White House, which was rebuilt after the British had burned it in the War of 1812. Weekly open house followed. As a Washington newspaper commented:

> The secretaries, senators, foreign ministers, consults, auditors, accountants, officers of the army and navy of every grade, farmers, merchants, parsons, priests, lawyers, judges, auctioneers and nothingarians—all with their wives and some of their gawky offspring, crowd to the President's house every Wednesday evening; some in shoes, most in boots and many in spurs . . . longing for their cigars . . . left at home.

A Formal White House

It was a democratic time. But James Monroe ran the business end of the White House in a strictly formal manner. Under Jefferson and Madison, the presidential office usually had been open to visitors at any time. Now those who wished to see the President had to be invited or make appointments. Either way the audiences were stiff and usually brief.

Full name: James Monroe

Born: April 28, 1758

Birthplace: Westmoreland County, Va.

Died: July 4, 1831

Burial site: Richmond, Va.

Spouse: Elizabeth Kortright

Occupation: Lawyer

Political party: Democratic-Republican

Terms: 1817–1825

Vice-President: Daniel D. Tompkins

Runner-up: Rufus King; no opposition

Electoral votes: 183; 231

Runners-up: 34; 1 (for John Quincy Adams)

At White House dinners, even with a few guests, the Monroes entertained in the "French style." James Fenimore Cooper, author of *The Last of the Mohicans,* said those occasions had "rather a cold than a formal air."

Although Dolley Madison came to dislike the task, the warm, outgoing former first lady had always tried to make the first call on Washington's social leaders. Failing that, she promptly returned calls.

Not so the aloof Elizabeth Monroe. She announced that she would neither make calls nor return them. Elizabeth was applauded by some for having "the good sense to see that life would be intolerable to any woman in her place who undertook to return all the calls made upon her." But others in Washington society, among them the Cabinet wives, criticized her.

Elizabeth remained unaffected, but Washington socialites sought their revenge. Society columnist Sarah Seaton noted in December 1819: "The drawing room of the President was opened last night to a beggarly row of empty chairs. Only five females attended, three of whom were foreigners."

The final effrontery to Washington society came when Maria Monroe, 16, became the first President's daughter to be married in the White House. Elizabeth ran the show as she saw fit. No one who was anyone in Washington was invited.

Even Cabinet members were left out. At the March 9, 1820, ceremony only attendants, the relatives, and a few old friends of the groom [Samuel L. Gouverneur of New York] witnessed the ceremony. Washington society eventually recovered and relented, however, and White House receptions were better attended.

During the Monroe Administration, the United States continued to expand. Florida was acquired from Spain. The new states of Illinois, Mississippi, Alabama, Maine, and Missouri entered the Union. The question of Missouri's admission aroused the slavery issue, embroiling the government in bitter controversy. The Missouri Compromise of 1820 at last brought Missouri in as a slave state, balancing this with Maine, which came in free.

Monroe (standing), shown with his Cabinet, was a capable, experienced leader who entered the presidency after over 40 years of public service.

*James Monroe and Andrew Jackson in an 1819 British cartoon
protesting Jackson's execution of two Englishmen in Florida.*

James Monroe is best remembered for the Monroe Doctrine,
in which Secretary of State John Quincy Adams had a large
hand. The doctrine, issued as part of a message to Congress in
1823, warned European nations that the Western Hemisphere
would no longer be subject to European colonization or interference. The Monroe Doctrine became part of the bedrock of
American foreign policy.

Retiring from the presidency in March 1825, Monroe and
Elizabeth lived at Oak Hill, an estate near Leesburg, Va. Like
most planters, Monroe was land rich and cash poor. He had
trouble making ends meet and eventually sold many of his holdings to pay debts.

Elizabeth died Sept. 23, 1830. Monroe moved in with his
daughter Maria Gouverneur. President John Quincy Adams had
appointed her husband postmaster of New York City. There the
73-year-old Monroe, last of the Virginia dynasty of Presidents,
died on July 4, 1831. Thomas Jefferson and John Adams had
died on that same date five years before.

President Monroe's Times
1817–1825

The U.S. Flag had 15 stars when Monroe took office, even though there were 19 states. Five states joined the Union: Mississippi in 1817, Illinois in 1818, Alabama in 1819, Maine in 1820, and Missouri in 1821. Two territories were organized: Arkansas in 1819 and Florida in 1822. The U.S. population was about 11,300,000 in 1825.

1819	The *Savannah* was the first steamship to cross the Atlantic. It sailed from Savannah, Ga., to Liverpool, England.
1819	In February, the treaty that eventually gave the United States Florida was signed with Spain.
1819	Jethro Wood patented an improved cast-iron plow, which featured replaceable pieces at points of greatest wear.
1819	Bolívar became first president of Colombia.
1820–1821	Congress approved the Missouri Compromise in March 1820. Maine was admitted as a free state in 1820, Missouri as a slave state in 1821. Except in the state of Missouri, slavery was forbidden from the Louisiana Purchase north of the southern boundary of Missouri, the line of the 36° 30′ north latitude.
1820	Washington Irving completed "Rip Van Winkle." With this piece, he created a new literary form, the short story.
1821	The first public high school in the United States opened its doors in Boston, Mass.
1821	The Santa Fe Trail, blazed by William Becknell, opened the Southwest to trade.
1821	Spain ceded control of Florida to the United States.
1821	The Greek War of Independence began.
1821	Napoleon died.
1821	Central American republics separated from Spain.
1822	Brazil became independent of Portugal.
1823	The Monroe Doctrine, proclaimed before Congress, guaranteed independence of the Americas against any European interference.
1824	Mexico became a republic.

JOHN QUINCY ADAMS

6th President of the United States
1825–1829

John Quincy Adams had a reputation for sloppiness. His office was always littered with papers, and he left apple cores on the mantelpiece. He annoyed his wife Louisa by using her fine Waterford glass dishes for germination experiments with plum pits and acorns. A Philadelphia newspaper once complained that Adams often appeared in public without a neck scarf or a tie, and sometimes went barefoot to church.

Adams did not defend himself, but he was a stickler for accuracy. He confided in his diary about the newspaper story that only the part concerning the neck scarf was true. And while he might appear sloppy, nothing was out of place in his well-ordered mind. It was one of the more powerful ever to occupy the presidency.

John Quincy was born on July 11, 1767, in Braintree (now Quincy), Mass. He was the second child and oldest son of Abigail and John Adams. John was destined to be the second President of the United States. When he became one of America's commissioners to France in 1778, he took 10-year-old John Quincy with him. The boy studied French, Greek, and Latin in Paris. When Congress transferred Adams to The Netherlands, John Quincy continued his education in Leyden, adding Dutch to his store of languages. His father was posted at The Hague.

A dedicated student, the youth reported regularly on his studies to his father. But John Quincy was not entirely a stick-in-the-mud grind. In one letter, he said, all in one sentence: "I should be glad to have a pair of skates they are of various prices from 3 Guilders to 3 Ducats those of a Ducat are as good as need to be but I should like to know whether you would choose

John Quincy Adams

Louisa Johnson Adams was well versed in the classics and in music. Her personality matched John Quincy Adams' well.

Full name: John Quincy Adams

Born: July 11, 1767

Birthplace: Braintree (now Quincy), Mass.

Died: Feb. 23, 1848

Burial site: Quincy, Mass.

Spouse: Louisa Catherine Johnson

Occupation: Lawyer

Political party: Democratic-Republican

Term: 1825–1829

Vice-President: John C. Calhoun

Runner-up: Andrew Jackson

Electoral vote: Adams 84, Jackson 99, neither total a majority. In the House of Representatives vote, Adams won 13 states, Jackson 7.

to have me give so much." John consented to a purchase but added a warning about ice-skating: "provided you confine yourself to proper hours, and to strict moderation."

In 1780, Congress appointed Francis Dana, a friend of John Adams, minister to Russia. Dana spoke no French, the language of the Russian court, but 14-year-old John Quincy did. So he went to St. Petersburg in 1781 as Dana's secretary and interpreter.

When John Adams became minister to Great Britain in 1785, his son returned to America. He graduated from Harvard College in 1787 and became a lawyer. But John Quincy Adams practiced little law. The new federal government demanded his services, and President George Washington made him minister to The Netherlands in 1794. While on a special assignment to England, John Quincy met Louisa Catherine Johnson, daughter of the American consul in London.

Like John Quincy, Louisa was accomplished in French, English, Greek literature, and music, as well. Also like him, she had little gift for small talk. Those who knew her said "she was just too retiring and scholarly" for that. Louisa's personality and John Quincy's matched well, and they were married on July 26, 1797, in London. They had three sons and also raised three orphaned children of Louisa's sister, Nancy Johnson Hellen.

Over a period of 30 years, John Quincy held government posts under five Presidents. He was minister to The Netherlands, Great Britain, Russia, and Prussia, and he served in the U.S. Senate from 1803 to 1808. President James Monroe made him secretary of state in 1817, and Adams was mainly responsible for what became the Monroe Doctrine.

When John Quincy became President in 1825, the election went beyond the Electoral College. Four candidates ran for the presidency in 1824, and none received a majority of electoral votes. Adams was second to Andrew Jackson in both popular and electoral votes. Henry Clay, a member of the House of Representatives from Kentucky, ran last.

As the Constitution provides, in such a case the House of Representatives selects the winner from the top three candidates. That provision eliminated Clay, who threw his support to Adams. When the House chose Adams, Jackson's followers were furious. They were more so when Adams made Clay his secretary of state. They believed that Adams had rewarded Clay for helping Adams win. As a result, John Quincy Adams, the first son of a President ever to become president, entered the White House under a cloud of controversy and criticism.

In the White House, Louisa Adams was a charming, though reserved, hostess. She was, according to reports, always "elegantly but not gorgeously" dressed. Her headdresses with plumes were always "tastefully arranged." Louisa and the President held regular receptions every other Wednesday. John Quincy Adams hated these along with all other parties. He recorded in his diary on February 20, 1828:

> This evening was the sixth drawing-room [gathering]. Very much crowded; sixteen senators, perhaps sixty members of the House of Representatives and multitudes of strangers. . . . The heat was oppressive and these parties are becoming more and more insupportable to me.

As President, Adams was up every day at dawn or before, usually reading Greek or Latin or the Bible with commentaries before breakfast. After morning meals, he retired to letter writing and to official business matters. Solitary walks along the Potomac and swimming in that stream were his main forms of recreation. According to one story, Anne Royall, who wrote for newspapers and traveled widely in America, once trapped Adams as he swam. She wanted an interview, and she sat on his clothes, which were piled along the bank, until Adams agreed to talk. The President answered questions, his bald head glistening in the sun and his round, stubby figure waist deep in the water.

Adams did not get on well with Congress, mainly because he had too many Jacksonian enemies there. Congress refused money to build roads and other transportation systems. It would not establish a national university, which Adams wanted. The President wished to send delegates to a conference of nations in Latin America. After much wrangling, the Senate finally agreed. But the two delegates never got there. One died en route. The other arrived after the conference was over.

John Quincy Adams ran for re-election in 1828, but Andrew Jackson won by an overwhelming margin. Retirement was not for Adams. In 1830, Massachusetts voters elected him to the House of Representatives. "My election as President of the United States was not half so gratifying," he wrote in his diary. Adams remained in the House for 17 years, until he died at 80 on Feb. 23, 1848, after suffering a stroke. "Where could death have found him," asked Senator Thomas Hart Benton of Missouri, "but at the post of duty?"

President Adams' Times
1825–1829

The U.S. Flag had 24 stars when Adams took office. No new states or territories were organized. The U.S. population was 11,252,237 in 1825.

1825	The first women's labor organization in a trade was formed by women working in New York City's garment industry.
1825	The Erie Canal was completed.
1825	Czar Nicholas I of Russia crushed the Decembrist uprising, a revolt of discontented nobles.
1826–1828	Russia invaded Persia and won the land north of the Aras River.
1828	Webster's dictionary, called the finest English dictionary of its time, was published.
1828	The first passenger railroad in America, the Baltimore & Ohio, began laying track.

ANDREW JACKSON

7th President of the United States
1829–1837

Andrew Jackson was a President with many firsts—the first President born in poverty, the first elected from the West, the first to run as the candidate of the "common people," the first to be nominated by a national political convention, and the first to ride a train. Jackson almost became the first President to be assassinated.

His parents were Scotch-Irish who arrived in America from northern Ireland in 1765. Though no one is certain, they probably landed in Pennsylvania and journeyed southward, traveling 500 miles (805 kilometers) over traders' paths and trails to a settlement along Twelve Mile Creek, a short distance from Waxhaw Creek in the Carolina foothills. Andrew Jackson, Sr., built a rude cabin there and cleared land. But he was able to put in only one crop before he died in March 1767. The future President was born on March 15, 1767, a few days after his father was buried.

Elizabeth Jackson hoped her youngest son Andrew would be a Presbyterian minister, and she saw to it that he got some education. He attended school long enough to learn to read, write, and "cast accounts." The child never mastered spelling and grammar, though, and his mother finally resigned herself to the fact that Andrew would never join the clergy.

Jackson had reddish hair and blue eyes, and his face was freckled. His main interests lay in outdoor life and in rough-and-tumble activities. His courage and stubbornness, along with his daring, were apparent at an early age. Jackson never ran from a fight, and he never quit. A boyhood friend threw young Jackson in three out of four wrestling matches. But, this classmate

Andrew Jackson

Rachel Robards Jackson was slandered by Jackson's opponents in the 1828 election, which may have contributed to her death later that year.

Full name: Andrew
   Jackson

Born: March 15, 1767

Birthplace: Waxhaw
   settlement, S.C.?

Died: June 8, 1845

Burial site: Hermitage,
   Tenn.

Spouse: Rachel Donelson
   Robards

Occupation: Lawyer

Political party:
   Democratic

Terms: 1829–1837

Vice-Presidents: John C.
   Calhoun; Martin Van
   Buren

Runners-up: John Q.
   Adams; Henry Clay

Electoral votes: 178; 219

Runners-up: 83; 49

Popular votes: 642,553;
   701,780

Runners-up: 500,897;
   484,205

recalled, "He would never *stay throwed* [sic]. He was dead game and never would give up."

Young Patriot

In 1780, at 13, Andy Jackson left childhood behind. By then the Revolutionary War was five years old, and he and his 16-year-old brother Robert enlisted in a mounted militia unit to fight the British in the South. Jackson's older brother Hugh had died after the battle of Stono Ferry a year earlier.

Soon after the Battle of Camden in South Carolina in April 1781, Andy and Robert were captured by the British. A British officer ordered young Andrew to clean his boots. But Jackson refused, arguing that he had rights as a prisoner of war. He was furious that he should be considered a mere servant. The angry officer lashed out with his saber, and Jackson threw up an arm to ward off the blow. The scars on his hand and head that resulted from that sword cut became the first of several Jackson collected during his lifetime. Robert also took a saber blow on the head for refusing to scrape mud from British boots.

Besides suffering from wounds and lack of food, the Jackson boys came down with smallpox while they were British prisoners. Elizabeth Jackson finally rescued her sick sons and took them home. There were only two horses, so Robert, much the worse off, rode alongside his mother. Young Andrew walked the 40 miles (64 kilometers) to their frontier cabin.

Robert died of smallpox within two days of reaching home, and Andrew almost followed. He later recalled vividly his bout with that dread disease. "When it left me I was a skeleton—not quite 6 feet [183 centimeters] long and a little over 6 inches [15 centimeters] thick! It took me all the rest of that year to recover my strength and get flesh enough to hide my bones."

The fighting war ended at Yorktown, Va., in the fall of 1781, and in November Elizabeth Jackson died of cholera. Andrew was now an orphan at 14.

In 1784, Jackson left the Waxhaw settlement for Salisbury, a cluster of some 50 houses in North Carolina. He read law there in Spruce Macay's office for two years and became a lawyer.

Jackson acquired a reputation as a hard-drinking, hard-fighting youth. One person remembered him as "the most roaring, rollicking, game-cocking, horse-racing, card-playing, mischievous fellow that ever lived in Salisbury, . . . the head of the rowdies hereabouts." Upon hearing of Jackson's nomination for the presidency in 1824, one of the town's socialites exclaimed:

> What! Jackson up for President? *Jackson? Andrew* Jackson? The Jackson that used to live in Salisbury? . . . Well, if Andrew Jackson can be President, anybody can!

By this time, however, Jackson was no longer the wild, roistering youth that woman remembered. He was a respected lawyer and politician in Tennessee, and the owner of a large plantation, the Hermitage, near Nashville.

When he was 21, Jackson packed a half-dozen or so law books in a saddlebag and rode out of Salisbury. He settled for a time in Jonesborough, then in North Carolina, to practice law.

In the fall of 1788 Jackson left Jonesborough for Nashville, Tenn., crossing the Cumberland Mountains with a group of pioneers. He was appointed attorney general for the western district of Tennessee in 1791. He received no pay but was occasionally reimbursed by the legislature for his services. Jackson practiced law on his own, however, and bought land. He also met Rachel Donelson Robards.

Rachel had "lustrous dark eyes" and was considered "irresistible," "the best storyteller, the best dancer, the sprightliest companion, the most dashing horsewoman in the western country." She had migrated with her parents to Nashville from Virginia and at 17 had married a jealous and at times mean army officer, Lewis Robards. They separated and Rachel thought she had been divorced. She and Jackson fell in love and were married in Natchez, Miss., in 1790 or 1791.

But Andrew and Rachel learned later that her marriage to Robards did not end officially until September 1793. They quickly went through another wedding ceremony. Still, their misunderstanding would plague Jackson for years.

During the War of 1812 Jackson led troops against Indians on the southern frontier and against the British. He commanded the defense of New Orleans against the British in January 1815, winning a smashing victory.

Two years later, President James Monroe sent U.S. troops

Emily Donelson, Mrs. Jackson's niece, served as White House hostess for the widowed Andrew Jackson. Mrs. Donelson's husband was the President's private secretary.

This 1870's lithograph, "The Brave Boy of the Waxhaws," shows young Jackson defying a British officer's order to clean his boots.

under Jackson against the Seminole Indians in Florida, then owned by Spain. Jackson burned some Seminole towns, and he captured and executed two Britons who were accused of inciting and aiding Seminole raids on American settlements in the South. This caused an international uproar, which ended when the United States acquired Florida from Spain in 1819.

By now, Jackson enjoyed a national reputation as "Old Hickory" and the "Hero of New Orleans." He was known as a resourceful and daring commander, and also as a person quick to anger, one who never forgave enemies.

Though Jackson could be a bitter foe, he was unswervingly loyal to friends. He also had a kind and compassionate side. Jackson was fond of all his relatives and took care of them when needed. He and Rachel were childless, and they took on responsibility for several wards, including a young Indian boy.

In 1824, Jackson ran in a four-way race for the presidency. He won more popular and electoral votes than any other candidate, but he did not have a majority of all votes cast. Following the Constitution, the U.S. House of Representatives chose the President. The members selected John Quincy Adams, who had come in second in the voting. Jackson and his followers immediately began to prepare for the next election.

The 1828 presidential campaign pitted Jackson against John Quincy Adams. It was one of the bitterest campaigns in American history. Democrats played up Jackson's military record and his frontier experience. They touted him as one of the common people, sensitive to their needs. Opponents painted Rachel as immoral and a crude, pipe-smoking product of the frontier. The campaign's viciousness may have contributed to her death—at least Jackson blamed his enemies for it. She suffered a heart attack and died in December 1828, soon after Jackson had won the presidency. Grief-stricken and enraged, he buried her on Christmas Eve in the garden of the Hermitage.

A Wild Inauguration

Thousands of persons attended Jackson's inauguration in March 1829, and just about all of them jammed into the White House reception afterward. Fine china and crystal were smashed, boots muddied carpets and upholstery, and the surge of admirers threatened to smother the President. He finally escaped to his boarding house. Servants lured the guests outside by transferring ice cream, cake, punch, and other refreshments to the White House lawn.

Up to a point, Jackson believed in states' rights—the less federal government, the better. He vetoed a bill providing federal money to build roads and another to recharter the Bank of the United States. These actions angered his Whig opponents, who saw federal support for internal improvements and a national bank as a means to help the nation grow economically.

On the other hand, Jackson disagreed with South Carolinians who declared that a state had the right to nullify, or declare void, any federal law that it found unconstitutional. A law providing for a tariff, or a tax on imports from other countries, was at issue, and many Southerners opposed such a tax. Nullification could destroy the Union, which Jackson held above all else. When he threatened to send troops to collect the tariff in South Carolina if necessary, the state's leaders knuckled under.

As President, Jackson also presided over the removal of thousands of Cherokee Indians from their ancient homeland in Georgia. The Cherokee had lived in peace there as farmers for many years. But Georgians wanted the Indians' land, some of which contained gold. The Supreme Court of the United States declared a Georgia law asserting authority over the Cherokee Nation unconstitutional as a violation of a federal treaty with those Indians. Jackson ignored the decision, and in the 1830's, 7,000 federal troops resettled Indians to a reservation west of the Mississippi. Fully 4,000 died on the journey that became known as the Trail of Tears.

The attempt on Jackson's life was the work of an unemployed house painter. Richard Lawrence stuffed two single-shot pistols in his pockets on Jan. 30, 1835, and set out for the House of Representatives, where Jackson was attending a funeral. When the President appeared, Lawrence suddenly stepped out, raised one pistol, and pulled the trigger within several yards of his target. The gun misfired. Jackson lunged toward Lawrence, his walking cane upraised. Lawrence brought out the other pistol. Miraculously, that one also misfired. Dampened powder on a rainy day may have saved the President. Even so, someone estimated the odds against both pistols failing at 125,000 to 1.

Many people concluded that Lawrence was part of a Whig

Andrew Jackson (seated on the white horse) directing troops at the Battle of New Orleans, Jan. 8, 1815.

An artist depicts crowds gathered outside the White House for the boisterous reception that followed Jackson's 1829 inauguration.

plot. But this was not the case. Periodic outbursts of rage disturbed Lawrence's otherwise mild and quiet life, and he imagined that Jackson had conspired to deprive him of a fortune in England. The jury returned a verdict of not guilty by reason of insanity. However, Lawrence remained in jail or mental institutions until his death in June 1861.

The final public reception at the Jackson White House took place on Feb. 22, 1837—Washington's Birthday. A 1,400-pound (635-kilogram) wheel of cheddar cheese from New York City, 2 feet (61 centimeters) thick and 4 feet (122 centimeters) in diameter, was the center of attention. The guests demolished the wheel, eating there or carrying away pieces wrapped in newspaper. The smell of cheese lingered for weeks in the White House.

Andrew Jackson, still tough and unbreakable as hickory, and still the people's hero, retired to the Hermitage in March 1837. He died there at 78 on June 8, 1845.

President Jackson's Times
1829–1837

The U.S. Flag had 24 stars when Jackson took office. Two states joined the Union: Arkansas in 1836 and Michigan in 1837. Wisconsin became a territory in 1836. The U.S. population was about 15,900,000 in 1837.

1829	The postmaster general became a member of the President's Cabinet.
1829–1831	Great Colombia was divided into Ecuador, Venezuela, and New Granada (now Colombia).
1830's	Troops drove thousands of Indians from the Five Civilized Tribes from their homes and west across the Mississippi River on a "Trail of Tears."
1830	Webster and Hayne held their famous debate on states' rights. The two Senators clashed over whether a state could nullify a law passed by Congress.
1830	Louis Philippe seized the French throne.
1830	Peter Cooper builds the "Tom Thumb," the first American-made steam locomotive to operate on a common carrier. It pulls one of the first passenger trains.
1831	William Lloyd Garrison began publishing his antislavery newspaper, *The Liberator.*
1831	The reaping machine, invented by Cyrus McCormick, brought sweeping changes to agriculture.
1832	The Democratic Party met in Baltimore for its first national convention.
1832	Illinois settlers defeated the Sauk and Fox Indians in the Black Hawk War.
1833	Benjamin Day founded the *New York Sun,* the first successful penny newspaper.
1833	Slavery was outlawed in British colonies.
1836	Texas declared its independence from Mexico during the Battle of the Alamo.
1836	Samuel Colt began manufacturing the Colt revolver, which became famous as the "six-shooter."
1836	Massachusetts passed the first law limiting child labor in the United States.
1836	Alonzo D. Phillips patented the first phosphorus matches in the United States.

MARTIN VAN BUREN

8th President of the United States
1837–1841

Martin Van Buren made three tries for the presidency. And the one time he won he probably wished he had not. Van Buren had scarcely been inaugurated in 1837 when economic depression struck the country. He was blamed for the hard times that quickly spread throughout the land, and he spent a troublesome four years in office.

The eighth President's ancestors were Dutch, his great-great-great-grandfather having come from The Netherlands in the 1630's to settle in New Netherland, part of which became New York State. Martin was born on Dec. 5, 1782, in a Dutch community along the Hudson River. The British explorer Henry Hudson had named the spot *kinder-hoeck,* meaning *children's corner,* in 1609. By Van Buren's time it was called Kinderhook, and years later as a political leader he became known as "Old Kinderhook." The American expression "OK" may have come from this term.

Van Buren attended school in Kinderhook for a time. When he was 14, he began to study law in Francis Sylvester's office. Court cases then were loosely run, judges often presiding in taverns. Rough justice usually satisfied those appearing in cases concerning land claims, disturbing the peace, and petty thievery. Still, it was somewhat unusual for a young law student to take an active part in a case, as Van Buren did when he was only 15. With testimony completed one day, the lawyer from Sylvester's office who was handling the matter turned to the youth and said: "Here, Mat, sum up. You may as well begin early." Van Buren did. Awkward and fumbling at first, he soon warmed to his task and performed well. He earned a silver half dollar for his work that day.

M. Van Buren

Angelica Singleton, who married the President's oldest son, Abraham, assumed the role of White House hostess for the widowed Martin Van Buren.

In 1803, Van Buren was able to open his own law office in Kinderhook, and four years later he was a married man. Little is known about Hannah Hoes, the distant cousin and childhood sweetheart who wed Van Buren on Feb. 21, 1807. They had four sons. Then Hannah died in 1819, shortly after her fourth son's second birthday.

Politics attracted Van Buren at an early age. He was approaching 30 when he was elected to the New York legislature in 1812. He became a U.S. senator at 38.

Van Buren was part of what was then a new breed in the United States—the professional politician, one devoting full time to political activity, drawing income mainly from public office. He helped to form the new Democratic Party in New York in the 1820's, and he soon became one of its stars. Van Buren's political ability eventually brought him nicknames such as the "Little Magician" and the "Sly Fox of Kinderhook."

Then, as now, it was difficult for many people to believe that the words *honest* and *politician* could go together. Politicians were considered tricky by definition. According to Davy Crockett, a member of Congress from Tennessee, Van Buren "could take a piece of meat on one side of his mouth, a piece of bread on the other, and cabbage in the middle, and chew and swallow each severally while never mixing them together."

The record shows that Van Buren was generally honest, though, and usually direct. And he contributed much to the development of party politics in America.

In 1828, Van Buren and New York Democrats supported the Hero of the West, Andrew Jackson, for the presidency. When Old Hickory became President in 1829, he made Van Buren his secretary of state. Van Buren was elected Vice-President in 1832, and, with Jackson's blessing, the Democrats nominated him for the presidency in 1836. Van Buren easily won election that year over the main Whig candidate, William Henry Harrison.

Full name: Martin Van Buren

Born: Dec. 5, 1782

Birthplace: Kinderhook, N.Y.

Died: July 24, 1862

Burial site: Kinderhook, N.Y.

Spouse: Hannah Hoes

Occupation: Lawyer

Political party: Democratic

Term: 1837–1841

Vice-President: Richard M. Johnson

Runner-up: William H. Harrison

Electoral vote: 170

Runner-up: 73

Popular vote: 764,176

Runner-up: 550,816

The "Little Magician," Martin Van Buren, takes the presidential oath of office in the Senate, March 1837.

President Van Buren entered a White House holding furniture well worn after eight years of the Jackson Administration. He had much of it auctioned off, collecting about $6,000. He obtained $27,000 from Congress for redecorating, spending it on new china, rugs, glassware, upholstery, and general housecleaning. Van Buren made his eldest son Abraham, a West Point graduate, his secretary. Not having remarried, though, the new President was without a White House hostess. Dolley Madison, the fourth President's widow and still a star in Washington society, fixed that.

Dolley had a young relative, a South Carolinian named Angelica Singleton, who was a graduate of a fashionable Philadelphia school. Angelica was strikingly pretty, and her full lips, wide mouth, and impish look belied her inhibiting name. Dolley introduced Abraham to Angelica. About a year later they were married. Angelica became the presidential hostess and did well.

Even without the depression, Van Buren would have found Andrew Jackson hard to follow. The Democrats nominated Van Buren for re-election in 1840. But the Whigs' "Log Cabin and Hard Cider" campaign for Harrison and John Tyler snowed Van Buren under.

Martin Van Buren retired alone to Lindenwald, his 200-acre (81-hectare) estate along the Hudson River near Kinderhook. He ran unsuccessfully for the presidency again in 1848, as the anti-slavery Free Soil Party candidate. America's eighth president died at Lindenwald on July 24, 1862, and was buried alongside Hannah at Kinderhook.

Hannah Hoes Van Buren died after a prolonged illness in 1819 at the age of 35. Her husband became President 18 years later.

President Van Buren's Times
1837–1841

The U.S. Flag had 25 stars when Van Buren took office. No new states joined the Union. Iowa became a territory in 1838. The U.S. population was about 17,700,000 in 1841.

1837–1838	Rebellions broke out in Upper and Lower Canada.
1837	The first great depression paralyzed the U.S. economy.
1837	Queen Victoria succeeded to the British throne.
1839	Goodyear discovered how to vulcanize rubber.
1839	The first state-supported normal school organized in the United States opened in Massachusetts.
Late 1830's	The Underground Railroad, a system that helped slaves flee the South, became increasingly active.
1840	Britain issued the world's first postage stamp.
1840	The Act of Union joined Upper and Lower Canada.

WILLIAM HENRY HARRISON

9th President of the United States
1841

William Henry Harrison had three distinctions. At age 68 he was the oldest President yet to be inaugurated. He was also the first to die in office. And his death within a month of inauguration made him the President with the shortest term on record.

Harrison was a Virginian, born at Berkeley plantation along the James River in Charles City County, Virginia, on Feb. 9, 1773. The Harrisons traced their American lineage back to early Jamestown, and Harrison's father Benjamin was a signer of the Declaration of Independence.

A tutor taught Harrison at Berkeley. He entered Hampden-Sydney College in Virginia in 1787, but he did not complete his courses. After studying medicine for a time in Richmond and Philadelphia, in 1791 Harrison joined the army at 18 as a junior officer. Posted to Fort Washington, near Cincinnati, he was in the Battle of Fallen Timbers against the Shawnee Indians in 1794.

At about that time Harrison met a North Bend, Ohio, belle, the dark-eyed and sedate Anna Symmes. She was the daughter of John Cleves Symmes, a judge and land speculator in Ohio. Knowing Symmes might disapprove of their marriage, Anna and Harrison eloped on Nov. 25, 1795, and were married by a North Bend justice of the peace. When Symmes learned of this, he confronted the young lieutenant: "How do you expect to support my daughter?" the judge inquired.

"My sword is my means of support, sir!" Harrison replied. He probably meant that he intended to make the army his career. This was not what Judge Symmes liked to hear. He would have preferred a doctor, a lawyer, or a minister—even a farmer.

Harrison and the judge later became good friends, and Wil-

Anna Symmes Harrison was too ill to join her husband at the White House during his ill-fated presidency.

Full name: William Henry Harrison

Born: Feb. 9, 1773

Birthplace: Charles City County, Va.

Died: April 4, 1841

Burial site: North Bend, O.

Spouse: Anna Symmes

Occupation: Soldier

Political party: Whig

Term: 1841

Vice-President: John Tyler

Runner-up: Martin Van Buren

Electoral vote: 234

Runner-up: 60

Popular vote: 1,275,390

Runner-up: 1,128,854

liam Henry and Anna named their first son John Cleves Symmes after him. The Harrisons had four girls and six boys. The last child, James, died at age three. One son, John Scott, was the father of Benjamin Harrison, who was elected as the nation's 23rd President in 1888.

In 1798, William Henry Harrison, then a captain, resigned from the army. He had already bought 160 acres (65 hectares) of land along the Ohio River, and he gradually added to his holdings. Under President John Adams he served as secretary of the Northwest Territory, and later as territorial delegate to Congress and as governor of the Indiana Territory.

Rejoining the army in 1811, Harrison placed his name in military history when his outnumbered forces won the Battle of Tippecanoe, once again against Shawnee. He went on to fight in the War of 1812. For several years after the war, Harrison served as a member of Congress from Ohio.

Known by now as "Old Tippecanoe," Harrison began to express interest in the presidency in 1835. Ignoring tradition, he campaigned publicly for the Whig Party nomination. After about a year of speeches and appearances, in 1836 he became one of three sectional Whig candidates who ran against Democrat Martin Van Buren. Harrison lost the race by nearly 100 electoral votes. "Old Tip" made a decent showing in the popular votes, however, and the Whigs chose him to run again in 1840. They nominated John Tyler of Virginia as his running mate.

President Van Buren had been politically hurt by an economic depression that started in 1837. As the 1840 campaign began, he was hurt more, perhaps, because of a remark that appeared in an article in a Baltimore newspaper. The article was actually favorable to Van Buren. It said that Harrison should withdraw from the race. "Give him a barrel of hard cider and a pension of two thousand a year . . . he will sit the remainder of his days in a log cabin . . . and study moral philosophy."

The Whigs did not let opportunity slip by. They had presented "Old Tip" as a war hero. Now they could also offer Harrison as the candidate of the common people, reared in a rude dwelling, able to afford nothing but the poor person's drink, hard cider. So the "Log Cabin and Hard Cider" campaign was born. Until then Americans had seen nothing like it.

The 1840 campaign featured stump speeches, torchlight parades, clambakes and picnics, slogans, and endless attempts at poetry. Whigs sang to the tune of "The Old Oaken Bucket": "The iron-armed soldier, the true hearted soldier, the gallant old soldier of Tippecanoe." Poking fun at Van Buren, allegedly the candidate of the well-to-do, Whigs sang to a tune long forgotten: "Let Van from his coolers of silver drink wine, and lounge on his cushioned settee; our man on his buck-eye bench can recline, content with hard cider is he." And: "Old Tip he wears a homespun coat, he has no ruffled shirt-wirt-wirt. But Matt he has the golden plate, and he's a little squirt-wirt-wirt." Unlike previous presidential candidates, Harrison made numerous public appearances. He delivered nearly two dozen speeches.

Stimulated by all the hoopla, about 2.4 million voters turned out on election day. About 1.25 million voted for "Tippecanoe and Tyler too," giving Harrison 234 of 294 electoral votes.

Anna became too ill to travel just before Harrison left for Washington. Jane Irwin Harrison, his widowed daughter-in-law, accompanied him. She served as White House hostess for the short time that Harrison was President.

Only a week after Harrison took office, the United States faced a serious crisis with Great Britain. Over three years earlier, a member of the American crew of the steamboat *Caroline* had been killed while carrying supplies to Canadian rebels. Much later, police in Buffalo, N.Y., arrested a visiting Canadian who had been one of the party that attacked the *Caroline*.

The British waited until Van Buren had left office, then demanded the prisoner's release on threat of war. Harrison turned the problem over to Daniel Webster, who apologized. But tension was not eased until Webster negotiated the Webster-Ashburton Treaty in 1842.

Little more can be said about William Henry Harrison's life in the White House. Fate granted Anna insufficient time even to settle in. The President delivered a long inaugural address outside in chilly weather in March 1841. Later that month he came down with pneumonia and he died on April 4, 1841. Anna Symmes Harrison lived until 1864, never having come to the White House.

Jane Irwin Harrison, the President's widowed daughter-in-law, served as White House hostess during his short term.

President William H. Harrison's Times
1841

The U.S. Flag had 26 stars when Harrison took office. No new states or territories were organized. The U.S. population was about 17,700,000 in 1841.

1841   Daniel Webster apologized to Great Britain in the *Caroline* Affair, when Great Britain demanded the release of a Canadian prisoner on threat of war. The case was finally resolved in October when a New York jury acquitted the prisoner.

1841   The United States was at peace during Harrison's one-month term. Louis Philippe, known as the *bourgeois king,* ruled in France. Great Britain had begun its great period of colonial expansion under Queen Victoria. Isabella II was queen of Spain, and Austria continued to rule much of the Italian peninsula.

JOHN TYLER

10th President of the United States
1841–1845

In April 1841, when John Tyler of Virginia became President upon William Henry Harrison's death, old-time southern hospitality returned to the White House. Tyler was old-family Virginian, his ancestry running back to early Jamestown days. He placed a high value on proper appearances. When he assumed the presidency, he told his daughter Elizabeth and her two sisters: "You are now occupying a position of deep importance. I desire you to bear in mind three things; show no favoritism, accept no gifts, receive no seekers after office." For all his propriety, however, Tyler would shock Washington society by the end of his only term.

The 10th President was born on March 29, 1790, in Charles City County, Va. His father, John Sr., was a respected judge, state legislator, and governor.

As a schoolboy Tyler was described as having "a slender frame, a very prominent thin Roman nose, silky brown hair, a bright blue eye, a merry, mischievous smile and silver laugh." To many observers he seemed easy to manage. Yet, the story goes, at about age 10 or 11, he led his classmates in rebellion against the harsh discipline of their schoolmaster, a Mr. McMurdo. The boys tied McMurdo hand and foot, leaving him in the classroom. And there the unfortunate Scot lay until late afternoon, when a passerby heard his cries and released him.

McMurdo complained to Tyler's father, demanding that he punish John. The judge simply reminded the outraged teacher of Virginia's motto: *Sic Semper Tyrannis* (Thus Always to Tyrants).

Completing William and Mary College at 17, Tyler studied law under his father. While still in his teens he also met Letitia

John Tyler

Letitia Christian Tyler, who suffered a stroke in the late 1830's, remained an invalid in the White House until her death in 1842.

Christian of the Cedar Grove plantation, near Richmond. The courtship lasted several years. At last, though, Tyler could write to a friend in March 1813: "On the 29th instant I lead my Letitia to the altar. I had really calculated on experiencing a tremor on the near approach of the day, but I believe I am so much of the old man already as to feel less dismay at a change of situation than the greater part of those of my age." John and Letitia Tyler had seven children that survived infancy and childhood. Elizabeth, the third daughter, became the second child of a President to be married in the White House. She wed William Waller in the East Room on Jan. 31, 1842.

Tyler served in the Virginia legislature, as governor, and in Congress. He was in the Whig Party and had been elected Vice-President as a Whig in 1840. Yet he opposed principles that other Whigs held dear. Among these were federal aid for business and internal improvements such as roads and canals. He also came out against a high protective tariff, which taxed imports to help American industry.

No sooner had Tyler become President than he was in trouble with the Whigs in Congress, who were led by Henry Clay. Tyler vetoed bill after bill, including one for a national bank. Infuriated Whigs called him "Old Veto," but Tyler firmly believed that he acted in the best interests of the country. Relations became so strained that in March 1845, Congress overrode a presidential veto for the first time in history.

Besides his constant squabbling with Congress, John Tyler is remembered for bringing the Lone Star State into the Union. Just before he left office in March 1845, he signed a congressional resolution approving the annexation of Texas, then an independent nation.

In Tyler's time, Washington, D.C., held more than 35,000 persons. It had still not become a pleasant place in which to live. The English author Charles Dickens called it a community "of spacious avenues that begin in nothing and lead nowhere." Pennsylvania Avenue had been paved with macadam, which consisted of small, broken stones. The avenue got street lighting with gas lamps in 1842, but for years it was the only Washington thoroughfare with lights. The Capitol remained the city's most imposing building, but it, too, had shortcomings. Near the spot where Congress met lay a cow pasture, a mosquito-breeding swamp filled with croaking frogs, a slaughterhouse, and pigpens.

Life in the White House was more genteel, although Letitia Tyler, who had suffered a stroke in the late 1830's, remained an invalid. Priscilla Cooper Tyler, wife of the President's son Robert, served as White House hostess. Letitia died in September 1842.

Not long after that, the beautiful young socialite, Julia Gardiner of New York City, met the President and charmed him. At 54, John Tyler became the first President to be married while in office.

Tyler and Julia, then 24, were married in New York City on June 26, 1844, and tongues wagged furiously at this May-December match. Former President John Quincy Adams, then a member of Congress from Massachusetts, recorded in his diary

Full name: John Tyler

Born: March 29, 1790

Birthplace: Charles City County, Va.

Died: Jan. 18, 1862

Burial site: Richmond, Va.

Spouses: Letitia Christian; Julia Gardiner

Occupation: Lawyer

Political party: Whig

Term: 1841–1845

that the couple was the laughingstock of Washington. Nevertheless, the marriage was a happy one and resulted in seven children. This made Tyler the father of 15 offspring, the oldest born in 1815, the youngest in 1860. He had more children than any other President.

Thoroughly unpopular with the Whigs by 1844, John Tyler stood no chance of nomination in his own right for the presidency. In March 1845, he and Julia retired to plantation life at Sherwood Forest in Charles City County.

Tyler remained loyal to his native state when Virginia seceded from the Union in 1861. Elected to the Confederate Congress, he died in Richmond on Jan. 18, 1862, before he could take his seat.

At age 24, Julia Gardiner became the youngest first lady up to that time upon marriage to John Tyler in June 1844, causing much talk among Washington socialites.

President Tyler's Times
1841–1845

The U.S. Flag had 26 stars when Tyler took office. Florida became a state in 1845. No new territories were organized. The U.S. population was about 20,200,000 in 1845.

Early 1840's Settlers began to follow the 2,000-mile (3,219-kilometer) Oregon Trail, which opened the way for settlement of the Pacific Northwest.

1842–1843 China opened its ports to world trade.

1842–1845 Kit Carson and John C. Frémont explored vast parts of the western United States, traveling as far west as California.

1843 The Hudson's Bay Company founded Camosun (later Fort Victoria) in Canada.

1844 Samuel Morse successfully demonstrated his electric telegraph before the members of Congress.

JAMES K. POLK

11th President of the United States
1845–1849

James K. Polk was a workaholic. As President, he put in long hours every day, personally overseeing almost every detail, just as he had done in every other position he had held. He was absent from Washington, D.C., for only about six weeks during his four years in office. His wife, Sarah, kept up with him. Not only was she White House hostess, she was her husband's personal secretary as well.

Polk's ancestors were Presbyterian Scotch-Irish. Robert Pollok (or Polke) migrated from northern Ireland to Maryland in 1687. James was born Nov. 2, 1795, on a farm in Mecklenburg County, N.C. He was Samuel and Jane Polk's first child, and nine others followed him. When Polk was about 11 years old, the family moved to Tennessee.

Sam Polk considered his eldest son too frail and sickly to go to school, so the boy learned to read and write at home. Then, when he was 16, it was discovered that Polk suffered from gallstones. After what was then a daring operation to remove the stones, his life changed completely. Energy and ambition now flowed in the youth, and at 17 he entered an academy to prepare for the University of North Carolina. He graduated from the university at the head of his class in 1818. Polk then studied law in Felix Grundy's office in Nashville, and Grundy introduced the young man to Andrew Jackson. When Polk was 26, he became reacquainted with Sarah Childress, the sister of a classmate.

Ambition drove Sarah as hard as it did Polk. Scarcely had they met than Sarah was urging James to run for the Tennessee legislature. He considered himself too young, poor, and inexperienced. But Sarah prevailed, and with Andrew Jackson's approval and support, Polk entered the race in 1823.

Sarah Childress Polk, who matched her husband in hard work and ambition, was his personal secretary as well as hostess in the White House.

Full name: James Knox Polk

Born: Nov. 2, 1795

Birthplace: Near Pineville, N.C.

Died: June 15, 1849

Burial site: Nashville, Tenn.

Spouse: Sarah Childress

Occupation: Lawyer

Political party: Democratic

Term: 1845–1849

Vice-President: George M. Dallas

Runner-up: Henry Clay

Electoral vote: 170

Runner-up: 105

Popular vote: 1,339,494

Runner-up: 1,300,004

Polk was then 5 feet, 7 inches (170 centimeters) tall. His physique was slender. He was an earnest speaker, and he developed into a forceful one during the campaign, earning the nickname "Napoleon of the Stump," referring to the fact that speeches on the frontier often were delivered from tree stumps. Polk won election to the legislature, and he and Sarah were married on Jan. 1, 1824.

From then on the Polks' life was almost entirely politics. He was elected to the U.S. House of Representatives from Tennessee in 1825. He served there 14 years, some of the time as speaker of the House. Polk's ambition for the presidency grew, and to further it he ran for and won the Tennessee governorship in 1839.

As a member of the House and as governor, Polk displayed the same avid attention to work and detail that would characterize him as President. In Washington, D.C., and in Nashville, he and Sarah gave little time to social life. Declining a dinner invitation, Polk once asserted: "I cannot lose half a day just to go and dine." Church was another matter. Nothing kept the Polks from services every Sunday.

James K. Polk's chance for the nation's highest office came in 1844. Former President Martin Van Buren was the favorite at the Democratic convention in Baltimore that year. Lewis Cass of Michigan also enjoyed support. But neither could muster sufficient votes. The nomination went to Polk on the ninth ballot. He won the 1844 election with 170 electoral votes to Whig candidate Henry Clay's 105.

Inauguration day 1845 was miserable. Contrary to expectations, rain fell without letup. For many people the inaugural ball that night was equally dismal, at least as long as the Polks remained there.

The Polks brought to the presidency a strong Calvinistic heritage upholding the value of hard work. They also carried an equally strong distaste for alcohol, card-playing, and dancing. Arriving at the inaugural ball, Polk ordered dancing stopped. He and Sarah greeted each guest in turn. The dancing started again when the Polks left two hours later.

Under the Polks, no liquor was served in the White House and no food was served at the twice-weekly public receptions. The ban on dancing continued. Once asked why she opposed it in the White House, Sarah Polk replied: "To dance in these rooms would be undignified, and it would be respectful neither to the house nor to the office."

Yet the presidential mansion was no drab and cheerless place during the Polk Administration. The President and first lady presided over interesting parties. Both kept abreast of affairs of the day through newspapers and books, and there was plenty to talk about at dinners. Sarah often became so engrossed in table conversation that she forgot to eat.

James K. Polk had run for the presidency on a program of territorial expansion. He promised a strong and growing America, one that other nations would need to reckon with. He kept his word. After threatening war with Great Britain over the northern boundary of what is now the state of Washington, Polk settled the dispute peacefully and to America's advantage. War with Mexico between 1846 and 1848 gained a sizable por-

This cartoon of the 1840's shows that the President did not fear England — the lion — during the Oregon boundary dispute.

tion of western territory for the United States. James K. Polk rests in history as the most expansionist of all Presidents.

Polk said when he entered office that he would not run for a second term. He wanted to work for the good of the country and not be distracted by the politics of preparing for a second race. He kept that promise, too.

Sarah and James Polk left Washington in March 1849. But in a little more than three months, Polk died of cholera. Childless, Sarah Polk retired to the family home in Nashville. Her 42 years of life as a widow ended on Aug. 14, 1891. She was almost 88.

President Polk's Times
1845–1849

The U.S. Flag had 26 stars when Polk took office. Three states joined the Union: Texas in 1845, Iowa in 1846, and Wisconsin in 1848. Two territories were organized: Oregon in 1848 and Minnesota in 1849. The U.S. population was about 22,700,000 in 1849.

1845	The U.S. Naval Academy was founded by Congress.
1846	The sewing machine was patented by Elias Howe.
1847	The first U.S. postage stamps were issued.
1847	Liberia became the first black republic in Africa.
1848	The Treaty of Guadalupe Hidalgo ended the war with Mexico.
1848	Marx and Engels issued *The Communist Manifesto.*
1848	Gold was discovered in California.

ZACHARY TAYLOR

12th President of the United States
1849–1850

At any time other than the late 1840's, Zachary Taylor may
have seemed an unlikely presidential candidate. His short, ungainly frame, usually draped in rumpled clothing, hardly in-
spired public confidence. Although he became a major general,
Taylor had not gone to West Point. He had furthermore spent
most of his career at obscure frontier army posts. Taylor had
never voted for President, and most people figured he knew
nothing about politics.

Still, the 63-year-old Taylor had one important achievement
in the summer of 1848. He was "Old Rough and Ready," hero
of the Battle of Buena Vista in the Mexican War, which had
ended in February. And after he became the Whig Party candidate for President that year, Taylor showed that while he might
be simple, he was no simpleton. As for politicians, no one at
that time rose in army ranks without knowing how to deal with
them. The major general proved deft at politics.

Most of Zachary Taylor's forebears were from Virginia, although he traced one family branch back to New England and
the *Mayflower.* His father, Colonel Richard Taylor of Virginia,
had fought in the Revolutionary War. James Madison, the
fourth President, had been Taylor's second cousin. Robert E. Lee,
to become famous in the Civil War, was also a relative.

Taylor was born in Orange County, Va., on Nov. 24, 1784.
He was a third son and he had five brothers and three sisters.
The Taylor family moved to Kentucky when he was an infant,
and Zachary grew up on a farm near Louisville. He had practically no formal education, but he learned to read and write.

In 1808 Taylor joined the army, his family having enough

Z. Taylor.

Margaret Smith Taylor lived the rugged life of a frontier army officer's wife. Her poor health made her avoid many White House functions.

Full name: Zachary Taylor

Born: Nov. 24, 1784

Birthplace: Orange County, Va.

Died: July 9, 1850

Burial site: Louisville, Ky.

Spouse: Margaret Mackall Smith

Occupation: Soldier

Political party: Whig

Term: 1849-1850

Vice-President: Millard Fillmore

Runner-up: Lewis Cass

Electoral vote: 163

Runner-up: 127

Popular vote: 1,361,393

Runner-up: 1,223,460

political connections for him to begin service as a first lieutenant. Two years later, he married Margaret Mackall Smith, daughter of a prominent planter family in Calvert County, Md.

For Margaret, life on the frontier military posts was a far cry from her genteel upbringing, but she put up with inconvenience and unfamiliar hardship as an army wife. And there were off-duty times when the Taylors could spend weeks at their home in Baton Rouge, La., or on the cotton plantation they bought in Mississippi, upriver from Baton Rouge.

Two Taylor daughters died in infancy. Three others, Ann, Sarah, and Mary Elizabeth (Betty) all married army officers. Sarah became the wife of the future President of the Confederacy, Jefferson Davis, only to die of malaria three months after the wedding. The Taylors sent their son Richard to Harvard and Yale, and he later became a general in the Confederate Army.

Zachary Taylor was on the Indiana frontier during the War of 1812. He fought in the Black Hawk War in what are now Wisconsin and Illinois in 1832. Between 1837 and 1840, he campaigned in Florida in the Second Seminole War. From 1840 to 1845 the Taylors moved to Fort Smith in Arkansas, to Fort Gibson in Oklahoma, and to Fort Jesup in Louisiana. President James K. Polk then sent Taylor to command troops in territory in dispute between Mexico and the United States south of the Nueces River in southern Texas. Mexican forces had fired on U.S. soldiers there, killing 11. Congress declared war on Mexico May 13, 1846.

Taylor led his army south, fighting battles at Palo Alto and Resaca de la Palma in southern Texas and at Monterrey, Mexico. Taylor's forces then made the Mexican army withdraw from a mountain pass near Buena Vista, Mexico. That battle made Taylor a national hero.

The Whigs believed they needed a national hero to take the 1848 election. Taylor won, beating his Democratic opponent, Lewis Cass of Michigan, by 163 to 127 electoral votes.

Taylor's victory dismayed Margaret. Only reluctantly did she leave their comfortable home in Baton Rouge to move to Washing-

General Taylor at the Battle of Buena Vista in 1847.

ton, D.C. Gossips said Margaret avoided public appearances because she liked to smoke a corncob pipe. This had no foundation in fact, and Margaret never responded to the stories.

Taylor ran an open and friendly administration. He usually appeared at summer receptions on the White House lawn, greeting guests and shaking hands while his favorite army horse, Old Whitey, placidly cropped grass off to the side. For relaxation, Taylor took morning strolls along Washington streets, his high black hat perched on top of his head.

Mary Elizabeth Bliss, the youngest daughter of the Taylors, assumed her mother's duties as first lady.

The controversy over extending slavery reasserted itself during the Taylor Administration. Although he himself owned more than 100 slaves, he did not favor slavery's extension. The Compromise of 1850 did not suit him. It allowed the lands won from Mexico that were organized into the territories of Utah and New Mexico to decide the question of slavery for themselves. Before the issue was settled, though, Zachary Taylor was dead. The President attended the capital's celebration on July 4, 1850, a hot and humid day. He sat on a platform near the Washington Monument, then under construction. Returning to the White House, Taylor drank cold water and iced milk and ate some raw food—some sources say cherries. He fell ill and died on July 9 in the White House. Vice-President Millard Fillmore became President. Margaret Taylor died two years later.

In 1991, Taylor's body was exhumed in an effort to determine the 12th President's cause of death. The exhumation was prompted when a Florida author researching Taylor's life pointed out that Taylor's symptoms at the time of his death were consistent with acute arsenic poisoning. This observation fueled the theory that Taylor may have been murdered because he opposed the spread of slavery. However, a medical examiner determined beyond doubt that Taylor was not poisoned.

President Taylor's Times
1849-1850

The U.S. Flag had 30 stars when Taylor took office. No new states or territories were organized. The U.S. population was about 23,300,000 in 1850.

1849-1850	Debates over slavery in Congress came close to bringing about a civil war. President Taylor opposed any compromise with slave states.
1849	The California Gold Rush began. Thousands of gold seekers, or "Forty-Niners," hurried westward by covered wagon, train, and ship.
1849	The Department of the Interior was created.
1849	Uprisings swept central Europe. Austria crushed revolution in Hungary.
1849	Lajos Kossuth, leader of the Hungarian revolt, toured the United States and was hailed a hero.

MILLARD FILLMORE

13th President of the United States
1850–1853

A year or so before Millard Fillmore's birth, his parents were victimized in an ill-advised land deal in New York state. All the Fillmores had been New Englanders since the first, John, came to Massachusetts in 1704. Then about 1798, tired of scraping for a living, trying to wrench a crop from reluctant Vermont soil, Phoebe and Nathaniel Fillmore headed farther west. Visions of fertile land of their own and a better life in central New York sustained them on their journey. But instead of prosperity, they found only continued poverty.

Nathaniel had bought the acreage from a land promoter without seeing it. The soil turned out to be poor, and a streak of clay that hampered drainage lay beneath it. The weather was worse, and the Fillmore title to the land proved defective. Within a few months Nathaniel and Phoebe gave it all up and moved south to what is now Niles, in Cayuga County, N.Y. There they settled into a farm life as perpetual renters. All that cheered them through this entire ordeal was the birth of their son on Jan. 7, 1800. They named him Millard, his mother's maiden name.

Millard Fillmore was born in a cabin, and he grew up poor. He learned to plow, hoe corn, mow hay, reap wheat, and perform other backbreaking farm chores. He did not cherish that life, and he broke away from it as soon as he could.

Fillmore went off to an academy in New Hope, N.Y. for a brief time when he was 19, but he gained most of what he learned from books on his own. More important for his future, he met Abigail Powers, a minister's daughter, at New Hope. She was 21.

Abigail Powers, who saw promise in the young Millard Fillmore, encouraged him to study law and married him in February 1826 after a courtship lasting several years.

Abigail's gentle nature attracted the raw farm youth, as did her dark eyes and long black hair drawn tightly to her head in a bun. She was equally taken by this dignified handsome young man, 6 feet (183 centimeters) tall. They saw each other often, but there would be no marriage until he proved himself.

He did, by a means common at the time to those wishing to rise in the world. By 1823, while teaching in an elementary school, Fillmore learned enough law to call himself a lawyer. The way upward was far from easy, though, and the young couple did not marry until Feb. 5, 1826, in Moravia, N.Y. Their son, Millard Powers, was born in April 1828. A daughter, Mary Abigail, was born in March four years later.

After his marriage, Fillmore's path to fortune smoothed. He won admission to practice before the state supreme court, and he built up a good law business in East Aurora, N.Y.

Fillmore got into politics with the Anti-Masonic movement in New York in the late 1820's. As an Anti-Mason, he won a seat in the state legislature. There he became acquainted with such future Whig Party leaders as Thurlow Weed and William Seward. As Anti-Masonic feeling petered out, Fillmore attached himself to the Whigs and worked his way up in that party. Eventually, in the 1830's, Fillmore became a Whig member of the U.S. House of Representatives. Then in 1848, he was elected Vice-President on a Whig ticket headed by Zachary Taylor.

Fillmore favored the Compromise of 1850, which was to settle the issue of extending slavery once and for all. The compromise passed Congress soon after Fillmore became President upon Taylor's death in 1850. Another significant event of the Fillmore Administration was Commodore Matthew C. Perry's expedition to Japan in 1852–1854. This marked the beginning of America's role as a power in the Pacific Ocean.

Abigail Fillmore installed a stove of "small hotel size" in the White House basement kitchen, replacing the open fireplace that had been used for preparing food. The Fillmores served no liquor in the White House—Fillmore was known even to avoid hotels where it was served. Finding no Bible, no dictionary, nor any other book in the mansion, Abigail had the President ask Congress for a library. Congress voted $250 to buy books.

Full name: Millard Fillmore

Born: Jan. 7, 1800

Birthplace: Locke, N.Y.

Died: March 8, 1874

Burial site: Buffalo, N.Y.

Spouse: Abigail Powers

Occupation: Lawyer

Political party: Whig

Term: 1850–1853

Daniel Webster (standing at right) spoke for the preservation of the Union during a Senate debate on the Compromise of 1850.

The Whigs passed over Fillmore in 1852, nominating instead General Winfield "Fuss and Feathers" Scott, who was, like Taylor, a hero of the Mexican War. Topping Fillmore's political disappointment, Abigail died of pneumonia on March 30, 1853, less than a month after they had left the White House. Mary died of cholera at 22 the following year.

Facing a lonely retirement, Fillmore devoted his time to practicing law. He also gave attention to the University of Buffalo, of which he was honorary chancellor; to Buffalo General Hospital, which he had helped found; and to the Buffalo Historical Society.

Fillmore tried for the presidency again in 1856. He was nominated by both the Whig Party and the American, or Know-Nothing, Party, an ultra-conservative group. But he was scarcely an also-ran. To most Americans, slavery had become the most important issue by that time.

In 1858, Fillmore married a wealthy widow, Caroline Carmichael McIntosh. Her wealth, plus his income from investments, enabled them to purchase a huge, ornate mansion on Niagara Square in Buffalo. They entertained often there, among the numerous portraits and busts of her husband that Caroline installed. Entertainment fell off, however, after Caroline fell ill in the late 1860's. She eventually became a chronic invalid.

In January 1874, Fillmore wrote: "My health is perfect, I eat, drink and sleep as well as ever, and take a deep but silent interest in public affairs, and if Mrs. F's health can be restored, I should feel that I was in the enjoyment of an earthly paradise."

Then fortune frowned. Fillmore suffered a stroke in the middle of February, while he was shaving. Another hit him two weeks later, and he died on March 8, 1874.

Mary Abigail Fillmore, the Fillmores' only daughter, often served as White House hostess due to her mother's poor health.

President Fillmore's Times
1850–1853

The U.S. Flag had 30 stars when Fillmore took office. California became a state in 1850. Three territories were organized: New Mexico in 1850, Utah in 1850, and Washington in 1853. The U.S. population was about 25,700,000 in 1853.

1850–1851	Amelia Bloomer wore long pantaloons to draw attention to the woman suffrage movement. Her followers became known as "Bloomer Girls."
1852	Direct rail service began between New York City and Chicago.
1852	The slavery issue flared after the publication of *Uncle Tom's Cabin.*
1852	Henri Giffard flew the first successful airship.
1852	Commodore Perry left for Japan to open that country to world trade.

FRANKLIN PIERCE

14th President of the United States
1853–1857

"Everything in that mansion seems cold and cheerless," a White House visitor during the Franklin Pierce Administration wrote. "I have seen hundreds of log cabins which seemed to contain more happiness." There was good reason for that gloom.

In January 1853, having won election the previous November, Pierce was on a train returning to New Hampshire after a visit in Massachusetts. With him were his wife Jane and their son Benjamin. The train derailed. Pierce and Jane escaped injury, but 11-year-old Bennie was killed. He had been the last son. One boy had died shortly after birth, another of typhus at age 4. To Jane Pierce, Bennie's tragic end was a final blow. The loss preyed on Pierce's mind for months, too.

The Pierces of Franklin's line traced to Thomas, who emigrated from England to Charlestown, Mass., in the mid-1630's. Franklin's father Benjamin served in the Revolutionary War. Later he was a member of the New Hampshire legislature and, in the 1820's, was that state's governor. Franklin was born on Nov. 23, 1804, in what was Hillsborough Lower Village, N.H.

After elementary school, Pierce attended several academies, entering Bowdoin College in Brunswick, Me., at 15. There he found the rules strict, though probably not insurmountable.

"No students shall . . . attend any theatrical entertainment or any idle show in Brunswick or Topsham, nor frequent any tavern or any house or shop after being forbidden by the president," one rule said. Another forbade students to "play at cards, billiards, or any game of hazard nor at any game whatever for money or other things of value." And, finally, "Students must be in their rooms Saturday and Sunday evenings and abstain

Tragedy struck Jane Pierce when her only surviving son, Benjamin, died in a train accident at 11, before his father's inauguration.

Full name: Franklin Pierce

Born: Nov. 23, 1804

Birthplace: Hillsboro, N.H.

Died: Oct. 8, 1869

Burial site: Concord, N.H.

Spouse: Jane Means Appleton

Occupation: Lawyer

Political party: Democratic

Term: 1853–1857

Vice-President: William R. D. King

Runner-up: Winfield Scott

Electoral vote: 254

Runner-up: 42

Popular vote: 1,607,510

Runner-up: 1,386,942

from diversions of every kind. They who profane the Sabbath . . . may be admonished or suspended."

Pierce mastered the Greek, Latin, mathematics, and science curriculum at Bowdoin and graduated close to the top of his class in 1824. Next he studied law. Between 1829 and 1842, he served in the New Hampshire legislature, the U.S. House of Representatives, and the Senate.

Pierce met Jane Means Appleton, daughter of a former Bowdoin president, in the 1820's. She was pretty, with dark curly hair framing fine facial features. She was also shy and had suffered from tuberculosis. Jane and Franklin were married in November 1834.

The match was not the best. She hated Washington, D.C., a town much too dirty and primitive for her taste. Pierce loved politics and life in Congress. Jane also hated liquor. Drinking went with politics there, and Pierce drank with the rest. At last, in 1842 Jane persuaded her husband to resign from the Senate. They moved to Concord, N.H. where he practiced law.

Pierce enlisted in the U.S. Army as a private when the Mexican War began in 1846. His Democratic friend, President James K. Polk, soon made him a brigadier general. Pierce saw some action under General Winfield Scott during the American advance on Mexico City.

In June 1852, Pierce appeared at the Democratic convention in Baltimore as a possible presidential contender from New Hampshire. No one gave him much of a chance. Stephen A. Douglas of Illinois, Lewis Cass of Michigan, James Buchanan of Pennsylvania, and William L. Marcy of New York far overshadowed him. But the frontrunners deadlocked, and Pierce won the nomination on the 49th ballot.

Thinking of Andrew Jackson, someone during the 1852 campaign dubbed Pierce "Young Hickory of the Granite Hills"— meaning New Hampshire. He won 254 of 296 electoral votes, beating his old commander, General Scott. Pierce at 48 became the youngest President up to that time.

Pierce did not read his inaugural address. He had memorized it, so he could gaze out and constantly address his audience directly. Jane was not there to witness the warm applause her husband received, however. Almost a month passed before she could force herself to come from Baltimore, where she was staying with friends, to live once more in Washington—even as first lady. Her Aunt Abby Kent Means would serve as White House hostess part of the time.

In a campaign biography in 1852, Pierce's good friend and New England author Nathaniel Hawthorne had written that Pierce had in him "many of the chief elements of a great ruler . . . he has a subtle faculty of making affairs roll onward according to his will, and of influencing their course without showing any trace of his action." As it turned out, Pierce influenced few domestic events during his term. Centered on the increasingly bitter slavery controversy, affairs rolled on without much help or hindrance from him.

Fiery speeches filled Congress early in 1854 during debate over the Kansas-Nebraska Act, a measure designed to form two new territories out of Indian land in the West. The act would allow settlers there to decide whether to permit slavery, and slavery and anti-slavery forces soon began fighting in armed clashes for control of Kansas. The Democratic Party split over slavery, and the Whig Party disintegrated. A new group, the Republican Party, formed in 1854.

Pierce was bold and somewhat successful in foreign affairs. Though the plan fell through, in 1853 he advocated the annexation of Hawaii. The Gadsden Purchase of 1853 provided the country with a southern railroad route to the Pacific Coast and settled the boundary question with Mexico. At Pierce's insistence, the Senate ratified a trade treaty with Japan in 1854. This treaty opened Japan to American trading interests.

Acts of this kind fit well with the attitude of the American people, who believed in national expansion. But when three of Pierce's diplomats claimed in 1854 that the United States had the right to seize Cuba from Spain, the public reacted against the President.

When Pierce's troubled term ended, he did not get a chance at a second. In 1856 the Democrats nominated James Buchanan instead. Buchanan had been out of the country serving as minister to Great Britain, and thus had not been identified with the controversial Kansas-Nebraska Act.

After leaving the White House in 1857, the Pierces traveled widely in the United States and Europe. They settled in Concord once again in 1860, and Franklin Pierce died there on Oct. 8, 1869.

President Pierce's Times
1853–1857

The U.S. Flag had 31 stars when Pierce took office. No new states joined the Union. Two territories were organized: Kansas in 1854 and Nebraska in 1854. The U.S. population was about 29,000,000 in 1857.

1853–1856	Turkey, and later Britain, France, and Sardinia, fought against Russia in the Crimean War.
1853	The Gadsden Purchase was signed.
1854–1856	The Republican Party was organized.
1854	About 400,000 immigrants arrived in New York City.
1855	The Soo Canal opened to shipping.
1856	Bleeding Kansas became a battleground between slavery and anti-slavery forces.
1856	Henry Bessemer patented the Bessemer converter.

JAMES BUCHANAN

15th President of the United States
1857–1861

James Buchanan's presidency was not a fitting end to his decades of public service. The increasingly bitter slavery controversy damaged every presidential administration in the 1850's, his most of all. Buchanan's efforts to hold the Union together failed, and his reputation as a leader suffered.

Buchanan's father James immigrated to America from Ireland in 1783, just as the Revolutionary War ended. He established a farm and a trading post at Stony Batter, near Mercersburg, Pa. In 1788, he married Elizabeth Speer. They had 11 children, three of whom died in infancy. The younger James, born on April 23, 1791, was the first son and second child.

Elizabeth Buchanan provided her children with their early education, along with training in the Presbyterian religion. She was a great storyteller, and among her favorites were tales of American heroes, especially George Washington.

At 16, Buchanan entered Dickinson College in Carlisle, Pa. Dickinson needed much improvement in the eyes of Jeremiah Atwater, its new president. Atwater complained of scandalous behavior among the students. He said they were "indulging in the dissipation of the town, none of them living in the college," and he prayed: "I hope that as God has visited other states, he will yet visit Pennsylvania."

Young Buchanan entered into the spirit of the place. As he later wrote: "Without much natural tendency to become dissipated, and chiefly from the example of others, and in order to be considered a clever and spirited youth, I engaged in every sort of extravagance and mischief." Still, he did well in Latin, Greek, mathematics, history, and other courses.

James Buchanan

Harriet Lane, James Buchanan's niece, served as White House hostess for the only bachelor President.

After graduation in 1809, Buchanan studied law in Lancaster, Pa. He opened his own practice in 1812 and in 1814 won election to the state legislature. Five years after that the tall, broad-shouldered young man with blue eyes and wavy blond hair became engaged to Ann Caroline Coleman.

Ann Coleman was rich as well as beautiful. Her father Robert, a strong-willed and hot-tempered person, was one of America's earliest millionaires through success in the iron manufacturing business. His wealth made him wary of young men's attentions to his daughters, including James Buchanan's.

Lancaster gossip soon had it that James was interested mainly in Ann Coleman's money. Coleman persuaded Ann that this was so. The final straw came when James paid a casual visit to another young woman. Ann broke off the engagement, a bitter blow to Buchanan. But a more dreadful event was yet to come.

While visiting a sister in Philadelphia in December 1819, Ann Coleman died. Grief-stricken, Buchanan sent a note to her parents: "It is now no time for explanation, but the time will come when you will discover that she, as well as I, have been much abused. God forgive the authors of it . . . I may sustain the shock of her death, but I feel that happiness has fled from me forever." The letter was returned unopened. The cause of Ann Coleman's death was never clear, and James Buchanan never married.

Buchanan plunged into politics and government service between 1821 and 1861. He was a Federalist member of the U.S. House of Representatives but became a Democrat in 1828. He served as minister to Russia from 1831 to 1833 and as a U.S. senator from Pennsylvania from 1834 to 1845. He was also secretary of state under President James K. Polk and minister to Great Britain under President Franklin Pierce.

The Democratic presidential nomination in 1856 may have been a reward to Buchanan for faithful service. More importantly, however, he had been serving as U.S. minister in London and had taken no stand on the Kansas-Nebraska Act in 1854. Leading Democrats had lost popularity as a result.

The measure added two new territories from land in the West and allowed settlers there to decide whether to allow or ban slavery. Violence quickly broke out in Kansas as forces favoring and opposing slavery fought for control. When the election came, Buchanan failed to win a popular majority but posted a large electoral majority over Republican John C. Frémont.

Buchanan installed his niece, Harriet Lane, as White House hostess. He had been her guardian since she was 9. Harriet received a good education and she spent time with Buchanan in London. She knew Washington society and was well prepared to guide White House social affairs smoothly. Among other events, she oversaw the reception for the first Japanese diplomatic delegation to Washington, D.C., in May 1860. "They take down notes of everything," Buchanan wrote. "Nothing escapes them. They've got a long description of how I looked."

Although opposed to slavery himself, President Buchanan tried to steer a compromise course on this issue. He sought some middle ground on the question of whether Kansas should enter the Union as a slave or a free state. But from all political quar-

Full name: James Buchanan

Born: April 23, 1791

Birthplace: Stony Batter, Pa.

Died: June 1, 1868

Burial site: Lancaster, Pa.

Occupation: Lawyer

Political party: Democratic

Term: 1857–1861

Vice-President: John C. Breckinridge

Runner-up: John C. Frémont

Electoral vote: 174

Runner-up: 114

Popular vote: 1,836,072

Runner-up: 1,342,345

Southerners who left regular Democrats to form a sectional party
gather at St. Andrew's Hall in Charleston, S.C., in 1860.

ters his efforts brought charges such as his being "pro-Southern"
and a "conspirator." Kansas came in as a free state as Buchanan's term ended—about the time that seven Southern states seceded to form the Confederacy.

Buchanan sought to confine the Confederacy to those seven.
By patiently avoiding rash action, he hoped to retain the loyalty
of the eight slave states still in the Union. But some Southerners
thought Buchanan was too hard on the South and some Northerners criticized him for being too soft.

In 1861 Buchanan retired from the presidency much ma-
ligned. He spent his remaining years at Wheatland, an estate
near Lancaster, and died there at 77 on June 1, 1868.

President Buchanan's Times
1857–1861

The U.S. Flag had 31 stars when Buchanan took office. Three
states joined the Union: Minnesota in 1858, Oregon in 1859, and
Kansas in 1861. Three territories were organized: Colorado in
1861, Nevada in 1861, and Dakota in 1861. The U.S. population
was about 32,400,000 in 1861.

1858	The first Atlantic cable was laid but soon failed.
1858	The Lincoln-Douglas debates, held in Illinois, focused attention on the question of slavery.
1859	Construction began on the Suez Canal.
1859	John Brown seized Harper's Ferry.
1859	Darwin published his theory of evolution.
1860	The Pony Express system was established.
1861	The Confederate States were organized with Jefferson Davis as President.

ABRAHAM LINCOLN

16th President of the United States
1861–1865

At the hands of the press, Abraham Lincoln fared badly during much of his presidency. Referring to him as "Honest Ape," *The New York World* stated: "his instincts are vulgar, his education narrow, his manners a cross between a boor and a buffoon. As a statesman, he selects the unfittest instruments for the most important functions." The *World* then went on to criticize Lincoln's choices for his Cabinet. In 1864 James Gordon Bennett of the *New York Herald* wrote:

> President Lincoln is a joke incarnated. . . . The idea that . . . he should be the President of such a country as this is a very ridiculous joke. . . . His début in Washington society was a joke; for he introduced himself and Mrs. Lincoln as "the long and short of the Presidency. . . ." His conversation is full of jokes. . . . His title of "Honest" Abe is a satirical joke.

During the dark days of the Civil War, as incompetent generals lost vital battles, sacrificing the lives of thousands, Lincoln himself had strong doubts. "I claim not to have controlled events," he told a newspaper reporter in 1864, "but confess plainly that events have controlled me."

Yet the people of the North stayed with Lincoln. They reelected him President in 1864 by a solid majority. And today Lincoln's greatness is clearly seen. He never wavered from his primary goal—to save the Union—and he saw the nation through its most dreadful experience, war between Americans.

A. Lincoln

Mary Todd Lincoln, a native of Kentucky, married the Illinois lawyer in 1842.

Full name: Abraham Lincoln

Born: Feb. 12, 1809

Birthplace: Hardin (now Larue) County, Ky.

Died: April 15, 1865

Burial site: Springfield, Ill.

Spouse: Mary Todd

Occupation: Lawyer

Political party: Republican

Terms: 1861–1865

Vice-Presidents: Hannibal Hamlin; Andrew Johnson

Runners-up: Stephen A. Douglas; George B. McClellan

Electoral votes: 180; 212

Runners-up: 12; 21. In the first election, two nominees, John C. Breckinridge of the Southern faction of the Democratic Party and John Bell of the Constitutional Union, both finished ahead of Douglas in electoral votes. Breckinridge received 72 and Bell 39.

Popular votes: 1,865,908; 2,218,388

Runners-up: 1,380,202; 1,812,807

With the Emancipation Proclamation, he took the first great step toward ridding the nation of slavery.

The Lincoln line that produced the 16th President came early to America. Samuel Lincoln, a weaver of Hingham, England, settled in Hingham, Mass., in 1637. Descendants scattered throughout New England, and south and west. Abraham Lincoln, of the fifth generation, moved his family from Virginia to Hughes Station, near Louisville, Ky., in 1782. He was killed by Indians while at work on his farm.

Thomas, Abraham's youngest son, eventually settled in Hardin (now LaRue) County, Ky. There he married Nancy Hanks in June 1806. Sarah was born to them the following year and Abraham, the future President, was born on Feb. 12, 1809. A third child, Thomas, who was born in 1811 or 1812, died in infancy.

As they grew, Sarah and Abraham kept busy at farm chores and managed to squeeze in a little time at a log schoolhouse 2 miles (3.2 kilometers) from home. Their father, like many pioneers, had trouble with title to his land. So the family set out in December 1816 to cross the Ohio River for a new home in Indiana. "It was a wild region, with many bears and other wild animals still in the woods," Abraham Lincoln remembered as an adult. The Lincolns settled along Little Pigeon Creek, 16 miles (26 kilometers) north of the Ohio River. With the help of neighbors, Tom Lincoln and 8-year-old Abe threw up an 18- by 20-foot (5- by 6-meter) log cabin.

In the fall of 1818 Nancy Lincoln came down with the "milk sick"—a progressive coating of the tongue, with high fever and ever slower pulse. She died on October 5, only 34 years old. Thomas went back to Kentucky the following year and returned with a new wife, Sarah Bush Johnston. A widow with three children, Sarah saw to it that Abe got a little more schooling until, as he himself said later, he could "read, write, and cipher to the Rule of Three." Young Lincoln now also hired out as a hand on neighboring farms. Sandwiching in time between chores at home and elsewhere, he read a lot. Years later, a cousin remembered:

> I never seen Abe after he was twelve 'at he didn't have a book some'ers 'round. He'd put a book inside his shirt an' fill his pants pockets with corn dodgers, an' go off to plow or hoe. When noon come he'd set down under a tree, an' read an' eat. In the house at night, he'd tilt a cheer by the chimbly, an' set on his backbone an' read. I've seen a feller come in an' look at him, Abe not knowin' anybody was 'round, an' sneak out agin like a cat an' say, "Well, I'll be darned." It didn't seem natural, nohow, to see a feller read like that. Aunt Sairy's never let the children pester him.

On to Illinois

The Indiana farm with all its backbreaking work barely yielded a living, and in 1830 Thomas Lincoln decided to move west to Illinois. The family settled along the Sangamon River, west of Decatur. The next year, Abe got a job as a clerk in a general

This 1868 painting shows the young Abraham Lincoln educating himself as he reads a book by firelight in his log cabin home.

store in nearby New Salem. By then he had reached his full height, 6 feet, 4 inches (193 centimeters) and carried about 180 pounds (82 kilograms) on his ungainly, slightly stooped frame.

In 1832, as captain of a militia company, Lincoln went off to the Black Hawk War, which was fought against Sauk and Fox Indians in northwestern Illinois and what is now Wisconsin. He saw no action and within three months was back in New Salem.

Lincoln ran for the Illinois legislature and lost. With a partner, he opened his own general store and went broke. He worked as a surveyor and as postmaster in New Salem. Then in 1834, as a Whig, he was elected to the legislature and served four terms. In the meantime, he read enough law to become a lawyer, and in 1837 he moved to Springfield. There he attended legislative sessions, practiced law, and met his future wife.

Mary Todd had come from Kentucky to live with a married sister. The pretty belle of Springfield society was a plump 5-foot 2-inches (157 centimeters). She was 21 and Abe was 31.

The Lincoln-Todd courtship was not entirely smooth. At one point, they broke off the engagement. At last, though, they were married by an Episcopal minister on Nov. 4, 1842. They lived in a single room that Lincoln had rented for $4 a week over the Globe Tavern in Springfield. After their first child, Robert, was born in 1843, they moved into a frame house. Edward, born in 1846, died in 1850, shortly before his fourth birthday. William, called Willie, was born that same year, and Thomas in 1853.

Playing down his ability and reputation, Lincoln once wrote that he was not an accomplished lawyer. But he held honesty in the highest esteem. Lincoln's legal business grew. His fees averaged about $5 a case. In tune with the time and place, the family lived fairly well. During the 1840's, Lincoln's income ranged from $1,200 to $1,500. In the 1850's it was somewhat higher.

In 1846, Lincoln won election to the U.S. House of Representatives. There he served until 1849, when he returned to Springfield, choosing not to run for re-election.

A National Figure

Lincoln returned to politics in the 1850's as the issue of extending slavery into new territories heated up. He spoke out against slavery's extension, and in 1856, satisfied with the new Republican Party's stand on that question, he became a Republican. Lincoln received 110 votes for the party's vice-presidential nomination in 1856. Two years later, he ran for the U.S. Senate, losing to the Democratic incumbent, Stephen A. Douglas. However, the two met in a series of debates that made Lincoln a national figure. He argued in the seven debates that slavery was wrong.

Lincoln's supporters were well organized and ready at the Republican convention in Chicago in May 1860. He won the presidential nomination on the third ballot. He sat out election

The Lincoln-Douglas debate depicted here features Lincoln in action with his rival, Stephen A. Douglas, seated at his right.

night, November 6, awaiting returns in the Springfield telegraph office. As he later said to a friend:

> I told my wife to go to bed, as probably I should
> not be back before midnight. . . . On my arrival I
> went to my bedroom and found my wife sound
> asleep. I gently touched her shoulder and said,
> "Mary." She made no answer. I spoke again, a lit-
> tle louder, saying "Mary, Mary! we are elected!"

Lincoln had not received one vote in 10 from the Southern States. Southerners considered the Republican Party antislavery and anti-South. Rather than exist under a Republican adminis-tration, Southerners chose to secede from the Union. By the time Lincoln was inaugurated on March 4, 1861, seven Southern States had formed the Confederate States of America. They elected Jefferson Davis President. The Civil War began as Con-federates bombarded Fort Sumter, in the harbor at Charleston, S.C., on April 12.

The Lincolns gave their first dinner in the White House on March 28, for Vice-President and Mrs. Hannibal Hamlin and members of the Cabinet. The next was on June 4, 1861, for the diplomatic corps. One observer noted that in addition to the usual toasts and glasses of wine, all the diplomats and ladies were given fancy snuff boxes as souvenirs of the occasion.

President and Mrs. Lincoln also entertained the famous midget, General Tom Thumb, and his wife Lavinia at the White House. They greeted the tiny couple in the East Room.

The public New Year's reception in 1862 was more charac-teristic of White House gatherings at that time. As one person noted: "The striking feature was the great number of uniforms visible—generals, colonels and majors were plentiful as blackber-ries, while captains and lieutenants were multitudinous."

The press often criticized the Lincolns for holding social gatherings during wartime. Newspapers ignored the fact that such events were part of every presidential life, and that for the Lincolns, they provided respite from the worries of war.

Newspapers found other things to criticize Mary Todd Lin-coln for, and they spared her no more than her husband. Mary tended to be extravagant, and she overspent by $7,000 the allot-ment Congress had voted for redecorating the White House. The President also lost patience with her on this, but the bills were paid by the Commissioner of Public Buildings. Mary often shopped just for recreation, sometimes going to New York City and Boston to buy clothes and other items. The press was al-ways quick to note any examples of what it believed to be ex-travagance on her part.

Even in tragedy, the Lincolns came under attack. In the White House in February 1862, Willie died of typhoid at age 11. This drove Mary nearly wild with grief. Cruelly, a newspaper printed a letter from a Confederate mother whose son had been killed in action. At least Mrs. Lincoln had been with her son when he died, the letter said.

Mary's background was Southern, and for this the press and many citizens punished her. She also had relatives—including a brother and three half brothers—who served in the Confederate Army. She was accused of sympathizing with the Southern cause and even called a Confederate spy. Finally, to quiet rumors, the President stood before a joint House and Senate committee to read this statement: "I, Abraham Lincoln, President of the United States, appear of my own volition before this committee of the Senate to say that I, of my own knowledge, know that it is untrue that any of my family hold treasonable communication with the enemy."

Willie's death and the spy charges nearly crushed Mary Lincoln. Added to this was deep sorrow at the deaths of relatives in action, as well as recurrent headaches. Mary's behavior grew more and more erratic. Her secretary, William Stoddard, noted that on one day Mary could be kindly, considerate, generous, thoughtful, and hopeful. She "could, upon another day, appear so unreasonable, so irritable, so despondent, so even niggardly, and so prone to see the dark, the wrong side of men and women and events." A sad and weary President said to Emilie Helm, Mary's sister: "I feel worried about Mary, her nerves have gone to pieces; she cannot hide from me that the strain she has been under has been too much for her mental as well as her physical health."

One joy for Lincoln at this time was 8-year-old Thomas, an "only" child because his brother Robert was away at Harvard. Lincoln doted on the wriggling, nervous, active boy he called "Tad"—short for Tadpole. The child often appeared in Lincoln's office late at night. "[Tad] would lie around until he fell asleep," John Hay, Lincoln's secretary, recalled, "and Lincoln would shoulder him and take him off to bed." Like two other Lincoln children, Tad did not reach adulthood. He died in 1871 at 18.

An Uncharted Course

Abraham Lincoln came to the presidency facing a greater national crisis than ever even imagined—a ruptured Union. There were no precedents to guide the President in this circumstance. Lincoln for the most part had to feel his way, depending on good sense, a shrewd ability to judge people, and at times compromise and great patience. Perhaps more than anything else, his wry humor kept him balanced, even though at times he fell into depression and near-despair.

The first two years of the war saw few Union victories. Then came the fall of Vicksburg, Miss., and triumph at Gettysburg, Pa., both early in July 1863. Nearly two years of terrible fighting still lay ahead, but the war had reached its turning point. The Confederacy would be broken.

In November 1863, Lincoln dedicated the Gettysburg battlefield, where Union and Confederate armies had surged and fought and where thousands had died. In a short speech, to be known as the Gettysburg Address, he summed up the Civil War and its meaning to Americans. Lincoln asked that "we here highly resolve that these dead shall not have died in vain—that the nation under God, shall have a new birth of freedom—and that government of the people, by the people, and for the people, shall not perish from the earth."

After Vicksburg, Lincoln found a general who would fight and who could win. Ulysses S. Grant took command of the

Army of the Potomac in the East. For almost a year, beginning in 1864, Grant slugged it out with Confederate General Robert E. Lee and the Army of Northern Virginia. Gradually, Grant wore Lee's forces down.

The Emancipation Proclamation, issued by Lincoln on Jan. 1, 1863, played a big part in the North's resurgence. It declared that slaves in the Confederacy were free, and thousands of those who fled to freedom joined the Union Army or Navy. About 200,000 black soldiers and sailors helped the North win the war. General William T. Sherman took Atlanta and cut a 60-mile (97-kilometer)-wide swath of devastation through Georgia from Atlanta to the sea. The end came at Appomattox Court House in

Lincoln joins commanding General George B. McClellan and officers in 1862, shortly after the Battle of Antietam in Maryland.

A photograph of Lincoln's coffin passing along Broadway in New York City on April 25, 1865, on the way to Illinois.

Virginia, west of Richmond, where Lee surrendered to Grant on April 9, 1865. The Civil War, lasting almost four years to the day, was over.

His sad face now deeply lined and his eyes gaunt, Lincoln slept badly in those closing weeks. Dreams disturbed his rest, and he was exhausted. He told Mary about one dream in which the sound of muffled sobs awakened him. He went downstairs in the White House to investigate. In the East Room, he related, "I met with a sickening surprise."

> Before me was a catafalque, on which rested a corpse wrapped in funeral vestments. Around it were stationed soldiers who were acting as guards; and there was a throng of people, some gazing mournfully upon the corpse, whose face was covered, others weeping pitifully. "Who is dead in the White House?" I demanded of one of the soldiers. "The President," was his answer; "he was killed by an assassin!"

Actor John Wilkes Booth shot Lincoln as he and Mary watched a play in Ford's Theatre on April 14, 1865. Lincoln died at 7:22 A.M. the following day. As the President's eyes were closed, Secretary of War Edwin M. Stanton said: "Now he belongs to the ages." Lincoln lay in state in the East Room and in the Capitol rotunda. The funeral train began its slow journey to Illinois on April 21. As it passed, thousands of people lined the track along the way in silent mourning. Lincoln was buried in Springfield on May 4, 1865.

President Lincoln's Times
1861–1865

The U.S. Flag had 33 stars when Lincoln took office. Eleven Southern States, with over 9,000,000 persons, seceded from the Union and were returned to it as a result of the Northern victory in the Civil War. Two new states joined the Union: West Virginia in 1863 and Nevada in 1864. Three territories were organized: Arizona in 1863, Idaho in 1863, and Montana in 1864. The U.S. population was about 32,351,000 in 1861.

1861   On April 12, the Civil War began when Confederate guns fired on Fort Sumter.

1861   The transcontinental telegraph line was completed.

1861   French troops invaded Mexico.

1862   The first paper money was issued by the government of the United States.

1862   Congress created the Department of Agriculture.

1862   President Lincoln signed the Homestead Act. It allowed any settler to obtain 160 acres (65 hectares) of public land without charge.

1862   Bismarck became prime minister of Prussia.

1863   On Jan. 1, the Emancipation Proclamation was issued by President Lincoln. It declared slaves to be free in areas of the Confederate States that were still in rebellion.

1863   The world's first successful subway was opened in London.

1863   On March 3, the first draft law in U.S. history was passed. It gave the President authority to take men from 20 to 45 years for army service.

1863   On Nov. 19, President Lincoln delivered the Gettysburg Address.

1863   Free mail delivery was established in cities. Service started in 49 cities and soon spread throughout the country.

1864   Napoleon III made Maximilian of Austria the Emperor of Mexico.

1865   On April 9, General Robert E. Lee surrendered the Confederate troops to General Ulysses S. Grant at Appomattox Court House.

ANDREW JOHNSON

17th President of the United States
1865–1869

Andrew Johnson once said: "I have grappled with the gaunt and haggard monster called hunger"—and he had. Like his hero Andrew Jackson, Johnson grew up in poverty. Though he achieved high office, he never forgot his humble beginnings. Even in the White House, he and his wife, Eliza, preferred to think of themselves as just plain folks from Tennessee. Johnson developed into a tough and courageous political leader. His opponents thought of him as mule-headed and cantankerous. Johnson insisted that he always acted out of principle.

The 17th President's forebears in America went back probably no further than his parents, Jacob Johnson and Mary McDonough. Jacob arrived in America from England in about 1795. He and Mary—called Polly—lived in Raleigh, N.C., when their second son, Andrew, was born on Dec. 29, 1808. A daughter had already been born. What little income the family had came from Jacob's odd jobs and laundry and mending that Mary took in.

Neither parent could read or write, and Andrew never went to school. Somehow he learned to read. Later, his wife, Eliza McCardle, would teach him to write.

When Andrew was 3 his father died and was buried in the "citizens' cemetery"—a potters' field set aside for the poor. Mary Johnson remarried, but into no better circumstances than before. When Andrew was 13 his mother made him an apprentice. A court document dated Feb. 18, 1822, in Raleigh, reads: "Ordered that Andrew Johnson . . . the son of Jacob Johnson, deceased, . . . be bound to James J. Selby until he arrives at lawful age, to learn the trade of a tailor."

Andrew Johnson

Eliza McCardle Johnson was an invalid for many years. She was unable to serve as hostess at most official White House functions.

Johnson learned how to cut, stitch, bind, and finish clothing. Then, after two years, a childish prank got him into trouble. One night on a lark, he and one or two others tossed pebbles against the windows of two sisters to get their attention. The girls' mother threatened the boys with arrest and, fearing the worst, the boys left Raleigh for Carthage, 50 miles (80 kilometers) to the south. They set up their own tailor shop. From there they went on to Laurens, S.C., where they set up shop again.

Leaving an apprenticeship was considered a serious offense, and the three lived in fear of being caught, brought back, and punished. Johnson later tried to make amends with Selby, but without success. Finally, concluding that his future lay outside North Carolina, Johnson left for Tennessee.

While working for a tailor in Columbia, Johnson brought his mother and stepfather to live with him. He eventually settled in Greeneville, in eastern Tennessee, and established a tailor shop that did well. When he was 17, he met Eliza McCardle. She, at 15, was attractive, with large hazel eyes and light brown hair. Eliza and Andrew were married in May 1827, and they had five children.

People's Politician

Johnson's political career began in Greeneville. He served on the town council and was mayor. Then he took a seat as a Democrat in the Tennessee legislature. He served as governor and as a member of the U.S. House of Representatives and Senate. He drew his main support from farmers and residents of small towns in eastern Tennessee.

In the Senate, Johnson opposed Tennessee's secession from the Union in 1861 and became the only Southern senator not to leave the federal government. Abraham Lincoln rewarded that loyalty by making Johnson military governor of Tennessee in 1862. Two years later, though still a Democrat, he was elected Vice-President when Lincoln, a Republican, won re-election. Then early in the morning of April 15, 1865, Lincoln died after being shot by John Wilkes Booth. Johnson was sworn in as President.

Andrew and Eliza Johnson allowed Mary Todd Lincoln all the time she wanted to leave the White House. Johnson moved in in May 1865. The rest of the family, including Eliza, two sons, two daughters, a son-in-law, and five grandchildren moved in gradually.

Eliza stayed out of sight in the White House. She suffered from tuberculosis and by then was a semi-invalid. Besides, she felt out of place in the presidential home. She told Colonel W. H. Crook, who was a member of the White House staff, that she did not like public life at all. What she wished to do was return home, where she felt she and her family belonged.

Martha Johnson Patterson assumed White House duties in her mother's place. Then 36, Martha was married to David T. Patterson, senator from Tennessee, and she had spent some time in Washington, D.C., when her father was in Congress during the Polk Administration. She ran the White House with a firm and confident hand, free of the severe criticism Mary Lincoln

Full name: Andrew Johnson

Born: Dec. 29, 1808

Birthplace: Raleigh, N.C.

Died: July 31, 1875

Burial site: Greeneville, Tenn.

Spouse: Eliza McCardle

Occupation: Tailor

Political party: Democratic (National Union)

Term: 1865–1869

had attracted. Under Martha's guidance, the mansion once again became the prime attraction for Washington society. People drew favorable comparisons with the days when Harriet Lane, President James Buchanan's niece, had presided there.

Martha bought two cows that grazed on the White House lawn. Early each morning, a newspaper reported, Martha was up and dressed in a calico gown "and spotless apron" to "descend to skim the milk and attend the dairy before breakfast."

Johnson's governmental life was nonetheless dismal, particularly with respect to Congress. Reconstructing the South after the Civil War was the main issue during the Johnson Administration. Disagreements with Congress over how to do so soon gave way to bitterness and heated words. Johnson, like Lincoln, wanted to bring the South back into the Union quickly. In May 1865, he announced a plan offering pardons to all Southern whites except the main leaders and wealthy supporters of the Confederacy. The defeated states were to form new governments, abolish slavery, and vow loyalty to the nation before being readmitted to the Union. Under his plan, the states would determine the role of blacks.

Johnson's plan quickly ran into trouble. The new state governments passed black codes, packages of laws designed to keep control over blacks. In addition, many of the newly elected representatives and senators from Southern States who appeared when Congress reconvened had been Confederate officials or

Martha Patterson, the Johnsons' eldest daughter, served on many occasions as White House hostess in place of her mother.

Secretary of State Seward (seated) and Russian chargé d'affaires de Stoeckl (at globe) sign the Alaska purchase treaty, 1867.

sympathizers. Republican members of Congress became convinced that Johnson's plan had failed, and radical members demanded a new Reconstruction policy. They favored strong action to protect blacks and whites in the South who had remained loyal to the Union. Neither side would budge from its position. The controversy reached its climax early in 1868 with Johnson's impeachment and trial.

Impeachment

The House of Representatives charged Johnson with violating the Tenure of Office Act, along with other misdeeds. That law forbade the President to dismiss any federal officeholder without the Senate's consent if that officeholder's appointment had been confirmed by the Senate. In the summer of 1867, Johnson had suspended Secretary of War Edwin M. Stanton, who sided with the President's opponents in Congress. In February 1868, Johnson dismissed Stanton.

The Constitution provides that after impeachment the Senate shall try a President accused of "high crimes and misdemeanors." The trial of Andrew Johnson opened on March 5, 1868. Evidence to support any counts against him became increasingly unclear. Finally, the Senate voted on May 16 on one article of impeachment. Conviction required 36 votes, a two-thirds majority of the Senate. When Senator Edmund G. Ross of Kansas voted "not guilty," the chance for a two-thirds majority on any of the charges collapsed. By that one vote, Andrew Johnson escaped becoming the only President to be removed from office by means of impeachment by the House and conviction by the Senate. The vote saved the power and prestige of the presidency.

Although Johnson had hoped to receive the Democratic nomination for President in 1868, he did not. Instead, Governor Horatio Seymour of New York was chosen. He lost the election to General Ulysses S. Grant.

On Christmas Day, 1868, Johnson proclaimed a complete pardon for all Southerners who had taken part in the Civil War. This was his last important official act. Congress had reserved for itself the authority to grant amnesty with the 14th Amendment, proclaimed in July 1868. But Johnson's proclamation showed his desire to end the sectional bitterness that divided the nation during the Civil War.

For the Johnsons, the remaining months in the White House were quiet. They left Washington and returned to Tennessee in March 1869 without attending the inauguration of the incoming President, Ulysses S. Grant.

Andrew Johnson, however, was not through with politics. He was again elected to the Senate from Tennessee in 1874, proving to him that he had never lost the people's support. "If you would continue in public life," he advised a young politician at the time, "be sure of one thing . . . that you always strive to keep in touch with the common people. With them for you, corporations and combinations may organize against you . . . but they will war in vain. . . . Keep the common people on your side and you will win." When Johnson appeared in the Senate in March 1875, the gallery and the floor applauded him.

Andrew Johnson's impeachment trial was a popular event in Washington. Spectators needed tickets to witness it in the Senate.

The former President did not live out his term in Congress. While visiting on the Tennessee farm of his daughter, Mary Stover, 6 miles (10 kilometers) from Carter's Station, he had a stroke in July 1875. Andrew Johnson died on July 31, 1875. He was buried on a hilltop overlooking Greeneville.

President Johnson's Times
1865–1869

The U.S. Flag had 35 stars when Johnson took office. Nebraska joined the Union in 1867. Wyoming became a territory in 1868. The U.S. population was about 39,100,000 in 1869.

1865	The Reconstruction Era began.
1865	The 13th Amendment freed all remaining slaves.
1867	The Bureau of Education was established.
1867	The British created the Dominion of Canada.
1867	Alaska was purchased from Russia.
1867	Emperor Maximilian of Mexico was executed.
1867	Alfred Nobel of Sweden invented dynamite.
1868	The railroad refrigerator car was developed.
1868	The first practical typewriter was patented.
1868	The 14th Amendment made former slaves U.S. citizens.

ULYSSES S. GRANT

18th President of the United States
1869–1877

Leadership in war made Ulysses S. Grant one of America's greatest heroes since George Washington. And, as in Washington's case, that popularity propelled Grant into the presidency. George Washington, however, proved as great a leader in civilian life as he had been in war. Grant did not.

The 18th President was born on April 27, 1822, at Point Pleasant, O., the eldest son of Jesse and Hannah Grant. He was named Hiram Ulysses, but the name was erroneously listed as Ulysses S. on West Point admission papers, and Grant never changed it. Grant's father was a tanner and a farmer. The boy attended elementary school in Georgetown, O., where the family moved when he was 18 months old. He became acquainted with work at an early age.

Grant did not like the tanning business, which meant boiling hides in acids, smelly and unpleasant work. Nor did he care for farming. "When I was 7 or 8 years of age," Grant recalled later, "I began hauling all the wood used in the house and shops. I could not load it on the wagons, of course, at that time, but I could drive, and the choppers would load, and someone at the house unload." He was guiding a horse and plow at 11, turning over sod for planting. Grant liked horses. He learned to gentle and control them, and he became an excellent rider.

In 1839, Grant secured an appointment to the U.S. Military Academy at West Point. He then was 17, stood 5 feet 1 inch (155 centimeters) tall, and he weighed 117 pounds (53 kilograms). A shock of sandy brown hair topped his freckled face. At West Point, Grant joined cadets who, like him, would become well-known during the Civil War—James Longstreet,

Julia Dent Grant brought her two children, an aged father, and other relatives to live in the presidential mansion in March 1869.

Full name: Ulysses S. Grant

Born: April 27, 1822

Birthplace: Point Pleasant, O.

Died: July 23, 1885

Burial site: New York City, N.Y.

Spouse: Julia Dent

Occupation: Soldier

Political party: Republican

Terms: 1869–1877

Vice-Presidents: Schuyler Colfax; Henry Wilson

Runners-up: Horatio Seymour; Horace Greeley

Electoral votes: 214; 286

Runners-up: 80; 3

Popular votes: 3,013,650; 3,598,235

Runners-up: 2,708,744; 2,834,761

George B. McClellan, William T. Sherman, Thomas J. Jackson, and George H. Thomas.

The young Ulysses was an average student at the Point. "I never succeeded in getting squarely at either end of my class, in any one study during the four years," he later wrote. His greatest pleasure as a cadet was riding the horse his father gave him after his second year. He graduated from West Point a second lieutenant in 1843.

During his last year there, Grant roomed with Frederick Tracy Dent. After graduation they both were posted to Jefferson Barracks in Missouri. That area was home to Dent, and Grant met the young man's sister, Julia, at the Dent house near St. Louis. Julia Dent was then 17. A lively, pleasant person, she displayed a tough and determined personality. Best of all to Grant, she liked to ride. And when Grant went back to Ohio on leave after a few months, the two found they greatly missed each other.

Ulysses and Julia became engaged, but the army sent Grant to Louisiana in 1844 and to Texas in 1845. Then came the Mexican War, which kept him away until 1848. When the war ended, he and Julia were married in St. Louis on Aug. 22, 1848.

The next four years were fairly pleasant for the Grants. He was stationed at army posts in New York and Michigan, and they could be together. A son, Frederick, was born in 1850, and in 1852 Julia was pregnant again. But Grant was transferred to Fort Vancouver, along the Columbia River in what was then the Oregon Territory. Although he became a captain in 1853, his pay was too low to have his wife and family with him, and he sorely missed them. "I am almost crazy sometimes to see Fred," he wrote to Julia. He had still to see Ulysses, Jr., born after he had left for the West. Lonely and bored, Grant began to drink. Finally, he resigned from the army in July 1854.

During the next few years, the Grants' main joys were the births of Ellen—called Nellie—in 1855 and Jesse in 1858. There was almost no relief from hardship and poverty.

Grant tried farming in Missouri. The land was not especially productive—he called the farm "Hardscrabble"—and at times he had to peddle firewood in St. Louis to make ends meet. He worked for a time as a rent collector for a St. Louis firm. Then he moved to Galena, Ill., where his brothers ran a leather goods store. Grant became a clerk in the shop, but he displayed no head for business.

A Winning Commander

The Civil War saved him. When it began in 1861, Grant helped organize companies of Illinois volunteers and he led one outfit against Confederates in Missouri. In August 1861, President Abraham Lincoln made Grant a brigadier general, and he became the North's most successful commander. In January 1862, he moved against two forts at the center of the Confederate line. As he prepared to attack Fort Henry on the Tennessee River, Confederate forces withdrew and Union gunboats seized the fort. Grant then moved on nearby Fort Donelson, where he demanded unconditional and immediate surrender. Grant became a national hero, and happy Northerners declared that his initials stood for "Unconditional Surrender." He ended his successes in the West with the capture of Vicksburg, Miss., on July 4, 1863.

President Abraham Lincoln made him a lieutenant general and commander of all Union armies early in 1864. Grant moved east to make his headquarters with the Army of the Potomac. He faced the Army of Northern Virginia, under the command of General Robert E. Lee, a fellow officer in the Mexican War.

Attacking, Grant took heavy losses while inflicting great casualties on Lee's forces, and he attacked again and again. At last, with southern resources in soldiers and materiel exhausted, Lee surrendered to Grant on April 9, 1865, at Appomattox Court House, Va.

Republicans immediately began to consider Grant for the presidency in 1868. The general had never expressed much interest in politics, but he was willing to run. He decisively defeated Democrat Horatio Seymour 214 to 80 electoral votes. Nearly 500,000 popular ballots for Grant came from southern blacks, freed from slavery and possessing the right to vote.

Moving into the White House, the Grant family included the new President, Julia, and the two youngest children, Jesse and Nellie. Fred was at West Point and Ulysses, Jr., at Harvard College.

Julia became an enthusiastic White House hostess, and Washington society described the weekly receptions as "gala," "brilliant," "elegant," and "stately." The marriage of Nellie Grant to the Englishman Algernon Sartoris on May 21, the first White House wedding since Elizabeth Tyler's in 1842, highlighted the 1874 season.

Habits of regularity ingrained during army days stayed with

President Grant (third to the left of the man waving) at the opening ceremonies of the Centennial Exposition in Philadelphia in May 1876.

*After leaving the presidency in 1877, Ulysses S. Grant made a
two-year world tour, including a visit to an Egyptian pyramid.*

Grant in the White House. He arose at 7, read newspapers, and
breakfasted on a hearty meal with the family at 8:30. He usually
then took a walk, settling into his office around 10. The official
day ended at 3 P.M.

Grant won re-election with little trouble in 1872, but inauguration day turned out cold, windy, and raw, and the ball that
evening in an unheated building was a disaster. By then, so was
the Grant Administration, in many respects. Widespread corruption had gradually come to light.

The President was not involved in any corruption, but he
trusted his friends too much and then stuck with them even
after their misdeeds had become obvious. William W. Belknap,
secretary of war, took bribes in exchange for granting rights to
run trading posts on Indian reservations. Grant's secretary, Or-
ville Babcock, profited from whiskey taxes that went into the
pockets of whiskey distillers, not to the federal Treasury. Abel
Corbin, Grant's brother-in-law, became involved in a scheme to
corner the gold market on Wall Street. Government officials and
members of Congress engaged in shady financial operations with
the builders of the Union Pacific Railroad. Examples of wrongdoing and questionable practices in high places multiplied.

The Republicans denied Grant nomination for a third term
in 1876, honoring the two-term tradition Washington had established. Leaving the White House in March 1877, Ulysses and
Julia Grant made a world tour lasting more than two years.

Financial troubles plagued Grant's final years. Shares of railroad stock that admirers had placed in a trust fund for him on
his return from the world tour ceased bearing interest when the

railroad fell on hard times. Grant invested money in a business venture with his son, Ulysses, Jr., and lost it all.

Personal Memoirs

Deeply in debt but determined to pay it off, Grant began to write his memoirs in 1884, concentrating on the Civil War period. Mark Twain agreed to publish the work and Grant hoped to earn income from royalties.

Near the end of his writing, Grant found himself working against death. He had cancer of the throat, but he doggedly kept at his memoirs. He finished in July 1885 and died a few days later in a cottage near Saratoga, N.Y.

The *Personal Memoirs* which rank among the most popular writing on war ever published, became an immediate best seller and brought in nearly $500,000 in royalties, which kept Julia comfortably until her death on Dec. 14, 1902. Aside from his Civil War exploits, the *Memoirs* stand as Ulysses S. Grant's monument, perhaps more impressive even than the tomb along Riverside Drive in New York, where he and Julia were buried.

President Grant's Times
1869–1877

The U.S. Flag had 37 stars when Grant took office. Colorado became a state in 1876. No new territories were organized. The U.S. population was about 47,141,000 in 1877.

1869	The first transcontinental railroad system was completed when the tracks of the Union Pacific and Central Pacific railroads met in Utah.
1869	The Suez Canal opened.
1870–1871	The Franco-Prussian War resulted in the unification of Germany.
1870	The 15th Amendment was proclaimed, insuring citizens the right to vote regardless of race.
1872	The Yellowstone area was set aside as the first national park.
1876	Alexander Graham Bell invented the telephone.
1876	Indians massacred Custer and his troops in the Battle of the Little Bighorn.

RUTHERFORD B.
HAYES

19th President of the United States
1877–1881

Rutherford B. Hayes was officially elected President at the last minute, almost literally. A special commission had to be formed to settle the issue, and when it ruled, Hayes had won by one electoral vote.

After the election of 1876, disputes arose over numerous electoral votes, most of them in Florida, Louisiana, and South Carolina. The Electoral Commission was appointed to decide whom those ballots should go to, Hayes or Samuel J. Tilden, the Democratic candidate. Tilden needed but one more electoral vote to win. Hayes needed all those in doubt. Congress finally gave all questionable ballots to Hayes, but not until 4 A.M. on March 2, 1877. Inauguration Day, March 4, fell on Sunday that year. There would be no inauguration until Monday, March 5.

Rutherford and Lucy Hayes dined at the White House on Saturday evening with the outgoing presidential family, Ulysses and Julia Grant. Before dinner, Chief Justice Morrison R. Waite swore Hayes in as 19th President. He took the oath of office again on Monday, this time in public.

Rutherford B. Hayes was born in Delaware, O., on Oct. 4, 1822. His ancestors had been New Englanders. Hayes' great-great-great-grandfather George Hayes, a Scot, had settled in Connecticut in 1680. His father, also named Rutherford, and his mother, Sophia, migrated with two young children from Vermont to Ohio in 1817. The father died in 1822, 10 weeks before his second son's birth. Lorenzo, the first son, accidentally drowned when Rutherford was 2. The surviving son grew up among two doting relatives, his mother and his sister Fanny.

Hayes attended private schools, Kenyon College in Ohio

Lucy Webb Hayes, who banned alcoholic beverages from the White House, became known as "Lemonade Lucy."

Full name: Rutherford Birchard Hayes

Born: Oct. 4, 1822

Birthplace: Delaware, O.

Died: Jan. 17, 1893

Burial site: Fremont, O.

Spouse: Lucy Ware Webb

Occupation: Lawyer

Political party: Republican

Term: 1877–1881

Vice-President: William A. Wheeler

Runner-up: Samuel J. Tilden

Electoral vote: 185

Runner-up: 184

Popular vote: 4,288,546

Runner-up: 4,034,311

and Harvard Law School. From 1845 until the Civil War he practiced law in Lower Sandusky (later Fremont), O., and in Cincinnati. In 1847, he met Lucy Ware Webb.

Lucy was an advanced, if not liberated, person for her time. She attended Wesleyan Female College in Cincinnati, one of the few colleges to accept women then. Her courtship with Hayes progressed over the months, and Lucy finally consented to marriage. The wedding took place in Cincinnati in December 1852. The Hayeses had seven sons and one daughter. Three of the children died in infancy.

As an officer, wounded in battle four times, Hayes made a distinguished record in the Civil War. He was elected to the U.S. House of Representatives from Ohio in 1864, while still in the army. Later he served two full terms and part of a third as governor of Ohio. In 1876, delegates to the Republican convention in Cincinnati nominated him for the presidency.

As mistress of the White House, Mrs. Hayes went down in history as "Lemonade Lucy." She was totally opposed to alcohol, and during her time, as one observer put it, "the water flowed like wine" in the presidential mansion. People tended to overlook one fact, however: Hayes himself was a teetotaler. He had a sense of humor about it.

At a speech he delivered on one occasion, people noticed that his face was ruddier than usual. "When your eyes met mine a suspicion arose in your minds which I assure you is without foundation," he began. "I have not forsaken my temperance principles and practice. Appearances, I admit, are against me. But in truth it is not whiskey but poison ivy which did it." The Hayeses were both responsible for a dry White House. They were also devoted churchgoers. Every Sunday they attended Foundry Methodist Episcopal Church in the capital.

Sophisticated Washingtonians made fun of Lucy and her lemonade, but she was a person of principle. While stern-faced toward drink, she was cheerful, friendly, and outgoing otherwise. As White House hostess, she presided over elegant dinners and receptions. And she made an exception on one occasion and served wine at a banquet given for the Russian Grand Dukes Alexis Alexandrovitch and Constantine on April 19, 1877.

On Saturday evenings, Washingtonians laid aside their jokes long enough to flock to the Hayeses' regular open house. According to *Harper's Weekly,* the "world took . . . liberal advantage of the [Hayeses'] hospitality and worked . . . havoc to the executive mansion, and its own persons and garments." These affairs began at 8 P.M. They ended promptly at 10 P.M. as the Marine band played "Home, Sweet Home."

Besides her temperance stand, Lucy Hayes is also remembered for opening the White House lawn to children and decorated eggs on Easter Sunday. The White House Easter egg roll she started in 1878 became an annual event.

The Hayes Administration is known for having ended Reconstruction, the 12-year period after the Civil War. In return for agreeing that disputed electoral votes in 1876 would go to Hayes, Southern Democrats exacted certain concessions. These included the removal of all federal troops from the South, the appointment of a Southern Democrat to the Cabinet, and a hands-off federal policy regarding Southern political affairs.

Militia units from Philadelphia go up against railroad strikers in Altoona, Pa., during one of many bloody labor disputes in 1877.

President Hayes made good on all these points.

Rutherford B. Hayes is also remembered for his support of civil service reform. He wanted government jobs awarded on the basis of merit, rather than political connections. He did not achieve his goal, but in an executive order Hayes forbade government employees from taking part in the management of a political party.

Hayes had promised at his inauguration not to seek a second term, and he did not. In March 1881, the Hayeses went back to Fremont. Lucy died in 1889, and Rutherford followed her on Jan. 17, 1893.

President Hayes' Times
1877–1881

The U.S. Flag had 37 stars when Hayes took office. No new states or territories were organized. The U.S. population was about 51,500,000 in 1881.

1877–1878	The Russo-Turkish War gave Russia control over important areas in the Balkans and near the Black Sea.
1877	Reconstruction ended.
1877	The Railroad Strike of 1877 caused so much violence that Hayes called out federal troops.
1877	The phonograph was invented by Thomas A. Edison.
1879–1883	Chile won mineral-rich land from Bolivia and Peru in the War of the Pacific.
1879	Cleveland, O., became the first American city to install electric street lighting.

JAMES A. GARFIELD

20th President of the United States
1881

Next to William Henry Harrison, James A. Garfield had the shortest term in the presidency. Harrison died in 1841 after only a month in office. Becoming President March 4, 1881, Garfield was shot in a Washington, D.C., railroad station on July 2. He died 11 weeks later.

Edward Garfield, the first of the line in America, emigrated from England to settle in Watertown, Mass., in 1630. Descendants moved to New York, then to Ohio. Edward's great-great-great-great-great-grandson James was born in a log cabin on a farm near Cleveland on Nov. 19, 1831.

When James was 17 months old his father Abram died. His mother Eliza raised Garfield and three other children. The family was poor, although Eliza always denied that they were ever in want. In later life Garfield was fond of saying: "Poverty is uncomfortable, as I can testify. But nine times out of 10 the best thing that can happen . . . is to be tossed overboard and compelled to sink or swim. . . . In all my acquaintance I never knew a man to be drowned who was worth the saving."

On the other hand, Garfield's mother recalled in later life that he was "rather lazy, did not like to work the best that ever was." She also said, however, that her son was "never still a minute at a time in his whole life."

Garfield was walking when he was 9 months old and climbing fences and ladders a month later. He was reading from the Bible at 3. Next to hunting, he liked reading best as a youth. He had to earn much of his own way, and he worked as a farmhand, a carpenter, and as a tender of horses pulling boats along the Ohio Canal. After elementary school Garfield attended

The dark-eyed Lucretia Rudolph, known as "Crete," was at first a classmate and later a student of James A. Garfield. She married him in Hiram, O., in November 1858.

Full name: James Abram Garfield

Born: Nov. 19, 1831

Birthplace: Orange, O.

Died: Sept. 19, 1881

Burial site: Cleveland, O.

Spouse: Lucretia Rudolph

Occupation: Lawyer

Political party: Republican

Term: 1881

Vice-President: Chester A. Arthur

Runner-up: Winfield S. Hancock

Electoral vote: 214

Runner-up: 155

Popular vote: 4,446,158

Runner-up: 4,444,260

Geauga Academy in Ohio, then the Western Reserve Eclectic Institute (now Hiram College).

At Geauga, Garfield met the demure, dark-eyed Lucretia Rudolph, a fellow student known to her friends as "Crete." They met again at the institute, where Garfield was a teacher as well as a student. Crete was in the Greek and Latin classes he taught. Both had gone separate ways romantically, and both had been disappointed in love.

By the end of 1853, Crete's name was appearing often in Garfield's diary. "For myself, I feel that under the proper circumstances I could love her, and unite my destiny to hers," one entry ran. And by the spring of 1854: "We love each other, and have declared it." Yet, Garfield was wary. "Time which changes all things may make changes in us or our circumstances," he added. "I feel inclined to be cautious and so does she."

In 1854, Garfield went to Williams College in Massachusetts to earn a bachelor's degree. Armed with that, he returned to the institute in 1856 as a teacher and became its president in 1857. By studying on the side he also became a lawyer.

James and Lucretia were married on Nov. 11, 1858. They had seven children, but two died in infancy.

Enlisting in an Ohio regiment as a lieutenant colonel when the Civil War began, Garfield rose to the rank of major general. His distinguished army service helped him win election as a Republican to the House of Representatives in 1862. He served until 1880. After the Civil War, Garfield favored the harsh Reconstruction measures that Radical Republicans wanted the nation to adopt. Both Radical and Moderate Republicans contended that Congress, not President Andrew Johnson, should determine Reconstruction policy. Garfield was among those who voted to impeach President Johnson.

Garfield became the dark-horse candidate for the 1880 Republican presidential nomination. Three favorites, including former President Ulysses S. Grant, deadlocked at the convention in Chicago that year. Finally, on the 36th ballot, the weary delegates turned to Garfield. He went on to capture the presidency with 214 electoral votes to Democrat Winfield S. Hancock's 155.

The 6-foot (183-centimeter), full-bearded Garfield took office in March 1881. Even before the inauguration, people besieged him for government jobs.

Since the nation's beginning, a person needed political connections to get a government job, regardless of ability. There were no civil service examinations. Usually, many government workers were dismissed when a new administration came in to make way for the winners' political friends and supporters. Things were no different with Garfield, and an observer described the scene in the White House in the spring of 1881 in this way:

> As I go up the stairs, the atmosphere is heavy and close on this stairway and affects one singularly. Perhaps the sighs of disappointed office seekers, who for more than half a century have descended the steps, have permeated the walls and give to the air a quality that defies ventilation. Crowds in the anterooms and crowds in the upper hall. All these people are eager-eyed, restless and nervous.

They want something which the great man in
that well-guarded room across the hall can give if
he chooses, but which they fear they will not get.

Garfield almost threw up his hands. "These people would take
my very brain, flesh, and blood if they could," he commented.
"They are wholly without mercy."

On July 2, 1881, President Garfield entered the Baltimore
and Potomac railroad station in Washington. He was to board a
train to go to commencement exercises at Williams College. As
Garfield crossed the waiting room, someone moved quickly toward him and fired two shots at point-blank range. One bullet
grazed Garfield's arm. The other lodged in his back. Had there
been X rays, or such an antibiotic as penicillin, the President
probably would have recovered. The bullet lay in a muscle, by
itself posing no vital threat. But doctors probing to remove the
bullet may have brought on infection. Garfield died on Sept. 19,
1881.

Vice-President Chester A. Arthur became President. Garfield's assailant, Charles J. Guiteau, a disappointed federal office
seeker, was tried for murder, convicted, and hanged.

President Garfield's Times
1881

The U.S. Flag had 38 stars when Garfield took office. No new
states or territories were organized. The U.S. population was
about 51,500,000 in 1881.

1881	A member of the terrorist group known as "People's Will" assassinated Czar Alexander II of Russia.
1881	The French established a protectorate over Tunis that would last until 1956.
1881	The American Red Cross was organized by humanitarian Clara Barton, known as the "angel of the battlefield."
1881	This year saw the last of the famous cattle drives to Kansas cow towns. Railroads reached Texas soon after Garfield's assassination.
1881	Garfield was shot on July 2 and died on Sept. 19.

CHESTER A. ARTHUR

21st President of the United States
1881–1885

Tall, elegant, and handsome, Chester A. Arthur was known as the "Gentleman Boss." The first to hire a valet, Arthur was one of the best dressed of all Presidents. He was also widely read and an excellent conversationalist.

William Arthur, Chester's father, came to America from Ireland in the early 1800's. He taught school and became a Baptist minister. In 1821 he married Malvina Stone, whose forebears have been traced back to New Hampshire in the 1760's. Chester Arthur, the fifth child and the first boy, was born in Fairfield, Vt., on Oct. 5, 1829.

When Arthur was 10, the family settled in Union Village, N.Y. At 15, he entered Union College in Schenectady, N.Y. He spent two winter vacations from college teaching in elementary schools for $15 a month. After graduating from Union in 1848, Arthur continued to earn a living by teaching. At the same time, he studied law. In 1853, Arthur moved to New York City to complete his law studies. He was admitted to the bar in 1854.

He met Ellen Lewis Herndon of Virginia, and they were married on Oct. 25, 1859. William Lewis, their first child, was born in December 1860, but died less than three years later of convulsions. The trouble, Arthur wrote to a friend, was "brought on by some [affliction] of the brain. It came upon us so unexpectedly and suddenly." The Arthurs had two other children— Chester, born in 1864, and Ellen, born in 1871.

Arthur joined the Republican Party soon after it was formed in 1854. He became prominent in party circles, although he did not hold elected office. In 1861, New York Governor Edwin D. Morgan put Arthur in charge of outfitting the state militia for

Ellen Lewis Herndon of Virginia, who married Chester A. Arthur in 1859 and bore him three children, did not live to be first lady, dying of pneumonia in January 1880.

service in the Civil War. In 1862, he became the militia's inspector-general, and later he was state quartermaster-general. President Ulysses S. Grant made Arthur head of the New York Custom House in 1871, where he oversaw the collection of taxes on imports.

By 1880, the Republican Party had split into two factions. One, called the Half Breeds, swung the presidential nomination to James A. Garfield that year. Then, with the hope of gaining support from Grant's followers, the delegates offered the vice-presidential nomination to Arthur, a member of the group called Stalwarts. When one Stalwart boss heard of this, he advised Arthur to "drop it as you would a red-hot [horse]shoe from the forge." Arthur replied: "The office of Vice-President is a greater honor than I ever dreamed of attaining." Ignoring the advice placed Arthur in the presidency when James A. Garfield died of a gunshot wound on Sept. 19, 1881. Arthur took the presidential oath the next day.

Chester A. Arthur entered presidential office a widower with two children. Ellen had died of pneumonia in January 1880, and Arthur never remarried.

A person of recognized good taste, Arthur regarded the presidential mansion as "a badly kept barracks." He insisted that it be redecorated and refurnished from top to bottom. Some 24 wagonloads of old furniture and what can best be described as junk were hauled away and auctioned off. People bid eagerly for such "historic" items as old stoves, cuspidors, moth-infested carpets, and hair-stuffed mattresses stored away since James Buchanan's time in the 1850's. Along with new furnishings, Arthur also had two new bathrooms and an elevator installed.

The Arthur White House averaged a dinner party a week. During the winter season Arthur's sister, Mary A. McElroy, acted as official hostess. One delighted guest noted that never had epicures so enjoyed themselves at Washington. Public receptions at the White House were something else again. One, at least, resembled the scene at Andrew Jackson's inauguration in 1829, according to the *Washington Republican.* As hordes gathered, the paper reported, "an hour after the opening people began climbing in the windows to lessen the jam on the portico. Others sought entrance through the basement doors." General Philip Sheridan of Civil War fame was one guest who entered through

Full name: Chester Alan Arthur

Born: Oct. 5, 1829

Birthplace: Fairfield, Vt.

Died: Nov. 18, 1886

Burial site: Albany, N.Y.

Spouse: Ellen Lewis Herndon

Occupation: Lawyer

Political party: Republican

Term: 1881–1885

Chester A. Arthur, who had the White House redecorated to suit his own tastes, is shown here fishing—a favorite recreation.

a window; two police officers boosted him in.

Chester Arthur described himself as a "night bird." He often worked in his office after dinner or enjoyed a late supper and conversation with close friends. Arising about 9:30 A.M., he breakfasted on coffee and rolls. After a stint at his desk came a lunch of oatmeal, fish, and fruit. The official day usually ended at 4 P.M., after which he often took a horseback ride or a carriage drive.

As a loyal party member, Arthur had always endorsed the spoils system. He considered the practice of granting federal jobs to the party faithful a normal part of government business. As President, Arthur changed. He supported civil service reform, partly out of conviction and partly as a response to widespread public demand for change following Garfield's death at the hands of a disappointed job hunter. During his presidency, Arthur signed the Pendleton Act, setting up the Civil Service Commission. This began the system of awarding federal jobs on merit shown by examination instead of on the basis of political connection.

Arthur's stand on civil service reform displeased some Republican leaders. So did his veto of two bills, one to spend federal money on rivers and harbors and another to exclude Chinese as immigrants to the United States. Congress overrode the first veto but modified the second bill, and Arthur signed it.

Unhappy with his performance and realizing that he did not intend to make a serious effort to gain its nomination, the Republican Party passed Arthur by in 1884. He retired to his law practice in New York City. He died there on Nov. 18, 1886.

Mary A. McElroy, Arthur's youngest sister, served as White House hostess for the widowed President. She won wide praise for her warm hospitality.

President Arthur's Times
1881–1885

The U.S. Flag had 38 stars when Arthur took office. No new states or territories were organized. The U.S. population was about 51,500,000 in 1881.

Early 1880's   Geologists in Ontario found the world's largest copper-nickel reserves.

1882   The German physician Robert Koch discovered the germ that causes tuberculosis.

1883   The Brooklyn Bridge was completed.

1883   Standard Time was adopted by the railroads. The public gradually adopted the railroad system of time zones.

1884   Construction began on the world's first skyscraper, the Home Insurance Building, in Chicago.

1884   The Linotype was patented by Ottmar Mergenthaler.

GROVER CLEVELAND

22nd President of the United States 1885–1889
24th President of the United States 1893–1897

When Grover Cleveland ran for the presidency in 1884, among other things he faced was:

"Ma Ma, where's my Pa?"
"Gone to the White House, ha, ha, ha!"

Cleveland and a widow in Buffalo, N.Y., had had a son. They were not married—which is what that rhyme was all about. This could have been politically disastrous. At least, Republicans hoped that it would be so for Cleveland. But Cleveland, a bachelor, defused the issue by advising his friends always to "tell the truth" if questioned. He, himself, made no public comments on the charge.

Most voters were not inclined to punish Cleveland for refusing to shed bachelorhood and "do the right thing" 10 years earlier. Besides, the Republican candidate, James G. Blaine of Maine, was hardly clean. Among other misdeeds, he had been accused of shady deals in railroad stocks as a member of Congress. Cleveland won in 1884, breaking a Republican string of Presidents that had run from Abraham Lincoln to Chester A. Arthur.

The original Clevelands in America were New Englanders, going back to Moses Cleveland, who arrived in Plymouth, Mass., from England in 1635. Grover was born on March 18, 1837, in Caldwell, N.J. He was the fifth of nine children of Richard and Ann Neal Cleveland, and the third son. His father was a Presbyterian minister.

When Grover was 4, Richard Cleveland moved the family to Fayetteville, N.Y., to accept a call from a church there. Cleve-

Frances Folsom became the youngest first lady when at age 21 she married the 49-year-old President Cleveland. Cleveland called his wife by her nickname, "Frank."

Full name: Grover Cleveland

Born: March 18, 1837

Birthplace: Caldwell, N.J.

Died: June 24, 1908

Burial site: Princeton, N.J.

Spouse: Frances Folsom

Occupation: Lawyer

Political party: Democratic

Terms: 1885–1889; 1893–1897

Vice-Presidents: Thomas A. Hendricks; Adlai E. Stevenson

Runners-up: James G. Blaine; Benjamin Harrison

Electoral votes: 219; 277

Runners-up: 182; 145

Popular votes: 4,874,621; 5,551,883

Runners-up: 4,848,936; 5,179,244

land attended grammar school in Fayetteville, and at 11 he entered secondary school. In 1850, the family moved to Clinton, N.Y., where Grover completed high school. His sister Margaret remembered him at that time as "a lad of rather unusual good sense, who did not yield to impulses—he considered well, and was resourceful—but as a student Grover did not shine. The wonderful powers of application and concentration which afterward distinguished his mental efforts were not conspicuous in his boyhood."

His father died when Grover was 16, and he was on his own. He worked at various jobs before going to Buffalo to work for an uncle, Lewis Allen, a well-known cattle dealer. After six months, with his uncle's help, Grover was accepted as a clerk and student in a Buffalo law firm. His future was set.

Reform and Public Life

By the time the Civil War began in 1861, Cleveland was earning $900 a year with the firm that had trained him. Later, with two different partners, he opened his own practice. He was not a brilliant attorney, but he was thorough, steady, and reliable: characteristics that marked him all his life.

Graft and corruption—bribes, kickbacks, favoritism, outright theft—were common in city, state, and federal governments at that time. Buffalo was no exception, and Cleveland, a Democrat, joined reform forces there. He was elected mayor in 1881. Displaying incorruptibility and unswerving integrity in office, Cleveland became governor of New York in 1883. Two years later, he became President. A writer for the *Boston Advertiser* described him this way:

Cleveland is stout, has a well-fed look, is indeed a good liver, has the air of a man who has made up his mind just how he ought to behave in any position where he may find himself. He is getting bald; he is getting gray—though his white hair does not show conspicuously, as his complexion is sandy. He dresses well, carries himself well, talks well upon any subject with which he is familiar, and upon subjects with which he is not familiar he does not venture to talk at all. He has the happy faculty of being able to refuse a request without giving offense. It has been my fortune to see him several times during the past winter. . . . He has impressed me always as one heartily desirous of getting at the bottom of any matter he may have in hand, and of acting wisely in it.

The Cleveland inaugural ball, held on the interior courtyard of the incompleted Pension Building, was the first to be brightened by electric lighting. Nearly 10,000 guests danced on the waxed floor that measured 360 by 116 feet (110 by 35 meters). About a year later, Cleveland made even bigger social news. At 48, he announced that he would forsake bachelorhood to marry Frances Folsom, known to her friends as "Frank." Frances was 21, and tongues clicked, of course, just as they had in 1844 when President John Tyler, a 54-year-old widower, married 24-year-old Julia Gardiner.

Frances Folsom was the daughter of Cleveland's law partner in Buffalo. After Oscar Folsom's death in a carriage accident in 1875, Cleveland had looked after her and the estate. He had proposed to Frances in 1885, around the time of her graduation from Wells College in Aurora, N.Y.

As a large crowd of people milled about outside the mansion, the first—and to date the only—wedding of a President in the White House took place in the Blue Room at 7 P.M. on June 2, 1886. The Marine band opened the short ceremony with the Mendelssohn wedding march. As the ritual ended, guns in the naval yard along the Potomac River boomed a 21-gun salute.

The unaffected and charming Frances became one of the most popular first ladies. The worst thing a Cleveland political enemy could say was: "I detest him so much that I don't even think his wife is beautiful." But W. H. Crook, who had served in the White House in Andrew Johnson's time and after, remarked: "I am an old man now and I have seen many women of various types through all the long years of my service in the White House, but neither there nor elsewhere have I seen anyone possessing the same kind of downright loveliness which was as much a part of Mrs. Cleveland as her voice, or her marvelous eyes, or her warm smile of welcome."

In his inaugural address in 1885 Cleveland had promised "reform in the administration of the government, and the application of business principles to public affairs." He certainly was businesslike in performing his duties. One observer described Cleveland as

> an emphatically working man. . . . The President rises early, shaves himself, dresses without assistance, and reads newspapers until breakfast. From the breakfast table he goes to the library. . . . At 1 o'clock the President goes downstairs to lunch. . . . After luncheon he returns to his desk and works steadily until 5 o'clock. Dinner is served at 7:00 and by 8:30 he is at work again, often remaining until midnight.

Traditional public receptions and state dinners interrupted the routine, and at times the receptions got a little out of hand. At some of them people lined up four abreast to enter the White House.

Cleveland's relations with Congress were not happy. He tried to strengthen the civil service and weed out political patronage abuses. But some Democrats faulted him for not going far enough. Others criticized him for not giving more jobs to party workers. Cleveland vetoed many veterans' pension bills that he considered undisguised raids on the public treasury and, at best, rewards to undeserving soldiers. This angered Democrats and Republicans alike.

Nominated again in 1888, Cleveland ran about 900,000 popular votes ahead of Republican Benjamin Harrison. But the New York Democratic Party failed to give its wholehearted support, and that state's 36 electoral votes and the election went to Harrison, 233 to 168.

The story goes that the departing Frances said to a servant in March 1889: "Now Jerry, I want you to take good care of all the furniture and ornaments in the house, for I want to find everything just as it is now when we come back again."

Split Terms

Whether Frances actually said that or not, the Clevelands returned in 1893. Cleveland became the the first and only President to serve two split terms after he defeated Harrison in 1892.

Although he made history with his comeback, Cleveland's second term was no happier than his first. Economic depression, with widespread unemployment, hardship, and suffering characterized those years. Cleveland insisted that the federal government bore no responsibility for relief measures in time of economic trouble, which made him appear insensitive and brought criticism. Yet this was an attitude common to the time, especially among industrialists and other business people. Cleveland also lost popularity when he ordered federal troops to Illinois to break the American Railway Union-Pullman strike in 1894. But he had concluded that strikers were interfering with the delivery of U.S. mail. To Cleveland, this was gross violation of law. "Grover Cleveland," said the *Atlanta Constitution,* "will go out under a greater burden of popular contempt than has ever been

President Cleveland and Frances Folsom were married in the White House Blue Room on June 2, 1886. A cartoon by Joseph Keppler celebrates the event.

Jacob S. Coxey marched an "army" of unemployed from Ohio to Washington, D.C., in 1894 to demand depression relief.

excited by a public man since the founding of the government."

The *Constitution* was right, but Cleveland soon assumed the role of an elder leader of state, and rancor and dislike faded. He and Frances settled in Princeton, N.J., where Cleveland became a university faculty member and later a trustee. Cleveland died on June 24, 1908.

President Cleveland's Times
1885–1889
1893–1897

The U.S. Flag had 38 stars when Cleveland took office in 1885 and 44 stars when he began his second term in 1893. Utah became a state in 1896. No new territories were organized. The U.S. population was about 61,800,000 in 1889, when Cleveland's first term ended. When his second term ended in 1897, the country had about 72,200,000 persons.

1886	The Statue of Liberty, a gift of France to the United States, was dedicated in New York City.
1894	Captain Alfred Dreyfus' first trial for treason was held in France.
1895	Guglielmo Marconi of Italy produced a practical wireless telegraph system.
1895	Wilhelm Roentgen of Germany discovered X rays.
1896	Henry Ford's first car appeared.

BENJAMIN HARRISON

23rd President of the United States
1889–1893

When Benjamin Harrison was introduced before a Republican Party gathering in 1856 as the grandson of President William Henry Harrison, he exclaimed: "I want it understood that I am the grandson of nobody. I believe that every man should stand on his own merits." Even if Harrison was sincere in what he said, he never persuaded the party to forget his ancestry. "Grandfather's Hat Fits Ben" was one slogan they attached to him when he ran for the presidency in 1888.

One newspaper praised Harrison during that campaign as "calm, cool, deliberate, polished, candid, dignified and strong." Many who knew him emphasized the "cool." Harrison's handshake, one person said, was "like a wilted petunia."

Benjamin Harrison was born on Aug. 20, 1833. He was named for his great-grandfather, a signer of the Declaration of Independence. His birthplace was the 2,000-acre (809-hectare) family estate his father managed at North Bend, O. Ben was the second of the 10 children of John Scott Harrison and Elizabeth Irwin Harrison. His father served two terms in Congress.

Ben, a short, stocky boy, spent his youth on the farm. He attended elementary school near home and at age 14 went to secondary school outside Cincinnati. He graduated from Miami University in Oxford, O., in 1852.

After studying law for about a year in Cincinnati, in 1853 Harrison married Caroline Scott, the daughter of his former chemistry and physics teacher. Her father, a Presbyterian minister, officiated at the wedding. Benjamin was admitted to the bar in 1854, and the Harrisons settled in Indianapolis, Ind., where he established a law practice.

Caroline Scott Harrison was an accomplished painter of china and lover of flowers. She graced the White House as hostess for "Old Tippecanoe's" grandson.

Indiana Governor Oliver P. Morton asked Harrison in 1862 to recruit and command a regiment of Indiana volunteers in the Civil War. Bearded "Little Ben" stood only 5 feet 6 inches (168 centimeters) tall, but he proved to be a firm disciplinarian and respected officer. He won a reputation for fearlessness and rose to the rank of brigadier general. After the war he became a leader in the Indiana Republican Party. He ran for governor in 1876 but lost. He was elected to the U.S. Senate in 1881 and won the party presidential nomination in 1888.

The 1888 election was one of those in which the candidate with the most popular votes lost. Harrison polled about 90,000 fewer ballots than Democrat Grover Cleveland, but he won majorities in the right states, such as New York, with its 36 electoral votes. Harrison finished ahead of Cleveland in the Electoral College by 65 ballots.

The Harrison White House resembled the mansion during the Grant Administration—there were usually several relatives in residence. Benjamin and Caroline moved in with their children, Russell and Mary, and their families, who lived there most of the time. The Harrisons were joined for long periods by assorted nieces and nephews as well. Caroline's father also lived in the White House until his death near the end of Harrison's term.

Life in the White House was thoroughly photographed for the first time during Harrison's term. Electric lights and bells were installed in the mansion in 1891. But the Harrisons, fearing shocks, often used the old-style gas lights, or asked the White House electrician to turn the switches on and off.

Despite poor health, Mrs. Harrison worked hard as official hostess. She once told a reporter that "there are only five sleeping rooms and there is no feeling of privacy." Members of the Harrison family usually occupied these rooms.

Caroline Harrison loved flowers, especially orchids, and she established a greenhouse in which to grow them. She was also an accomplished painter of china, and she decorated the White House with many of her pieces.

The Harrison Administration became known principally for the passage of the Sherman Antitrust Act of 1890. It outlawed trusts or other monopolies that hindered trade. Three other measures were passed in 1890. The Sherman Silver Purchase Act increased the amount of silver that could be purchased. The McKinley Tariff Act was designed to protect American manufacturers, and the Dependent Pension Bill broadened qualifications to include all Civil War veterans who could not perform manual labor. Construction of a two-ocean navy began during Harrison's term, and the first Pan American Conference got under way in Washington, D.C., in 1889.

Harrison probably did more than any other President to increase respect for the flag of the United States. By his order, the flag waved above the White House and other government buildings. Harrison also urged that the flag be flown over every school in the land.

The Republicans renominated Harrison in 1892 and chose Whitelaw Reid, editor of the *New York Tribune,* as his running mate. The Democrats again nominated Cleveland for President and named

Full name: Benjamin Harrison

Born: Aug. 20, 1833

Birthplace: North Bend, O.

Died: March 13, 1901

Burial site: Indianapolis, Ind.

Spouse: Caroline Lavinia Scott

Occupation: Lawyer

Political party: Republican

Term: 1889-1893

Vice-President: Levi P. Morton

Runner-up: Grover Cleveland

Electoral vote: 233

Runner-up: 168

Popular vote: 5,534,488

Runner-up: 5,443,892

Adlai E. Stevenson, a former Illinois member of Congress, for Vice-President.

Discontented farmers turned from the Republicans to the new Populist Party, which had been formed in protest against falling farm prices. Angry factory workers deserted the Republicans, charging hostile interference by the federal and state governments in the Homestead strike and other labor disputes. Opposition to the McKinley Tariff Act also lost Harrison votes.

Then personal tragedy struck the President just two weeks before the national elections of 1892. His wife Caroline died on October 25.

Grover Cleveland came back to defeat Harrison in 1892, winning 277 electoral votes to Harrison's 145. Harrison retired to his law practice in Indianapolis and earned additional income as a writer and lecturer. He died in Indianapolis on March 13, 1901.

President Harrison's Times
1889-1893

The U.S. Flag had 38 stars when Harrison took office. Six states joined the Union: North Dakota in 1889, South Dakota in 1889, Montana in 1889, Washington in 1889, Idaho in 1890, and Wyoming in 1890. Oklahoma became a territory in 1890. The U.S. population was about 67,000,000 in 1893.

1889-1890	Nellie Bly set a record by traveling around the world in 72 days.
1889	The Eiffel Tower was dedicated in Paris.
1889	The International Conference of Latin American States was held. It led to the founding of the Pan American Union.
1890	The Sherman Antitrust Act was passed to curb monopolies.
1891	Basketball was originated by James A. Naismith.
1891	The International Copyright Act was passed.

WILLIAM McKINLEY

25th President of the United States
1897–1901

William McKinley, said Robert M. La Follette of Wisconsin, "had an innate dignity and at the same time a warm, sympathetic nature. . . . He had a rare tact as a manager. Back of his courteous . . . manner was a firmness that never yielded. . . . While scarcely seeming to force issues he usually achieved exactly what he sought." In 1896, McKinley achieved his highest goal—the presidency.

The McKinley roots were Scotch-Irish. William's great-great grandfather, a weaver, settled in Pennsylvania in the early 1700's. William was born in Niles, O., on Jan. 29, 1843, the seventh of William and Nancy McKinley's nine children. An iron foundry provided the family income.

Though not well-schooled themselves, McKinley's parents valued education. "I put my children in school just as early as they could go alone to the teacher, and kept them at it," McKinley's mother recalled in later life. William was a serious student and liked to read. He was no grind, however, and he found plenty of time to play. "The thing he loved best of all was a kite," his mother said. "It seems to me I never went into the kitchen without seeing a paste pot or a ball of string waiting to be made into a kite." McKinley's favorite subject in high school was debate. This was also the case at Allegheny College in Pennsylvania, which he attended for less than a year when he was 17. "McKinley was a magnetic speaker," Robert M. La Follette once said. "He had a clear, bell-like quality of voice, with a thrill in it."

As the Civil War began in 1861, the teen-aged McKinley enlisted in an Ohio regiment. He served with distinction throughout the conflict, rising from private to major.

The deaths of her two daughters, one in infancy and the other in early childhood, left Ida Saxton McKinley ill for life with epileptic-type seizures.

Law studies in Albany, N.Y., followed the war, and McKinley opened a law office in Canton, O., in 1867. He also became active in local Republican politics, winning his first public office as prosecuting attorney of Stark County in 1869. At about this time he met Ida Saxton.

A member of a prominent Canton family, she worked as a cashier in her father's bank. The two were deeply attracted to each other almost immediately. They were married in 1871.

The McKinleys' first child, Katherine, was born on Christmas Day that year. Another daughter arrived in April 1873, but she died within five months. Mrs. McKinley took the death of their daughter exceedingly hard, wondering if the loss was a punishment from God. A few years later, Katherine came down with typhoid and died. This shattered Ida's world, and she was never well again. She developed an illness characterized by periodic seizures. These plagued her the rest of her life.

The death of their children drew the McKinleys closer together, and William afforded Ida every care. Despite her troubles, Ida did nothing to try to dampen his political ambitions, although she could do little to help him.

McKinley on the Move

McKinley was elected as a Republican from Ohio to the U.S. House of Representatives in 1876. He served until 1891 with one break of 10 months due to a contested election. He earned a reputation for hard work and conscientiousness, seldom missing a session or committee meeting. Then he was elected to the first of two terms as governor of Ohio in 1891. His success in that office and the executive experience he gained prepared him well for his next political step.

"The very air is full of McKinley," one observer noted just before the Republican convention in St. Louis in 1896. The McKinley organization, managed by Ohio industrialist Mark Hanna, moved smoothly and efficiently. The candidate from Ohio won the nomination on the first ballot. The Republican Party chose Garret A. Hobart of New Jersey as the vice-presidential candidate.

William Jennings Bryan, the Democratic nominee, made the 1896 campaign livelier than most. He outdid all other candidates, covering about 20,000 miles (32,187 kilometers) by train. On many days he delivered more than 30 speeches, most of them from the train at whistle stops along the way. Bryan campaigned against rule by the rich and for free coinage of silver.

McKinley stayed in Canton, conducting a "front porch" campaign. He greeted some 750,000 Republicans in almost 300 delegations there. As a member of Congress, McKinley had favored limited coinage of silver, but now he favored a gold standard. McKinley won by about 600,000 popular votes and got 271 electoral votes to Bryan's 176.

McKinley carried his habit of hard work with him to the White House. He put in long hours at his desk, reading letters and reports and dictating responses. He wrote his own speeches and messages to Congress.

Full name: William McKinley

Born: Jan. 29, 1843

Birthplace: Niles, O.

Died: Sept. 14, 1901

Burial site: Canton, O.

Spouse: Ida Saxton

Occupation: Lawyer

Political party: Republican

Terms: 1897–1901

Vice-Presidents: Garret A. Hobart; Theodore Roosevelt

Runner-up: William J. Bryan

Electoral votes: 271; 292

Runners-up: 176; 155

Popular votes: 7,108,480; 7,218,039

Runners-up: 6,511,495; 6,358,345

*In 1901, President McKinley rode to the Pan American Exposition
in Buffalo, N.Y., where his assassin, Leon Czolgosz, waited.*

Regular public receptions had by then become traditional.
On those occasions McKinley, dressed in a frock coat, greeted
guests at the White House door. During his political career he
had refined the act of shaking hands to an art, and without tir-
ing he could greet and shake the hands of 30 persons a minute
and nearly twice that many if he wished to increase the pace.
Along with the art of handshaking, McKinley also possessed a
prized politician's trait: the ability to connect people's faces and
names.

During working hours McKinley was always available to
visitors—the common as well as the mighty—although favor
seekers sometimes wearied him. Walking or driving a carriage
through the streets of Washington, D.C., were his favorite forms
of relaxation. Ida often accompanied him on drives.

Security at the White House was lax, as it had been throughout most presidencies. Secret Service attention to McKinley's
safety was spotty. One of the President's staff made the rounds
one evening and found many people at work, except for the Secret Service agent, "whom I discovered asleep on a lounge in one
of the bedrooms on the second floor." McKinley himself did not
worry about security.

Ironically, McKinley hated conflict but became a war President. He tried to maintain neutrality and avoid war with Spain.
But when the battleship U.S.S. *Maine* blew up in Havana harbor,
many Americans blamed that nation. The Spanish-American
War of 1898 lasted only a few months. When it ended, America
had a colonial empire: Puerto Rico, the Philippines, and Guam—
all former Spanish possessions.

A successful war and general prosperity brought McKinley
re-election in 1900. Vice-President Hobart had died in November 1899, and Governor Theodore Roosevelt of New York was

A yellow journalism cartoon aiming to stir American anger against Spain helped to bring on an American declaration of war in 1898.

now McKinley's running mate. McKinley again defeated Bryan, this time by 292 to 155 electoral votes.

Assassination

In 1901, President McKinley journeyed to Buffalo, N.Y., to attend the Pan American Exposition. Standing in the Temple of Music on September 6, he greeted and shook hands with a long line of admirers. One with what appeared to be a bandaged right hand approached the President. As he took McKinley's right hand with his left, Leon Czolgosz fired twice at the President with a revolver that the "bandage" concealed. William McKinley died eight days later, on September 14.

A self-styled anarchist, or foe of all government, Czolgosz gave no logical reason for his deed. Found guilty of murder, he was later put to death in the electric chair.

McKinley's body lay in state in the White House. Then a slow-moving train, watched by silent, grieving crowds in each town, city, and hamlet through which it passed, carried the body to Canton for burial.

President McKinley's Times
1897–1901

The U.S. Flag had 45 stars when McKinley took office. No new states or territories were organized. The U.S. population was about 77,600,000 in 1901.

Late 1890's The Klondike Gold Rush brought prospectors from all parts of the world to Alaska. The sudden influx threatened the area with famine.

Late 1890's Sir Ebenezer Howard's *Tomorrow,* later published as *Garden Cities of Tomorrow,* started modern city planning. Howard founded the Garden City Association.

1898 Germany embarked on a naval building program and began its "world policy."

1898 The Spanish-American War began after an explosion on board sank the battleship *Maine* in Havana Harbor, Cuba.

1898 Hawaii, Guam, Puerto Rico, and the Philippines became American possessions.

1898 In France, Pierre and Marie Curie observed radioactivity and isolated the element radium.

1899–1902 The Filipinos revolted against American rule.

1899–1902 The British and Dutch fought the Boer War, also known as the South African War.

1900–1901 Walter Reed helped conquer typhoid fever and yellow fever through the medical experiments he conducted in Cuba.

1900–1901 The Boxer Rebellion, an antiforeign movement, flared in North China.

1900 The American Baseball League was organized, but it did not gain recognition as a major league organization until 1903.

1900 The Currency Act of 1900 consolidated McKinley's gold standard policy in the United States.

1900 Sigmund Freud, an Austrian psychiatrist, published the *Interpretation of Dreams.* It marked the beginning of psychoanalysis.

1900 Max Planck evolved quantum theory.

1901 On Sept. 6, Leon Czolgosz, an anarchist, shot President McKinley, who died of his wounds on Sept. 14.

THEODORE ROOSEVELT

26th President of the United States
1901–1909

"I hear you are being groomed by the Republicans as my husband's successor in the coming election," Mrs. Garret Hobart, widow of William McKinley's deceased Vice-President, said to Theodore Roosevelt in 1900.

"No, by George!" Roosevelt replied. "I've had a good time as governor and I want to be governor again."

Republican Party bosses had other plans. They disliked the governor of New York, who had made his way politically without much help from them. He was uncontrollable, unpredictable, and he was a reformer. The bosses wanted Roosevelt out of the New York governorship. Mark Hanna, McKinley's campaign manager, protested against plans to nominate Roosevelt as Vice-President, and he worried after the nomination. "Don't any of you realize," he asked, "that there's only one life between this madman and the presidency?" Hanna told McKinley: "Your duty to the country is to live for four years from next March." When McKinley died from an assassin's bullet in September 1901, Hanna exclaimed: "Now look, that ——— cowboy is President of the United States!"

"Cowboy" was no figure of speech. Roosevelt had been a real cowboy—and more. Besides being governor of New York, he had been a New York state legislator and president of the New York City board of police commissioners. He was also a federal civil service commissioner and assistant secretary of the navy. Roosevelt furthermore had made a name as a writer. His *The Naval War of 1812,* published when he had barely reached his 20's, and his four-volume *The Winning of the West* had earned historians' praise and respect. Many other books and magazine arti-

Theodore Roosevelt

Alice Lee, whom Theodore Roosevelt married in 1880, died in childbirth on Valentine's Day 1884, the same day Roosevelt's mother died of typhoid.

Full name: Theodore Roosevelt

Born: Oct. 27, 1858

Birthplace: New York City, N.Y.

Died: Jan. 6, 1919

Burial site: Oyster Bay, N.Y.

Spouses: Alice Hathaway Lee; Edith Kermit Carow

Occupation: Author; rancher

Political party: Republican

Terms: 1901–1909

Vice-President: Charles W. Fairbanks

Runner-up: Alton B. Parker

Electoral vote: 336

Runner-up: 140

Popular vote: 7,626,593

Runner-up: 5,082,898

cles followed over the years.

Boundless enthusiasm and curiosity summed up Theodore Roosevelt, who was called "Teddy" or "T.R." Wanting to know everything wherever he went, he wore people out with questions. Much of the time he wanted to do everything, too, especially if in the meantime he was the center of attention.

Roosevelt's Dutch background ran deep. In the 1640's, Claes Maertenszen van Rosenvelt emigrated from Holland to America. He settled in what was then New Netherland, later New York. Claes married Jannetje Samuels Thomas. Their son Nicholas, who dropped the "van" and spelled the name Roosevelt, had three sons: Nicholas, Johannes, and Jacobus. From Johannes, five generations later, followed Theodore, second of the four children of Theodore and Martha Bulloch Roosevelt. He was born on Oct. 27, 1858, in New York City.

A Sickly Youth

Over the generations the Roosevelts had accumulated wealth. Theodore was born into comfort and privilege. Yet his health was poor, his body weak, and he suffered dreadful attacks of asthma that left him scarcely able to breathe. He was also terribly near-sighted.

Glasses corrected the visual problem. Strenuous exercise and rough and tumble activity built his puny body and, eventually, eliminated the asthma. Although of average height—5 feet, 8 inches (173 centimeters)—as an adult his overdeveloped chest and shoulders and bull-like neck muscles made Roosevelt seem taller.

That wide streak of curiosity and unquenchable desire to know appeared at an early age. As a youth, Roosevelt read and read. He was a collector and his dresser drawers often smelled of dead mice, bats, birds, and other specimens. So did Teddy.

Tutors educated him until he was 18, when he entered Harvard University. Graduating in 1880, he studied law at Columbia University in New York City. Then Roosevelt entered public service. At 23, he won the first of three terms in the New York legislature. By then he had married.

Alice Lee was 17 when she and Roosevelt met in October 1878. After Alice had accepted his proposal, he recorded in his diary early in 1880: "The aim of my whole life shall be to make her happy, and to shield her and guard her from every trial; and, oh, how I shall cherish my sweet queen! How she, so pure and sweet and beautiful can think of marrying me I cannot understand, but I praise and thank God it is so."

They were married in the Unitarian Church in Brookline, Mass., on October 27 that year. Twin tragedies struck in 1884. Roosevelt's mother died of typhoid on February 14. On that same day Alice died, 48 hours after giving birth to a daughter, named after her.

Roosevelt worked out his grief in Dakota Territory, on cattle ranches he had bought along the Little Missouri River. He learned to herd cattle, organize roundups, and otherwise run a ranch, and he won the respect of seasoned ranchers and cowboys. The terrible winter of 1886–1887, which wiped out three-fourths of the herds in the West, ruined Theodore Roosevelt as a rancher, just as it did many others.

In December 1886, Roosevelt married Edith Kermit Carow, a childhood friend. Edith was pretty, shy, and reserved. Yet her quiet presence and her good sense as well as her beauty attracted Theodore, and he later wrote: "Whenever I go against her judgment, I regret it." They had five children, and Edith reared Alice Roosevelt as her own child.

As a civil service commissioner under Presidents Benjamin Harrison and Grover Cleveland, Roosevelt established merit examinations for some federal jobs. As a New York City police commissioner in the 1890's, he battled corruption in the department. He personally patrolled streets at night, checking on police performance and on law enforcement, generally.

William McKinley made him assistant secretary of the navy in 1897, and Roosevelt enthusiastically supported increased spending to strengthen the fleet. He impatiently opposed McKinley's attempts to avoid war and greeted the outbreak of the Spanish-American War with joy. Roosevelt resigned as assistant secretary to raise a regiment of cavalry, drawing largely on former college athletes and cowboys. He led the Rough Riders in Cuba, proving as fearless and enduring in combat as in politics.

Roosevelt's war record helped him become governor of New York in 1898. There he added to his reputation as a reformer, supporting state civil service legislation. He also disturbed regular Republicans and business interests by approving a bill to tax corporations. Then came the vice-presidency, and six months later, the highest office. At 42, Roosevelt became the youngest person to assume the presidency.

The six Roosevelt children made the White House a playhouse, roller-skating in the corridors, moving through high-ceilinged rooms on stilts, and ignoring stairs to zip down bannisters. They brought their pets as well—dogs, cats, a black bear, an Australian kangaroo rat, and on one occasion the family calico pony, Algonquin.

Roosevelt often joined the games after a day in the Executive Office. The games usually ran from 8:30 A.M. to 5 P.M. or later. He was active in other ways, too. He exercised regularly and with enthusiasm—fencing, boxing, tossing a medicine ball, playing tennis. Teddy also walked, and briskly, often with puffing members of the Cabinet or Congress struggling to match his pace. His interest in the strenuous made good newspaper copy, as when he staged a match in the East Room between an American wrestler and a Japanese skilled in jujitsu.

Through it all, Edith Roosevelt remained calm. She redecorated and refurbished the White House and presided with grace, charm, and a firm hand over formal affairs. Edith also oversaw Alice's coming-out party in the mansion and her wedding there to Congressman Nicholas Longworth of Ohio on Feb. 17, 1906.

By the time of Alice's wedding, Theodore Roosevelt was well into the term of office he won in his own right in 1904. He trounced Democrat Alton B. Parker by about 2.5 million popular votes that year, the largest margin to that time.

Roosevelt was among the best-liked Presidents and, in many respects, the most interesting. As President, he supported business regulation. He endorsed legislation such as pure food and

The shy, reserved Edith Kermit Carow was a childhood friend who married Theodore Roosevelt in 1886. Her good sense and judgment aided him.

Theodore Roosevelt, who recruited the Rough Riders for the Spanish-American War, poses as their proud and ready commander.

drug laws. During his administration the Department of Justice won court orders to break up a number of trusts, or large business combinations, into smaller units. Many people of the time believed that this would bring price advantages through increased competition.

Roosevelt believed in justice for labor unions as well as business. Although not new, government intervention in labor disputes prior to this time had usually favored management. In 1902, his efforts at mediation ended a coal miners' strike on terms generally favorable to the union. Teddy also supported the conservation movement, adding more than 125 million acres (51 million hectares) to national forests.

In foreign affairs, Theodore Roosevelt wielded a "big stick," exercising power forcefully. He encouraged Panama's rebellion from Colombia in 1903. Colombia had rejected a treaty for the right to build a canal linking the Atlantic and Pacific oceans. When the rebellion occurred, Roosevelt stationed a warship off the isthmus, preventing Colombia from sending troops to put down the uprising. After Panama had gained independence, the United States negotiated a treaty and took over the Panama Canal project, completing the Big Ditch in 1914.

To the Monroe Doctrine, Roosevelt added the idea that the United States had the right to intervene in Latin American affairs to keep European countries from moving in. The United States took over tax collection in Santo Domingo in 1904 to pay debts that nation owed Europeans. In 1906, Roosevelt sent troops to Cuba to quiet political turmoil there.

Nobel Prize for Peace

Acting as mediator, in 1905 Roosevelt brought the Russo-Japanese War to a close. That effort won him the Nobel Prize for Peace in 1906. That same year he negotiated a "gentlemen's agreement" with Japan to halt the emigration of Japanese to the United States. To display U.S. naval power, the President sent 16 battleships—the Great White Fleet—to show the flag on a cruise around the world.

Teddy refused to seek another term in 1908. He did not leave a position of such action and power as the presidency gladly, however. The American public was sorry at his departure, too. The Roosevelt years had been exciting and, many people thought, good for the United States.

Roosevelt hand-picked his successor, Secretary of War William Howard Taft. After Taft's election in 1908, Teddy went off to hunt in Africa. Returning in 1910, Roosevelt soon found numerous reasons to fault his successor. Partly because Taft did not measure up to his expectations, and partly because he missed the limelight, Roosevelt tried for the Republican nomination in 1912. Failing that, he ran for the presidency on the Progressive Party ticket. He split the Republican vote, and the election went to Democrat Woodrow Wilson.

Against his will, Theodore Roosevelt sat out World War I.

Theodore Roosevelt, thoroughly in his element in the West, delivers one of his rousing speeches in New Castle, Wyo., in 1903.

His sons enlisted. Quentin, who had been born in 1897, was killed in action as an aviator in France in 1918.

Roosevelt picked up a form of jungle fever while on an expedition in Brazil in 1914. It left him weak and brought on recurrent abscesses, which required operations. Still, Teddy was thinking of 1920 and the presidency again. But a blood clot in his heart killed him suddenly on Jan. 6, 1919.

Both the Roosevelt home at Oyster Bay and his birthplace in New York City are national historic sites. His ranches in North Dakota are part of the Theodore Roosevelt National Memorial Park. Along with Lincoln, Jefferson, and Washington, Roosevelt's likeness carved in stone gazes out from Mount Rushmore in South Dakota.

For Theodore Roosevelt, it was a "bully" experience to inspect progress on the Panama Canal in person.

President Roosevelt's Times
1901–1909

The U.S. Flag had 45 stars when Roosevelt took office. Oklahoma became a state in 1907. No new territories were organized. The U.S. population was about 90,000,000 in 1909.

1901	The first wireless telegraph message was sent across the Atlantic.
1902	The British defeated the Dutch in the Boer War in South Africa.
1903	Congress established the Department of Commerce and Labor.
1903	Roosevelt sent a message over the newly completed cable across the Pacific Ocean.
1903	A six-person tribunal upheld U.S. claims in the Alaska boundary dispute with Great Britain. The dispute arose after the gold was discovered in the Klondike.
1903	The Wright brothers launched the air age when they made the first airplane flight at Kitty Hawk, N.C.
1904	Work on the Panama Canal to connect the Atlantic and Pacific oceans began.
1905	Albert Einstein, a 26-year-old physicist, published his theory of relativity.
1906	The San Francisco earthquake destroyed much of the city and killed about 700 persons.
1906	The Federal Food and Drugs Act protected the public against impure foods.
1906	Roosevelt won the Nobel Peace Prize for helping to end the Russo-Japanese War.
1907	Delegates from over 40 nations attended the second conference on world disarmament at The Hague in The Netherlands.
1907	A financial panic started when prices dropped suddenly on the New York City stock market. Prosperity returned in 1909.
1907	The "Great White Fleet" of U.S. warships began a 14-month good-will tour around the world.
1908	The first "Model T" Ford went on the market.

WILLIAM HOWARD TAFT

27th President of the United States
1909–1913

The Supreme Court of the United States pulled William Howard Taft one way. The presidency, with Helen Herron Taft tugging the string, pulled him the other. He finally went both ways, becoming the only person to serve in the White House and on the highest bench.

"I love judges," Taft once said, "and I love courts. They are my ideals, that typify on earth what we shall meet hereafter in heaven under a just God."

Helen was quoted as saying on March 4, 1909, "It always has been my ambition to see Mr. Taft President of the United States, and naturally when the ceremonies of the inauguration were in progress I was inexpressibly happy."

The Taft heritage was Puritan, and so was Helen's. Robert Taft settled in Braintree (later Quincy), Mass., in 1678. The Herrons went back even further, to an English family that helped found Weymouth, Mass., in 1640.

William Howard was born in Cincinnati on Sept. 15, 1857, the second son of Alphonso and Louisa Taft. He was a large child and although his family called him Willie, his playmates preferred "Big Lub." As an adult, Taft stood 6 feet (183 centimeters) tall and he often had to work hard to keep his weight down near 300 pounds (136 kilograms). He had a special bathtub built in the White House because he always got stuck in a normal-sized one and had to be pulled out. To demonstrate the tub's capacity, four workers once lay in it to pose for pictures. They were not crowded.

Alphonso Taft was a lawyer in Cincinnati and prominent in Republican party affairs. He served as secretary of war and as

Helen Herron Taft's ambitions for her husband were fulfilled when he accepted Theodore Roosevelt's blessing and campaigned successfully for the presidency in 1908.

Full name: William Howard Taft

Born: Sept. 15, 1857

Birthplace: Cincinnati, O.

Died: March 8, 1930

Burial site: Arlington, Va.

Spouse: Helen "Nellie" Herron

Occupation: Lawyer

Political party: Republican

Term: 1909–1913

Vice-President: James S. Sherman

Runner-up: William J. Bryan

Electoral vote: 321

Runner-up: 162

Popular vote: 7,676,258

Runner-up: 6,406,801

attorney general in Ulysses S. Grant's Cabinet. Alphonso and Louise, as she was called, treasured accomplishment, and they set high goals for their children.

As a youth, William Howard was popular with other children. He swam and ice-skated, and he was an enthusiastic and fairly good baseball player. He hit and threw well. He could not run fast, however.

Taft made good marks in school, but he was inclined to be somewhat lazy—at least from his parents' viewpoint. His father once wrote him that he agreed with one of Willie's high school teachers "when he said that you had the best head of any of my boys and if you [were] not too lazy you would have great success." William, it seems, was usually content to be runner-up. He graduated second in his high school class and second in his class at Yale in 1878. After Yale he earned a degree from Cincinnati Law School.

In February 1880 Helen Herron, called Nellie, daughter of a prominent Cincinnati lawyer, noted in her diary: "I was surprised immensely a week before by receiving an invitation from Will Taft. Why he asked me I have wondered ever since [as] I know him very slightly though I like him very much. . . . He sent me a lovely bouquet, too."

They had met the year before at a winter coasting, or sledding, party, when Nellie was 18. She was popular and pretty, with brown eyes and curly brown hair. Nellie was also intelligent, and she did not conceal it. She was outspoken. She loved music. And she was determined and ambitious.

The relationship progressed slowly. As late as April 1884, Will still addressed Nellie in letters as "My dear Miss Herron." A year later, though, he was writing of his hopes that they would be married.

"You know," Nellie said to her mother, "a lot of people think a great deal of Will. Some people even say he may obtain some very important position in Washington." Taft's mother encouraged the marriage, telling her son that a tall wife would show off his broad proportions to full advantage.

Marriage and Politics

Nellie and Will were married at last on June 19, 1886. They had three children, all of them to be successful. Robert Alphonso became a U.S. senator. Helen was a history professor and dean at Bryn Mawr College. Charles became a lawyer and served as mayor of Cincinnati.

The position his father held in the Republican Party helped edge Will toward politics and public service. He became, in turn, assistant county solicitor for Hamilton County, O., a superior court judge, and solicitor general of the United States under President Benjamin Harrison. He served as a federal judge for eight years, and he was also dean of the University of Cincinnati Law School.

William Howard Taft first made a national name as civil-governor of the Philippines, appointed by President William McKinley in 1901. He brought colonial rule to a high point of enlightenment and good work. This led to his appointment by

In the Philippines, William Howard Taft greets Datto Piang, father-in-law of the Filipino independence fighter Datto Ali.

President Theodore Roosevelt as secretary of war in 1904.

Taft had only one goal, really—the Supreme Court. He could have reached it in 1902, but he did not think his work in the Philippines was far enough along by then. Mrs. Taft liked the Cabinet position better. "This was much more pleasing to me than the offer of the Supreme Court appointment," she wrote, "because it was in line with the kind of work I wanted my husband to do, the kind of career I wanted for him and expected him to have, so I was glad there were few excuses for refusing to accept it open to him."

Another Court vacancy occurred in 1906, and Taft nearly had it that time. After a meeting with Roosevelt on March 9, 1906, Taft wrote in his diary: "I also explained . . . that Nellie is bitterly opposed to my accepting the position and that she telephoned me this morning to say that if I did, I would make the great mistake of my life. The President has promised to see her and talk the matter over with her and explain the situation. . . ." After a half-hour confidential conversation with Nellie, Roosevelt saw her point.

With Nellie's help, Theodore Roosevelt persuaded Taft to run as his successor for the presidency. At first Taft objected, preferring to wait yet longer for possible appointment to the Supreme Court. But after further prodding from Mrs. Taft and his brothers, he changed his mind at last. Taft won the Republican nomination on the first ballot at the national convention in 1908.

Representative James S. Sherman of New York received the vice-presidential nomination. They won the election easily, defeating Democrats William Jennings Bryan and John W. Kern 321 to 162 electoral votes.

President and Chief Justice

Nellie Taft took charge of the White House even before the Roosevelts were completely moved out. And she outraged Alice Roosevelt Longworth, Theodore's eldest daughter, whose strong-mindedness and outspokenness easily matched her own. When Alice was unable to attend the inaugural luncheon, Nellie assured her that she might have a ticket to enter the White House should she change her mind.

Washington gossips called Nellie Taft "pushy," criticizing her for promoting, guiding, and advising her husband. The *Washington Post* said, however, "In the matter of mental attainments she is probably the best-fitted woman who ever graced the position she now holds and enjoys."

Shortly after the inauguration, Nellie Taft suffered a stroke that left her a semi-invalid with impaired speech for some time. Even so, ignoring criticism, she attended White House conferences whenever possible. She listened, saying nothing, and later passed on reactions and ideas to the President. He always found her advice valuable.

It was Nellie Taft's idea to plant the cherry trees that now grace Washington's Tidal Basin. When she was unable to find the number she wanted, the mayor of Tokyo shipped 3,000 as a gift from his city.

William Howard Taft was the first President to be paid $75,000 a year—the salary had been raised to $50,000 during the Grant Administration. Taft was the last President to have a cow grazing on the White House lawn. Pauline Wayne, as she was called, kept the grass cropped and provided fresh milk for the family twice a day.

Taft found Teddy Roosevelt a hard act to follow. Anyone would. They had worked well together, but he suffered by comparison with Teddy's flamboyant, restless, and energetic style.

During Taft's presidency, Congress established the Postal Savings System, parcel post, and the Children's Bureau. Business interests extended U.S. influence in Latin America through loans and investment. The Taft Administration began more court actions to break up trusts—huge business combinations—than the government had under Roosevelt. But Taft did not get on well with liberals in Congress, who had considerable influence, and his lack of forcefulness in general did not please Theodore Roosevelt.

In 1910, Roosevelt returned from big-game hunting in Africa and soon took the stump again for the presidency. When the Republicans denied him the nomination in 1912, staying with Taft, Roosevelt ran on the Progressive Party ticket and received 88 electoral votes to Taft's 8. But Woodrow Wilson ran far ahead with 435.

William Howard Taft left the White House in March 1913 to become a law professor at Yale, and he served on the Na-

Before Dwight D. Eisenhower, William Howard Taft was the most famous golfer in the White House.

tional War Labor Board during World War I. Then in 1921, he achieved his highest goal—President Warren G. Harding appointed him Chief Justice of the United States. "The truth is," Taft wrote in 1925, "that in my present life I don't remember that I ever was President." Chief Justice Taft established an excellent record.

Ill health forced William Howard Taft to retire from the Court on Feb. 3, 1930. He died a month later, on March 8.

President Taft's Times
1909–1913

The U.S. Flag had 46 stars when Taft took office. Two states joined the Union: New Mexico in 1912 and Arizona in 1912. No new territories were organized. The U.S. population was about 97,200,000 in 1913.

1909	Admiral Robert E. Peary discovered the North Pole.
1910	The Union of South Africa was founded.
1910	The Mexican Revolution began.
1911	Roald Amundsen discovered the South Pole.
1912	The Republic of China was established, with Sun Yat-sen as provisional president.
1913	Parcel-post service began.
1913	The 16th Amendment to the Constitution gave Congress the legal power to levy income taxes.

WOODROW WILSON

28th President of the United States
1913–1921

From one point of view, Woodrow Wilson was a stiff-necked, intellectual snob given to moralizing, always certain he was right, loath to compromise. He struck many people as distant and aloof. On the other hand, as a college teacher Wilson was no dreary scholar. Like many good teachers, he sprinkled his lectures with humorous stories to make points, and he wrote well.

As a political leader Wilson was quick, intuitive, and at times inspirational. In political affairs he was not forever deaf to compromise—no politician who wishes to survive can be.

Wilson's grandfather, James Wilson, a Scotch-Irishman, emigrated to Philadelphia in 1807. There he married Anne Adams, the daughter of a Presbyterian minister. Wilson's father, Joseph, was also a minister, and he was pastor of a Presbyterian church in Staunton, Va., at the time of Woodrow's birth on Dec. 29, 1856. Before Wilson was 2 years old the family was living in Augusta, Ga., where his father had accepted a new pastorship.

As a boy, Wilson witnessed the effects of the Civil War, especially General William T. Sherman's march through Georgia in 1864. The war closed many schools, so Wilson had no formal education until he was 9. His father taught him a great deal at home, and he also grounded the boy firmly in Presbyterian principles and beliefs. Wilson's father also passed on a great respect for literature and for the spoken as well as the written word. As Wilson recalled years later: "I was swollen with pride as I listened to my father's preaching; and if he hesitated for a word I would, in my mind, supply it. I can still feel that exultant thrill of joy if I got the right word in my mind before he voiced it from the pulpit."

Woodrow Wilson

*Ellen Axson Wilson shared
academic life with the future
President and had a studio
installed in the White
House so that she might
pursue her interest in
painting.*

Full name: Woodrow
Wilson

Born: Dec. 29, 1856

Birthplace: Staunton, Va.

Died: Feb. 3, 1924

Burial site: Washington,
D.C.

Spouses: Ellen Louise
Axson; Edith Bolling
Galt

Occupation: Educator

Political party:
Democratic

Terms: 1913–1921

Vice-President: Thomas
R. Marshall

Runners-up: Theodore
Roosevelt; Charles E.
Hughes

Electoral votes: 435; 277

Runners-up: 88; 254

Popular votes: 6,293,152;
9,126,300

Runners-up: 4,119,207;
8,546,789

After a year at Davidson College in North Carolina, the 18-year-old Wilson entered Princeton University in New Jersey (then called the College of New Jersey). Upon graduation from Princeton in 1879, he studied law and then attended Johns Hopkins University in Baltimore for advanced study in history and government. Wilson received his Ph.D. there in 1886.

The year before, Wilson became a lecturer at Johns Hopkins at a salary of $500 a year and a professor of history at Bryn Mawr, a newly founded women's college near Philadelphia, at $1,500 a year. To a person brought up on the meager income of a minister, $2,000 a year seemed like a princely sum. Most important, it meant that Wilson could marry Ellen Louise Axson, whom he had met on a business trip to Rome, Ga., in 1883. She was, like him, the offspring of a Presbyterian minister. They were married on June 24, 1885, and Ellen became trusted adviser as well as wife. Wilson once described her as receptive, not aggressive, having what he called "a speaking silence." Their marriage was a happy one.

The Wilsons had three daughters—Margaret, Jessie, and Eleanor. This delighted Wilson, for he deeply enjoyed the company of women, especially those who were bright and educated.

The Wilsons moved from Bryn Mawr to Wesleyan University in Connecticut, then to Princeton. In 1902, Wilson became that university's president. He earned a nationwide reputation as a college administrator, and this helped move him into politics.

At the time, machine politics had given New Jersey a reputation as one of the more corrupt states in the Union. Democratic boss James Smith, Jr., casting about in 1910 for an honest candidate for governor to remove some of the taint, found the person he needed in Woodrow Wilson. And Wilson, who had studied and taught government and written books about it, was eager to run. He won election in the fall of 1910.

As governor, Wilson fooled and dismayed the bosses. He took it upon himself to clean up New Jersey. He pushed through the legislature reform measures such as a primary election law, a corrupt practices act, a law regulating and taxing public utility companies, and a law holding employers liable for workers' injuries on the job.

Wilson's reputation as a reformer—along with careful planning and organization—brought him the Democratic presidential nomination in 1912. With William Howard Taft and Theodore Roosevelt splitting Republican support, Wilson went on to win that fall with 435 electoral votes to his opponents' combined 96.

During his inauguration on March 4, 1913, Wilson noticed that a wide space had been cleared in front of the speaker's platform. He motioned to the police holding back the crowd and ordered: "Let the people come forward." His supporters said the phrase expressed the spirit of his administration.

In his inaugural address, the President accepted the challenge of the November landslide that had also swept a Democratic Congress into office. "No one can mistake the purpose for which the nation now seeks to use the Democratic Party," he declared. "It seeks to use it to interpret a change in its plans and point of view." Among the laws that needed to be changed,

Wilson named those governing tariffs, industry, and the banking system.

Wilson was the last President to ride to his inauguration in a horse-drawn carriage. Neither he nor his wife liked large social affairs, so the Wilsons did not give an inaugural ball. On March 15, only 11 days after his inauguration, Wilson held the first regular presidential press conference. He felt that the people were entitled to reports on the progress of his administration.

In the White House

Ellen Wilson turned the White House attic into guest rooms, reserving one with a skylight as a studio in which she could paint. After Congress voted money to restore the flower gardens on each side of the mansion's south portico, she designed and laid out one of them. Ellen made slum clearance in Washington, D.C., her main social project. The city of trash-filled alleys and dilapidated housing badly needed it. Congress was persuaded to appropriate money for the work.

There had been marriages in the White House before, but under Wilson there were two. Jessie married Francis B. Sayre on Nov. 25, 1913, in the East Room. Eleanor and William Gibbs McAdoo, Wilson's secretary of the treasury, followed on May 7,

Edith Galt Wilson married the widower President in 1915, and during his long illness in 1919 she took over many of the routine duties in the White House.

Woodrow Wilson delivered his war message to a joint session of Congress on April 2, 1917. America declared war four days later.

OCEAN STEAMSHIPS.

CUNARD

EUROPE VIA LIVERPOOL

LUSITANIA

Fastest and Largest Steamer
now in Atlantic Service Sails
SATURDAY, MAY 1, 10 A.M.
Transylvania, Fri.,   May 7, 5 P.M.
Orduna, - - Tues., May 18, 10 A.M.
Tuscania, - - Fri., May 21, 5 P.M.
LUSITANIA, Sat., May 29, 10 A.M.
Transylvania, Fri., June 4, 5 P.M.

Gibraltar—Genoa—Naples—Piraeus
S.S. Carpathia, Thur., May 13, Noon

NOTICE!

TRAVELLERS intending to
embark on the Atlantic voyage
are reminded that a state of
war exists between Germany
and her allies and Great Britain
and her allies; that the zone of
war includes the waters adja-
cent to the British Isles; that,
in accordance with formal notice given by the Imperial German Government, vessels flying
the flag of Great Britain, or of
any of her allies, are liable to
destruction in those waters and
that travellers sailing in the
war zone on ships of Great
Britain or her allies do so at
their own risk.

IMPERIAL GERMAN EMBASSY

WASHINGTON, D. C., APRIL 22, 1915.

*Nearly 1,200 people who
did not heed this notice lost
their lives when a German
U-boat torpedoed and sank
the liner Lusitania on May
7, 1915.*

1914. Eleanor's wedding was the smaller because her mother had become ill. Ellen's health continued to decline, and she died on Aug. 6, 1914.

The melancholy that overtook Wilson upon Ellen's death finally lifted when he met Edith Bolling Galt, the widow of a Washington, D.C., jeweler. They were married at her Washington home on Dec. 18, 1915.

As President, Wilson pushed reform programs just as he had when governor of New Jersey. Congress lowered tariff rates, established the Federal Reserve System and the Federal Trade Commission, and strengthened antitrust laws. It limited the working hours of children and set eight hours as the working day for railroad employees. Congress enacted a federal income tax after the 16th Amendment, which went into effect in 1913, made such legislation constitutional. The government under Wilson also had to deal with the problem of keeping the United States neutral while maintaining freedom of trade on the high seas after World War I began in August 1914.

Running under the Democratic slogan "He Kept Us Out of War," Wilson campaigned for re-election in 1916. On election night, the outcome was confused because of delays in receiving the election returns. Wilson went to bed believing his opponent, Republican Charles Evans Hughes, had won. Many newspapers carried stories of Wilson's "defeat." But the final count in California gave the state to Wilson by 4,000 votes. This insured his re-election. The victory was narrow, however. Wilson's margin over Hughes was only 23 electoral votes out of 531.

The United States did not stay out of the conflict much longer. Germany had declared all waters around the British Isles a war zone. On May 7, 1915, a German submarine sank the British passenger liner *Lusitania* off the coast of Ireland, and 128 of the 1,198 persons killed were Americans. This aroused great anger in the United States, but President Wilson insisted the U.S. would remain neutral. Many U.S. merchant ships were sunk in the following months, however, and the United States entered the war officially on April 6, 1917.

Aside from news of battle deaths, most Americans at home remembered World War I as a time of Liberty Bonds and conservation of food, energy, labor, and other resources. The Wilsons cut White House entertaining to a minimum and, to save the labor involved in keeping the lawn trimmed, agreed to turn a flock of sheep onto it. The flock multiplied and, besides keeping the grass neatly cropped, produced wool. About 98 pounds (44 kilograms) sold at auction brought $100,000, which was donated to the Red Cross.

During the war, President Wilson spoke repeatedly of the necessity of making a better world after the war. In a speech on Jan. 8, 1918, he listed his famous Fourteen Points, to be used as a guide for a peace settlement. They included freedom of navigation, an end to secret diplomacy and trade barriers, arms reductions, and the creation of an association of nations to work for permanent peace.

When the war ended in November 1918, President Wilson met in Paris with other Allied leaders. France, Great Britain, and Italy had never officially accepted Wilson's Fourteen Points. They refused to accept many of them in Paris. Wilson was forced to compromise on many points but did win acceptance of his plan to establish an association of nations—the League of Nations.

Wilson Rejected

Wilson returned home with high hopes that the Senate would accept the Treaty of Versailles without change, making the United States a member of the League. Here he met his greatest disappointment. Wilson's concessions in Paris weakened him politically, and he found opposition to the treaty growing. The Republican-controlled Senate refused to ratify the treaty without changes regarding the League of Nations, most of them aimed at maintaining United States sovereignty.

On Sept. 4, 1919, Wilson began a speaking tour through the Midwest and Far West, hoping to win public support for his stand. The tour ended on September 25, when the overworked and exhausted President collapsed from fatigue. On October 2, Wilson suffered a stroke that left him partially paralyzed with speech impaired, and during his illness Edith Wilson made many of the day-to-day decisions in the White House.

In the meantime, the Treaty of Versailles went down to defeat in the Senate. The League of Nations was established, but the United States never joined. On Dec. 10, 1920, Wilson was awarded the 1919 Nobel Peace Prize for his work in founding the League of Nations and seeking a fair peace agreement.

Woodrow Wilson believed that God guides all human activity. Shortly after his election in 1912 he declared to a Democratic Party official: "God ordained that I should be the next

The signing of the peace treaty in Versailles's Hall of Mirrors, June 28, 1919. President Wilson is seated, center left.

Wilson in Columbus, O., in 1919 during his national tour to gain support for U.S. participation in the League of Nations.

President of the United States. Neither you nor any other mortal could have prevented that!" On his last public appearance, on Armistice Day in 1923, he said in reference to the League and its defeat in the Senate: "I am not one of those who have the least anxiety about the triumph of the principles I have stood for. I have seen fools resist Providence before and I have seen their destruction. . . . That we shall prevail is as sure as that God reigns."

Regardless of whether Wilson was, as he believed, a chosen instrument of God, he was a strong, forceful President. His vision of U.S. participation in a world peacekeeping organization came to pass in 1945, when the United States took the lead in establishing the United Nations. Wilson died on Feb. 3, 1924. He was buried in Washington Cathedral, the only President to be interred in Washington, D.C.

President Wilson's Times
1913–1921

The U.S. Flag had 48 stars when Wilson took office. No new states or territories were organized. The U.S. population was about 108,600,000 in 1921.

1913	The 17th Amendment to the Constitution became law, providing for the election of U.S. Senators by popular vote instead of by state legislatures.
1913	The Federal Reserve System was created. It set up a central banking system for the United States.
1914	World War I began in Europe. The four-year conflict between the Allies and Central Powers would cost more than 37,000,000 military casualties.
1914	A passenger-cargo ship made the first complete trip through the Panama Canal.
1915	The first telephone line linking New York City and San Francisco began operating.
1915	A German submarine sank the British *Lusitania,* contributing to the rise of sentiment among Americans for entering World War I.
1917	The Virgin Islands were purchased by the United States from Denmark for $25,000,000.
1917	The United States entered World War I.
1918	Wilson proposed his Fourteen Points.
1918	The first airmail route was established between New York City, Philadelphia, and Washington, D.C.
1919	The 18th Amendment to the Constitution, banning the manufacture, sale, and transportation of alcoholic beverages, became law.
1919	British fliers made the first nonstop transatlantic flight.
1919	The Allies and Germany signed the Treaty of Versailles, which officially ended World War I.
1920	The League of Nations was established.
1920	The 19th Amendment to the Constitution, giving women the right to vote, became law.
1920	The first commercial radio broadcasts were made from Detroit and Pittsburgh.

WARREN G. HARDING

29th President of the United States
1921–1923

"Judge," said Warren G. Harding one day in 1921 to John Barton Payne, a golfing partner, "I don't think I'm big enough for the presidency." Yet the tall, handsome, silver-haired Harding looked like a President. And for many Americans weary of war, of Democrats, and of such forceful Chief Executives as Theodore Roosevelt and Woodrow Wilson, that was enough. The nation elected Harding overwhelmingly in 1920.

The first Harding, Richard, came to Braintree (now Quincy), Mass., from England in 1623. Warren, a member of the 10th generation, was born on a farm near what is now Blooming Grove, O., on Nov. 2, 1865. His father George was both a farmer and a doctor.

Life on the Hardings' farm was little different from what it had been for their ancestors: simple but hard. As one of Warren's Ohio contemporaries wrote:

> It was hard work in season and out. In summertime we were in the fields at sunrise; we came in for dinner at eleven o'clock, had supper at four o'clock and then followed the plow or the sickle until sundown. . . .
>
> The budget on the farm was rather simply conducted. The sale of lambs and wool usually took care of the June taxes. The December assessments were met by the sale of hogs. . . . Groceries . . . were purchased by the marketing of butter, eggs, and chickens. The early part of the winter was the clothing era. It was usually the sale of surplus wheat or corn that met this requirement.

Harding's mother, Phoebe, taught him to read, and he attended

WARREN GAMALIEL HARDING
PRESIDENT OF THE UNITED STATES OF AMERICA
1920   1923

Florence Harding, known as the "Duchess," enjoyed her life as first lady after fostering presidential ambitions in her husband.

Full name: Warren Gamaliel Harding

Born: Nov. 2, 1865

Birthplace: Near Blooming Grove, O.

Died: Aug. 2, 1923

Burial site: Marion, O.

Spouse: Florence Kling DeWolfe

Occupation: Publisher

Political party: Republican

Term: 1921–1923

Vice-President: Calvin Coolidge

Runner-up: James M. Cox

Electoral vote: 404

Runner-up: 127

Popular vote: 16,133,314

Runner-up: 9,140,884

grammar school in Blooming Grove. As a child, Warren learned to play the cornet, and he later mastered other instruments as well. One of his pleasures as a youth and adult was playing in community band concerts. He went to high school in Iberia, O., where he was active in debate and edited the high school newspaper.

After graduation Harding got into the newspaper business in Marion, O. In 1884, with two partners, he bought the *Marion Star,* a daily, for $300. Seven years later, he married Florence Kling DeWolfe, whom he called "Duchess." Florence belonged to a prominent Marion banking family. A divorcee with a son, she was intelligent, strong willed, and ambitious. She helped Harding build the *Star* into a prosperous daily.

In 1898, as a Republican, Harding won election to the Ohio legislature. He later became lieutenant governor, and in 1914 Ohioans elected him to the U.S. Senate.

Although popular, Harding made no record of note in Congress. His name was floated for possible presidential candidacy in 1919, a year before the Republican convention, although he was at best lukewarm to the idea. Harding enjoyed the comforts and privileges of the Senate. But Florence Harding had different ideas, and so did Harry Daugherty, an Ohio lawyer and politician who had helped Harding's career in the past. Events matched Daugherty's expectations at the convention in Chicago in June 1920. After nine ballots failed to break a deadlock among strong candidates, the delegates accepted Harding. As someone said, he "was everyone's second choice." Calvin Coolidge, governor of Massachusetts, became the vice-presidential candidate.

In his campaign, Harding promised to return the country to "normalcy," by which he may have meant the relatively untroubled, uncomplicated times he had known on the Ohio farm. He also promised no more turmoil over reform and no more high taxes. This pleased the majority of voters. In November 1920, when Americans heard election returns broadcast over radio for the first time, they learned that Harding had defeated James M. Cox by 404 to 127 electoral votes.

Florence Harding enjoyed her role as first lady. Her favorite entertainments were White House garden parties that attracted hundreds of people. Harding liked them, too. "I love to meet people," he told his secretary. "It is the most pleasant thing I do; it is really the only fun I have. It does not tax me, and it seems to be a very great pleasure to them."

Best of all, though, Harding enjoyed dinners with a few close friends. The 18th Amendment, prohibiting the manufacture and sale of alcoholic beverages in America, went into effect in 1920. Still, Harding's White House guests enjoyed cocktails before the evening meal of sauerkraut and sausage. After dinner, refreshments continued and the guests played bridge or poker.

During his campaign, Harding promised to work for an "association of nations." Like most Republicans, he felt that during World War I President Woodrow Wilson had taken powers that properly belonged to Congress. Harding depended on Congress and on his Cabinet to provide leadership from the beginning of his administration. He took a narrow view of his constitutional powers. During the "return to normalcy," Harding quickly ended the deadlock on the League of Nations. He signed peace treaties that did not include the League covenant with Germany and the other Central Powers.

In domestic legislation, Congress took the leadership. It placed quotas on immigration for the first time in 1921. It reduced taxes, and, in 1922, it raised tariffs to record heights.

The Harding Administration is best remembered for scandals involving charges of bribery, kickbacks, and theft. Harding, a poor judge of character, took many of his friends to Washington, D.C., with him. Some of them betrayed him. In perhaps the best-known case, the Teapot Dome scandal, Secretary of the Interior Albert B. Fall went to prison for accepting a bribe and leasing government oil reserves to private companies.

Harding may have gotten an inkling of wrongdoing by some of his friends shortly before leaving for a tour of Alaska and the Pacific Northwest in 1923. However, he fell ill in Seattle, Wash. Pneumonia set in, and he died on Aug. 2, 1923, in San Francisco. News of the scandals had not yet spread. As Harding's body was returned to Washington, mourning crowds gathered along the route.

Mrs. Harding burned as much of his correspondence as she could in an effort to protect his memory. She died the following year and was buried beside her husband in Marion, O.

President Harding's Times
1921–1923

The U.S. Flag had 48 stars when Harding took office. No new states or territories were organized. The U.S. population was about 111,900,000 in 1923.

1921–1922	The Washington Conference, held in both years by leading nations, agreed to limit naval arms.
1921	Peace treaties with Germany and Austria were signed by the United States.
1921	The Unknown Soldier of World War I was buried at Arlington National Cemetery.
1922	Benito Mussolini became dictator of Italy.
1922	The Union of Soviet Socialist Republics was formed by the Communists.
1923	The Teapot Dome scandal involving Cabinet members shocked the country.

CALVIN COOLIDGE

30th President of the United States
1923–1929

It was easy to make fun of stern-faced, Silent Calvin Coolidge. He rarely smiled, almost never laughed, and was apt to sit silently through official dinners. Mainly, he was quiet because he was shy. Even the social whirl of Washington did nothing to enliven him. At one affair, a woman told him she had bet that she could get more than two words out of him. "You lose," replied Coolidge. Years later, when asked to recall his first thought upon becoming President, he replied: "I thought I could swing it."

Coolidge was elected Vice-President in 1920. He became President upon Warren G. Harding's death in 1923. Political cronyism and scandal had marked the Harding years, but Coolidge's honesty was never questioned. Alice Roosevelt Longworth, daughter of Theodore Roosevelt, said about the Coolidge White House: "The atmosphere was as different as a New England front parlor is from a back room in a speakeasy." Another observer commented that it was as if a bowl of field flowers had replaced an ashtray full of cigar ends.

As President, Calvin Coolidge knew what he was doing. He fit his time. Americans liked him. They elected him President in his own right in 1924 and probably would have voted him into office again in 1928 had he chosen to run.

The Coolidge roots were strictly Puritan and Yankee. John Coolidge, who emigrated to Watertown, Mass., from England in about 1630, was the first to set them down in America. Calvin was born on July 4, 1872, in Plymouth Notch, Vt. His father John ran a general store, and he bought a farm across the road from it when Calvin was 4. John Coolidge also served four terms in the Vermont legislature.

Vivacious and talkative, Grace Goodhue Coolidge, a former teacher of the deaf, stood in sharp contrast to her tight-lipped husband.

Full name: Calvin Coolidge

Born: July 4, 1872

Birthplace: Plymouth Notch, Vt.

Died: Jan. 5, 1933

Burial site: Plymouth Notch, Vt.

Spouse: Grace Anna Goodhue

Occupation: Lawyer

Political party: Republican

Terms: 1923–1929

Vice-President: Charles G. Dawes

Runner-up: John W. Davis

Electoral vote: 382

Runner-up: 136

Popular vote: 15,717,553

Runner-up: 8,386,169

Calvin attended the Plymouth Notch grammar school and the nearby Ludlow, Vt., high school. He graduated with honors from Amherst College in Massachusetts in 1895. He studied law and passed the Massachusetts bar exam, but practiced little. After he won election to the Northampton, Mass., city council in 1898, politics became his life. And in 1904, he met the charming and pretty Grace Goodhue. She already knew of him.

Grace, a teacher in the Clarke Institute for the Deaf in Northampton, lived with other teachers in Baker Hall, next to the school. Coolidge stayed at a nearby house belonging to Robert N. Weir, a school official. One day while watering the flowers, Grace glanced through an open window and saw a man shaving—in a union suit (long underwear) and a hat. Grace let out a whoop of laughter everyone in the neighborhood heard, including the man in the hat and long underwear.

Coolidge later explained to Grace that an unruly lock of hair always got in his way as he shaved, so he wore the hat to hold it down. He did not need to explain the underattire, which was common among males at the time.

Fun-loving, talkative, and often given to laughter, Grace was quite the opposite of the thin-lipped Silent Cal, who kept quiet so much of the time. They were married on Oct. 4, 1905. The Coolidges had two sons, John and Calvin, Jr.

Steady Progress in Politics

Coolidge's political progress as a Republican was steady, though not spectacular. He served in the Massachusetts legislature, as lieutenant governor, and as mayor of Northampton. In 1918, he became governor of Massachusetts.

In 1919, the Boston police went on strike, demanding recognition of their union and higher pay. Chaos quickly overtook the city. Declaring that "there is no right to strike against the public safety by anybody, anywhere, any time," Governor Coolidge broke the strike. His action gained national attention and helped bring him the vice-presidential nomination in 1920. Under Harding, Coolidge was the first Vice-President to attend Cabinet meetings regularly.

While vacationing on his father's farm, he was awakened early on Aug. 3, 1923, and told that Harding had died. Coolidge dressed, prayed, and went downstairs. By the light of a kerosene lamp, Coolidge's father, a notary public, administered the presidential oath. Coolidge then went back to bed. Eighteen days later, Coolidge had a second oath of office administered by a justice of the Supreme Court of the District of Columbia. Attorney General Harry M. Daugherty had questioned the validity of the first oath because Coolidge's father had authority to swear in only state officials of Vermont.

Coolidge entered the White House just as the Teapot Dome and other scandals of the Harding Administration became public. The new President made no effort to shield the guilty. His personal honesty was never questioned. In 1924, he forced the resignation of Attorney General Daugherty and other high officials who had been connected with the scandals. He continued Harding's policy of supporting American business at home and

Taking action in the Boston police strike of 1919, Governor Calvin Coolidge ordered out units of the Massachusetts state troops.

abroad, favoring a program he called "constructive economy."

After a year in office, running on the slogan "Keep Cool with Coolidge," Silent Cal won his own term, gaining 382 electoral votes to John W. Davis' 136. The good economic times that had begun in America under Harding continued, known now as "Coolidge prosperity." Stock prices on Wall Street soared to new highs and kept climbing.

Personal tragedy struck the Coolidges in 1924. Their 16-year-old son Calvin developed a blister on a toe while playing tennis. The infection spread, and young Coolidge died of blood poisoning.

Throughout his term of office, President Coolidge was a pest to the White House staff. He liked to pop into the kitchen unexpectedly to inspect food supplies and menus and stress the wisdom of economy. He once wondered if six rather small Virginia hams were not too much for 60 dinner guests. He played practical jokes, such as pushing all the buttons on his desk and sitting back to laugh as all his aides appeared at his office door at once. Coolidge often punched the elevator button to summon the cage and its attendant, quickly walking down the stairs before the elevator arrived. He had his own nicknames for all members of the staff. According to the housekeeper's report, the houseman on the second floor became "The Frog." The front doorman was "Front Door Jack" and the back doorman, who took care of the dogs, was "Back Door Jack." The chambermaid was "That Person." Although she was incredibly neat, he liked to pretend that she was careless in her personal appearance.

Grace Coolidge was a charming and pleasant hostess and she enjoyed entertaining. The great and famous welcomed to the White House during the Coolidge years included Charles A. Lindbergh, just home after his epic solo flight across the Atlantic Ocean in 1927; the 30-year-old Edward, Prince of Wales, later King Edward VIII of England; and Queen Marie of Romania.

In March 1925, Americans listened for the first time to an inaugural address over radio, and Coolidge was quick to realize the political advantage broadcasting offered. "I am very fortunate that I came in with the radio," he told a senator one day. "I can't make an engaging, rousing . . . speech to a crowd as you can, . . . but I have a good radio voice, and now I can get my messages across . . . without acquainting them with my lack of oratorical ability."

Coolidge also recognized the value of newspaper publicity. He frequently held press conferences and seldom denied the press "photo opportunities." Probably the best-known Coolidge photo shows him in the feathered ceremonial headdress of a Plains Indian.

"Less Government"

Declaring that "the business of America is business," Coolidge supported high tariffs on imported manufactured goods to help American manufacturers. He also favored low taxes on business and strict economy in government. He contended that the less government, the better. Coolidge believed in economy and a simple way of life, but many Americans discarded all thoughts of thrift during this period of prosperity. The President did not try to stop the speculation that ended in the stock-market crash of 1929.

In 1927 Calvin Coolidge announced that he did not choose to run again for the presidency. There is evidence that he regretted the decision as nomination time approached that year, but he kept his position. In March 1929, saying to reporters, "Goodbye, I have had a very enjoyable time in Washington," he and Mrs. Coolidge left the capital for their home in Northampton. But the stream of tourists past their home made it impossible to enjoy a quiet life. In 1930, Coolidge bought an estate in Northampton called The Beeches. It had an iron gate to keep curious visitors at a distance.

During retirement Coolidge wrote his autobiography. He also turned out a daily newspaper column, "Thinking Things over with Calvin Coolidge." He wrote chiefly about government, economics, and politics. He had become a life trustee of Amherst College in 1921, and was named a director of the New York Life Insurance Company in 1929.

The stock-market crash in October 1929 and the resulting nationwide depression distressed Coolidge. He became increasingly unhappy as the depression deepened during the fall and winter of 1932.

Calvin Coolidge needed few words to announce the end of his presidency, saying "I do not choose to run for President in 1928."

On Jan. 5, 1933, Mrs. Coolidge found him lying on the floor of his bedroom, where he had died of a heart attack. He was buried beside his son and father in the Plymouth Notch cemetery. Mrs. Coolidge returned to Northampton where she lived until her death on July 8, 1957.

President Coolidge's Times
1923–1929

The U.S. Flag had 48 stars when Coolidge took office. No new states or territories were organized. The U.S. population was about 122,000,000 in 1929.

1924	The first round-the-world flight was made by two U.S. Army biplanes.
1926	The first flight over the North Pole was made by Richard E. Byrd and Floyd Bennett.
1927	Radiotelephony connected New York City and London.
1927	Charles Lindbergh flew nonstop across the Atlantic.
1927	The first "talking" motion picture, *The Jazz Singer,* was produced.
1928	The Kellogg-Briand Peace Pact was signed in Paris.

HERBERT HOOVER

31st President of the United States
1929–1933

Herbert Hoover enjoyed a reputation as a brilliant mining engineer, a humanitarian, and a first-rate administrator of government programs and agencies. Franklin D. Roosevelt in the 1920's called him a "wonder." He wished to see Hoover as President, saying there could not be a better one. Hoover was elected President in 1928, although not as a Democrat, as Roosevelt would have liked. Then, seven months after his inauguration, the stock market crashed, taking Hoover and his reputation down with it.

Hoover traced his ancestry in America to Andreas Huber, a Swiss-German who reached Philadelphia in 1738. The future President was born in West Branch, Ia., on Aug. 10, 1874. His father, Jesse, a blacksmith and a dealer in farm equipment, was by no means well-to-do. Jesse and Hulda Hoover were Quakers, and Herbert grew up in that faith. An aunt remembered him as a "mischievous, laughing boy," and his first grade teacher rated him an average student, good in arithmetic.

Hoover's father died in 1880. His mother died three years later. Now orphaned, young Herbert spent some time with an uncle in West Branch and then went to live with another uncle in Newberg, Ore. There, he completed high school at 15.

When he was 17, Hoover entered the newly opened Stanford University in Palo Alto, Calif. Working part-time and during the summers, he paid most of his own expenses. Hoover graduated with a degree in geology in 1895 and worked for a mining company in California for a time.

While at Stanford, Hoover met Lou Henry, a banker's daughter and, like him, a geology student. She spoke several languages and had a deep interest in other sciences, and in liter-

Herbert Hoover

Well-educated in languages, literature, and the arts, an excellent rider and lover of outdoor life, Lou Henry married future President Herbert Hoover in 1899.

Full name: Herbert Clark Hoover

Born: Aug. 10, 1874

Birthplace: West Branch, Ia.

Died: Oct. 20, 1964

Burial site: West Branch, Ia.

Spouse: Lou Henry

Occupation: Engineer

Political party: Republican

Term: 1929–1933

Vice-President: Charles Curtis

Runner-up: Alfred E. Smith

Electoral vote: 444

Runner-up: 87

Popular vote: 21,411,991

Runner-up: 15,000,185

ature and art as well. In addition, Lou was athletic and a fine rider. "I want a man who loves the mountains, the rocks, and the ocean like my father does," she once commented, and she found him in Herbert Hoover. They were married on Feb. 10, 1899, and had two sons.

Herbert Hoover fit himself to the American image of the self-made individual. Through diligence and ability, Hoover made a fortune in mining ventures in China, Australia, the United States, and elsewhere. He never forgot, though, that he had come up the hard way, and he felt that everyone should have the opportunity to do so.

Administrative Ace

As World War I began, Hoover directed relief measures in England that were aimed at getting food to Belgium, which had been overrun by German armies. After the United States entered the war, Hoover served as head of the Food Administration, the federal agency concerned with the pricing, production, and distribution of food in the United States. President Warren G. Harding made him secretary of commerce, and President Calvin Coolidge kept him on in the post. Hoover registered an outstanding record in all his public service. When Coolidge decided not to run in 1928, the Republican Party turned to Hoover. Millions of Americans felt the Republicans would keep the nation prosperous. Many others opposed the Democratic candidate, Alfred E. Smith, because he was a Roman Catholic. Hoover won 40 of 48 states and 444 electoral votes to Smith's 87.

The new first family set up housekeeping at the White House in style. With money of their own, the Hoovers did not need to rely on Congress to pick up the bill for presidential entertainment. They could and did entertain lavishly. It was said that they dined alone only on their wedding anniversaries. It was also said that Mrs. Hoover never questioned the cost of food, demanding only that it be the best. The White House had a cook for the family and guests, another who prepared meals for the staff of about 30, and a pastry chef.

Lou Hoover saw to it that the staff was equal to all emergencies. Ava Long, the housekeeper, purchased lamb chops one day for an expected luncheon for four, only to be put on a half-hour notice that plans had changed. There would be 40 guests. She came up with croquettes made of lamb and pieces of ham, beef, and other meats ransacked from White House refrigerators and put through a grinder.

President Hoover worked out each day on the White House lawn for a half hour before breakfast. Rain, shine, snow, or sleet, the aides who made up the "medicine ball cabinet" joined him. Hoover's favorite sport was trout fishing, and he and Mrs. Hoover often visited a fishing camp they had established on the Rapidan River in Virginia, about 100 miles (161 kilometers) from the capital.

Though farmers and other wage earners were having a tough time in the 1920's, American business prospered. During the 1928 campaign, Hoover had said, "We in America today are nearer to the final triumph over poverty than ever before in the history of any land. The poor house is vanishing from among us." After the election, he reflected:

> I have no dread of the ordinary work of the presidency. What I do fear is the result of the exaggerated idea the people have conceived of me. They have a conviction that I am a sort of superman, that no problem is beyond my capacity. . . . If some unprecedented calamity should come upon the nation . . . I would be sacrificed to the unreasoning disappointment of a people who expected too much.

Calamity came, and Hoover was blamed.

The prosperity of the 1920's proved top-heavy and thin, built mainly on stock speculation and wishes. Black Thursday, Oct. 24, 1929, brought ruin to the dream, the economy, and to Herbert Hoover. Wall Street posted stock losses in the billions of dollars that day, and stock values did not hit bottom for several years thereafter.

By early 1930, factories were closing. More than 1,300 banks closed by the end of the same year. Unemployment lists were growing—by 1932, 12 million Americans, one-fourth of the entire labor force, were out of work. The prices of corn, wheat, and cotton dropped drastically, and hundreds of thousands of desperate farmers glumly awaited foreclosure, the sheriff's sale, and the loss of their land. Families began to live in dumps of shacks that became known as Hoovervilles.

Future President Herbert Hoover (standing) with aborigine shield, spear, and boomerangs on a mining expedition in Australia.

Some people still could joke about it, but their humor cut with a bitter edge. According to one story, Hoover said to Secretary of the Treasury Andrew Mellon: "Andy, I came out without a cent in my pocket. Lend me a nickel, will you? I want to call up a friend."

Replied Mellon: "Here's a dime. Call up both of them."

Depression Stance

Herbert Hoover was sensitive to human suffering, but he believed in state and local government responsibility for relief to the needy. He took the position that "natural" economic forces would eventually overcome the depression without federal programs. Hoover agreed to federal loans to states for relief measures and to banks and businesses. He supported a few federal conservation projects that provided some employment. That was as far as he would go.

Hoover's administration saw the beginning of construction of Boulder Dam, now called Hoover Dam, on the Colorado River. The government worked to develop inland waterways for navigation and flood control and added about 3,000,000 acres (1,214,057 hectares) to national parks and monuments. It enlarged the national forests and built more than 800 public buildings. It helped states build about 37,000 miles (59,546 kilometers) of major highways.

During the early 1930's, unemployed workers staged hunger marches and demonstrations in several cities. The Bonus Expeditionary Force, an "army" of World War I veterans, was the most famous. The bonus law of 1924 had given every veteran a certificate that was payable in 1945. The veterans wanted the bonus paid immediately. The House of Representatives passed a bill to meet the demand, and in June 1932, about 15,000 veterans marched on the capital to bring pressure on the Senate to pass the bill. But the Senate did not. Troops finally drove the veterans out of Washington. Hoover himself opposed the bonus because he thought it was financially unsound.

Digging out after the Democratic landslide that buried him in 1932, Hoover still had four months left in his administration. The economy did not improve. Bank failures and unemployment increased. Congress largely ignored Hoover's recommendations, and the President-elect, Franklin Roosevelt, would not promise to support Hoover's policies.

In February 1933, the 20th Amendment, known as the "lame duck amendment," became law. It changed the last day of a President's term from March 4 to January 20. The provision did not go into effect until October 1933.

When he left office, Hoover had more than 30 years of public life ahead of him. He chaired the Famine Emergency Commission after World War II and served on two presidential commissions to reorganize government agencies. He became a director or a trustee of many educational, scientific, and charitable organizations. He also wrote several books.

Herbert Hoover died on Oct. 20, 1964, at the age of 90. By then he stood much higher in public esteem than when he had

Depositors besiege a closed New Jersey bank in 1929 as the stock market crash began the Great Depression.

left the presidency in March 1933. The country mourned him as a truly great American. Hoover was buried near his birthplace in West Branch.

President Hoover's Times
1929–1933

The U.S. Flag had 48 stars when Hoover took office. No new states or territories were organized. The U.S. population was about 125,600,000 in 1933.

1929	The stock market crash took place in October. It marked the start of the Great Depression of the 1930's.
1930	The London Conference limited the size of ships and navies.
1931	The United States declared a moratorium on World War I debts.
1932	The "Bonus Army" of unemployed war veterans marched on Washington, D.C.
1933	Adolf Hitler became chancellor of Germany.
1933	The 20th Amendment to the Constitution made Hoover the last "lame duck" President.

FRANKLIN DELANO ROOSEVELT

32nd President of the United States
1933–1945

After the Democrats chose Franklin D. Roosevelt as their presidential candidate in Chicago in 1932, he appeared at the convention to accept the nomination in person. No candidate had ever done so before. Furthermore, Roosevelt flew in from New York, at a time when air travel was in its infancy, making the event even more dramatic. But with the United States in the deepest economic depression in its history, unprecedented times called for unprecedented action. "You have nominated me and I know it," he told his fellow Democrats in Chicago, "and I am here to thank you for the honor. Let it . . . be symbolic that in so doing I broke traditions."

That was not to be the last time that Roosevelt, who became known by his initials, F.D.R., shattered tradition. His program for economic recovery and change in America—called the New Deal—broke many. He also became the first and last person to be elected to four terms as President.

F.D.R. traced his ancestry to the same source as his cousin Theodore Roosevelt: to Claes Maertenszen van Rosenvelt, the Dutch immigrant who arrived in New Netherland in the 1640's. The line from one of Claes' grandsons, Johannes, had run to Theodore. That of another, Jacobus, produced Franklin. He was born on Jan. 30, 1882, on the family estate at Hyde Park, N.Y. The son of James and Sara Delano Roosevelt, he, like Theodore, was born into wealth.

F.D.R. grew up in a life of ease under the watchful eyes of doting parents who had no other children. Starting at age 3, he accompanied his mother and father on several trips to Europe. He spent summers at the family home on Campobello, a resort

Eleanor Roosevelt won praise for her humanitarian work. In 1946, she was elected head of the United Nations' Human Rights Commission.

Full name: Franklin Delano Roosevelt

Born: Jan. 30, 1882

Birthplace: Hyde Park, N.Y.

Died: April 12, 1945

Burial site: Hyde Park, N.Y.

Spouse: Eleanor Roosevelt

Occupation: Lawyer

Political party: Democratic

Terms: 1933-1945

Vice-Presidents:
John N. Garner; Henry A. Wallace; Harry S. Truman

Runners-up: Herbert Hoover; Alfred M. Landon; Wendell L. Willkie; Thomas E Dewey

Electoral vote: 472; 523; 449; 432

Runners-up: 59; 8; 82; 99

Popular votes: 22,825,016; 22,747,636; 27,263,448; 25,611,936

Runner-up: 15,758,397; 16,679,543; 22,336,260; 22,013,372

island off the coast of New Brunswick, Canada.

Although he attended one public school in Germany for six weeks, Roosevelt was schooled for the most part by governesses and tutors. When he was 14, he entered Groton, a private school in Massachusetts. He played football there, although at 14 he stood only 5 feet 3 inches (160 centimeters) tall and weighed little more than 100 pounds (45 kilograms). He also played baseball, badly, earning a place only on the lowly BBBB team—the "Bum Base Ball Boys." As he wrote his parents after one game: "The only ball I received I nobly missed, and it landed biff! on my stomach, to the great annoyance of that intricate organ, and to the great delight of all present." Roosevelt also sang in the Groton choir, at first as a soprano because his voice had not yet changed.

After Groton, Roosevelt entered Harvard University in 1900. There he majored in history and for a year edited the college newspaper. He entered Columbia University Law School in New York City in 1904, and he was admitted to the bar in 1907. By then, F.D.R. had been married for two years to his distant cousin Eleanor, Theodore Roosevelt's niece.

Franklin and Eleanor had known each other since childhood and became more closely acquainted while Franklin was at Harvard. Eleanor, born in 1884, had had an unhappy childhood. She adored her father, an alcoholic, who died when she was 9. She was bright and well educated, but she had come not to expect much of life, especially in the way of male attention. She was tall, awkward, and shy. She had not yet had a date at 18 and was pleasantly surprised when Franklin asked her to dance at a Christmas party. The romance blossomed, and at the family Thanksgiving gathering in 1903 Franklin informed his mother that he and Eleanor were engaged.

The two were married on March 17, 1905, in New York City. Theodore, recently elected President of the United States, came up from Washington, D.C., to give the bride away. As might be expected, Teddy was more the center of attention than the bride and groom.

Eleanor was a warm, devoted person, and she helped her husband's political career more and had greater influence on him than he usually cared to admit. They had six children, one daughter and five sons. One son died in infancy.

Politics and Polio

Not interested in practicing law, Roosevelt soon turned to politics. He was elected to the senate in 1910. In 1912, he campaigned on behalf of the Democratic presidential nominee, Woodrow Wilson. Wilson won, and he rewarded Roosevelt with appointment as assistant secretary of the navy. In 1920, F.D.R. became the Democratic vice-presidential candidate. That was not a Democratic year, but the campaign gave him national exposure. Soon, though, it appeared that Roosevelt's political career was finished. He came down with poliomyelitis in 1921, and the disease left both his legs withered. He could never again walk without braces, canes, and assistance. Roosevelt restored his general health by hard exercise, which built up his body and arm muscles.

Despite his handicap, Roosevelt remained active in the Democratic Party. He won the New York governorship in 1928, and he was re-elected two years later by a record majority. The reputation he established as governor helped bring him the Democratic nomination for President in 1932.

Because of the Great Depression, few doubted a Democratic victory that year. Roosevelt defeated Herbert Hoover by about 22.8 million popular ballots to 15.7 million, and by 472 to 59 electoral votes.

Neither Franklin nor Eleanor were strangers to the White House, and both took to public and private entertainment with enthusiasm, displaying considerable stamina. Eleanor herself could greet and shake hands with more than a thousand guests in the afternoon, and repeat the performance in the evening without wilting. She preferred informality, however, and left formal planning and execution entirely to her staff. Food—which according to some observers was not so good in the Roosevelt White House—interested her only to the extent that it supplied

George VI and Elizabeth (the current Queen Mother) attend services at St. James Church, Hyde Park, New York, with Eleanor and Franklin Roosevelt, during the British King's visit to Canada and the United States in June, 1939. To the right of Queen Elizabeth stands the Rector of St. James, Frank Wilson. Between the President and Mrs. Roosevelt stand their eldest son, James, and the President's mother, Sara Delano Roosevelt.

the body with necessary fuel to keep one going. Eleanor endured public criticism when she fed King George VI and Queen Elizabeth of England hot dogs at a picnic at Hyde Park during their visit in June 1939. She also gave them a formal state dinner in the White House.

Eleanor Roosevelt was no stay-at-home first lady. She was very much in the public eye. She wrote a daily newspaper column, "My Day." She made regular radio broadcasts, discussing issues and Roosevelt Administration policies. She also traveled the country on fact-finding missions for the President, feeding him much useful information on conditions under which people lived and on government programs. During her first eight years, she covered an average of 40,000 miles (64,374 kilometers) annually. A cartoon in *The New Yorker* magazine showed a miner at the bottom of a deep shaft looking up and exclaiming to his fellow worker: "Why, it's Mrs. Roosevelt!"

Equality for blacks and women was a special concern to Eleanor Roosevelt, and her husband's failure to push civil rights irked her. She did what she could, even in segregated Washington, D.C. When the Daughters of the American Revolution refused permission for Marian Anderson, the gifted black singer, to perform in their Constitution Hall in Washington, Eleanor Roosevelt promptly announced her resignation from the organization. She then arranged for Ms. Anderson to sing before the Lincoln Memorial on Easter Sunday in 1939. Thousands lined the Mall to listen. Eleanor later invited Marian Anderson to sing at the White House before the king and queen of England.

The first lady was pleased when her husband appointed Frances Perkins secretary of labor, the first woman to hold a Cabinet position. She sympathized with the trouble she thought F.D.R. must have had with labor leaders over that appointment.

The President's wife was largely responsible for the creation of the National Youth Administration (NYA), a federal agency which among other things provided part-time jobs for college and high school students. FDR doubted the political wisdom of the move, but NYA proved highly popular. "It was one of the occasions on which I was proud that the right thing was done regardless of political considerations," Eleanor remarked.

The New Deal

In January 1932, the noted political pundit Walter Lippmann had written in the *New York Herald Tribune* that Roosevelt was a pleasant man who would very much like to be President. Lippmann also pointed out that Roosevelt was without any important qualifications for the office.

Qualifications aside, Roosevelt proved to have more than just the desire. He possessed great zest for the office, and through his New Deal he entirely changed the role of the federal government and its relationship to Americans.

By the time F.D.R. took office in March 1933, the U.S. economy had hit bottom. Banks and businesses had failed by the thousands. Farm prices had reached new lows, and hundreds of thousands of farmers faced the loss of their land through mortgage foreclosure. About 13 million Americans—one-fourth

Roosevelt often made informal reports to the nation and gained public support through radio broadcasts known as the "fireside chats."

of the work force—were without jobs and income of any kind. State, local, and private relief funds were practically exhausted. Some people feared revolution in America.

F.D.R. had no master plan to end the depression, and he was no revolutionary. His New Deal was largely a matter of try this, try that, and stick with what seems to work. But it represented confidence and action, which is what Americans wanted.

Five days after Roosevelt became President, Congress began a special session called the "Hundred Days." It passed nearly all the bills he submitted during this period. The measures were aimed at helping farmers, industry, labor, savers and investors, and the needy. Roosevelt, a superb speaker, also began a series of radio broadcasts called "fireside chats," explaining his administration's actions.

The New Deal established subsidies and conservation pro-

grams to aid farmers. It attempted to foster industrial recovery
through wage, price, and production agreements among businesses under the National Industrial Recovery Act. It set up the
Federal Deposit Insurance Corporation to insure bank deposits,
preventing losses such as had occurred when banks closed. The
government guaranteed farm and homeowner mortgage loans.
Under the Civilian Conservation Corps, the federal government
put thousands of youths to work in forests and on conservation
projects. The National Labor Relations Act, called the Wagner
Act, gave labor the right to organize and bargain collectively
with employers. A beginning was made in a social security program that would offer pensions to the retired. Various public
works agencies, such as the Works Progress Administration
(WPA), provided employment for an average of 2 million workers annually. The New Deal also greatly increased business regulation with agencies such as the Securities and Exchange Commission and the Federal Communications Commission.

Some pieces of legislation, like the National Industrial Recovery Act and the Agricultural Adjustment Act, fell by the
wayside as the U.S. Supreme Court declared them unconstitutional. Other programs, like the WPA, were often ridiculed as
make-work, "leaf-raking" endeavors benefiting ne'er-do-wells
who refused to get out and look for "real" jobs. Yet they produced schools and other public buildings, sewage systems, and
paved streets, and they built community swimming pools in
many localities. The WPA also helped painters, writers, compos-
ers, and other artists.

Federal programs cost money. They were financed largely
through borrowing, which meant an increase in the public debt
and unbalanced budgets.

F.D.R. was as much criticized as praised for increasing the
influence of the federal government in American lives, for big
spending and running up the public debt, and for appearing to
be antibusiness. He responded at one time by quoting a remark
Abraham Lincoln made during the Civil War: "I do the very
best I know how—the very best I can; and I mean to keep on
doing so until the end. If the end brings me out all right, what
is said against me won't amount to anything. If the end brings
me out wrong, 10,000 angels swearing I was right would make
no difference." Whether the New Deal was successful, and good
or bad for the country, has been thoroughly argued up and
down since Roosevelt's time. But despite criticism from various
quarters, Roosevelt kept the majority of Americans behind him.
He easily won re-election in 1936, carrying the electoral votes of
every state save Maine and Vermont.

By the late 1930's, Japan's attacks on China, the rise of dic-
tatorships, and approaching war in Europe brought foreign affairs to the forefront in the Roosevelt Administration. Isolation-
ist sentiment in the United States throughout the decade had
reflected the desire of many Americans to hold the nation apart
from other countries. Roosevelt wanted to give "all aid short of
war" to nations opposing Germany, Italy, and Japan because he
believed these aggressors were a threat to democracy throughout
the world.

When World War II started in September 1939, many
Americans still believed that the United States could stay out of

it. The nation stopped all arms shipments to warring nations. Later, it allowed the Allies to buy arms for cash, but by 1940 the United Kingdom and China were running out of funds. F.D.R. then urged the nation to become "the great arsenal of democracy." The Lend-Lease Act, passed in March 1941, allowed the U.S. to supply war materials through sale, loan, or lease.

War Leader

In the 1940 campaign for his third term, Roosevelt promised to try to keep the nation out of war. Then France surrendered to Germany, and the French defeat shocked Americans. Most voters opted to stay with experienced leadership, and Roosevelt won easily with 449 electoral votes to Wendell Willkie's 82.

When Roosevelt started his third term, the United States was giving the United Kingdom all aid short of war. In January 1941, F.D.R. declared that all people are entitled to freedom of speech and worship and freedom from want and fear—the Four Freedoms. In August 1941, he and British Prime Minister Winston Churchill agreed in the Atlantic Charter to respect every nation's right to choose its own form of government; to guarantee free-

In the 1930's, the Works Progress Administration employed over eight million Americans, such as these laborers widening a street.

Three world leaders—Churchill of the United Kingdom, Roosevelt, and Stalin of the Soviet Union—meet at the Yalta Conference in February 1945.

dom of the seas; and to conduct peaceful world trade. Then, on Dec. 7, 1941, Japan suddenly attacked U.S. naval and military forces at Pearl Harbor, Hawaii. The United States was at war.

To meet with Churchill, Soviet Premier Joseph Stalin, and Generalissimo Chiang Kai-shek of China, Roosevelt left the country many times during the conflict—the first President to do so during wartime. He and Churchill decided that the Allies should concentrate on winning the war in Europe first. In 1943, they named General Dwight D. Eisenhower as supreme commander of the Allied Expeditionary Force. Then in June 1944, Allied forces landed on the Normandy coast. The invasion of Europe was under way.

Roosevelt said in 1944 that he wanted to retire, but he believed that it was his duty to run again, for his fourth term. Democrats urged voters not to "change horses in midstream." Roosevelt handily defeated Thomas E. Dewey, governor of New York, with 432 electoral votes to Dewey's 99.

The President was by then ill and exhausted. On April 12, 1945, Franklin D. Roosevelt died of a cerebral hemorrhage at his retreat in Warm Springs, Ga. He was buried at Hyde Park.

Eleanor continued in public life. She served as a delegate to the United Nations. She worked for humanitarian causes. She traveled extensively and published several books. She remained truly America's first lady until her death in 1962.

President Roosevelt's Times
1933–1945

The U.S. Flag had 48 stars when Roosevelt took office. No new states or territories were organized. The U.S. population was about 140,000,000 in 1945.

1933	The "Good Neighbor Policy" was proclaimed. It sought to strengthen friendly ties among nations of the Western Hemisphere.
1933	The "Bank Holiday" closed banks and helped end the bank crisis.
1933	The New Deal began with the "Hundred Days."
1933	The 21st Amendment to the Constitution, permitting the sale of liquor, ended Prohibition.
1935–1936	Italian forces under Benito Mussolini conquered Ethiopia.
1935	The National Recovery Act was declared unconstitutional by the U.S. Supreme Court.
1935	The Social Security Act was passed by Congress.
1936–1939	Rebels led by Francisco Franco defeated the Loyalists in the Spanish Civil War.
1937	Roosevelt tried to "pack" the Supreme Court with justices of his own choosing. The unsuccessful attempt caused a national controversy.
1939	World War II began with the German invasion of Poland.
1940	Congress passed the Selective Service and Training Act, America's first peacetime draft law.
1940	The American people broke tradition by electing Roosevelt to a third term as President.
1941	The Lend-Lease law, providing arms for Great Britain, made America the "Arsenal of Democracy."
1941	Japan attacked Pearl Harbor, bringing the United States into World War II.
1942	In December, the first nuclear chain reaction was achieved at the University of Chicago.
1944	Allied armies landed in Normandy.
1944	Congress approved the Servicemen's Readjustment Act, or "GI Bill of Rights."
1945	The "Big Three" met at Yalta, in the Crimea.

HARRY S. TRUMAN

33rd President of the United States
1945–1953

Only with great reluctance did Harry S. Truman accept nomination to the nation's second highest office. After Democratic leaders picked Truman as Franklin D. Roosevelt's running mate in 1944, the senator from Missouri told Robert E. Hannegan, Democratic National Committee chairperson, that he did not want to be Vice-President, that few people could be found who could remember who many recent Vice-Presidents of the United States were. Truman preferred to remain in the Senate, but, at Roosevelt's insistence, he accepted the nomination.

Then, at 7:09 P.M. on April 12, 1945, shortly after Roosevelt's death, Harry S. Truman was sworn in to the nation's highest office, an event that left him humbled and awestruck. He soon recovered, however, and became one of the stronger and more forthright, scrappy, and quotable Presidents of all time.

Harry S. Truman's great-grandfather, William Truman, was born in Virginia in 1783. William's son Anderson moved to Missouri in 1846. Harry, Anderson's grandson, was born on May 8, 1884, in Lamar, Mo., the oldest of three children of Martha Young and John Truman, a farmer and mule trader.

Poor eyesight plagued young Harry, and he began wearing glasses when he was 8. "I was so carefully cautioned by the eye doctor about breaking my glasses and injuring my eyes," he later wrote, "that I was afraid to join in the rough-and-tumble games in the schoolyard and back lot. My time was spent in reading." When he was 13 or 14 years old, Harry had read all the books in the Independence Public Library, and the old family Bible three times through.

After graduation from high school in Independence in 1901,

Bess Wallace Truman, whom Harry referred to as "the Boss," shunned publicity and continued her plain Missouri ways in the White House.

Truman worked at several jobs before finally taking over the family farm. During World War I, he served as an army artillery officer, rising to the rank of major. Upon his return from France, Truman married Elizabeth "Bess" Wallace on June 28, 1919.

Harry and Bess had known each other since childhood. She had established a reputation as a tomboy. She beat all the youngsters at mumbly-peg, and Harry seldom won a game of tennis from her. Bess also liked to fish, and she often did so during their courtship while Harry sat nearby reading a book. As Mrs. Truman, Bess was a quiet person, always shunning the limelight, carefully guarding her private life.

Truman and a friend opened a men's clothing store in Kansas City in 1919, but the business failed in 1921. He then turned to politics. He gained the support of Tom Pendergast, the Democratic Party boss who led one of the largest political machines in the United States. With the Pendergast machine's support, Truman served several terms as a county judge, a post similar to county commissioner in other states. He became known for honesty and efficiency. In 1934, he was elected to the U.S. Senate. Later in the 1930's, a government study produced charges of vote fraud and shady financial deals against Pendergast's machine. Pendergast and others were sent to prison, but the charges did not touch Truman. He won re-election in 1940.

Perhaps Truman's greatest accomplishments as a senator came as chairperson of the Committee to Investigate the National Defense Program, established in 1941. The Truman committee uncovered waste and inefficiency, saving about $1 billion and speeding up war production.

Full name: Harry S. Truman

Born: May 8, 1884

Birthplace: Lamar, Mo.

Died: Dec. 26, 1972

Burial site: Independence, Mo.

Spouse: Elizabeth "Bess" Virginia Wallace

Occupation: Businessperson

Political party: Democratic

Terms: 1945–1953

Vice-President: Alben W. Barkley

Runner-up: Thomas E. Dewey

Electoral vote: 303

Runner-up: 189

Popular vote: 24,105,587

Runner-up: 21,970,017

Controversial President

Throughout his administration, Truman was often the center of controversy. A plain, outspoken individual, he tended to sprinkle his statements—and sometimes his correspondence—with salty comments. This offended many people who considered such language beneath presidential dignity. Mrs. Truman did not approve, either, and did her best to tone Harry down.

The story has been told that after he became President, Harry found Bess burning a pile of papers in a fireplace. Asked what she was doing, she replied: "I'm burning your letters to me."

"Bess, you oughtn't do that," he protested.

"Why not?" she responded. "I've read them several times."

"But think of history," said Harry.

"I have," Bess answered.

Truman aroused a howl of protest when he proposed that the executive offices in the west wing of the White House be extended. Congress refused to appropriate the necessary money (over $1.6 million) for the job. Truman's expenditure of $10,000 to build a balcony behind the pillars of the south portico in 1947 created an even greater stir.

Early in 1948, though, Truman persuaded Congress to vote $50,000 for a study of the mansion's safety and soundness. The results showed that only the outer walls were fit for preservation. All the rest constituted grave fire and safety hazards. During a four-year period, the interior and foundation of the White House were completely rebuilt at a cost of more than $5 million. In the meantime, the Trumans lived in Blair House, across the street.

Truman was always quick to defend his family from criticism, and this sometimes caused controversy, too. Their daughter Margaret studied voice and became a concert singer. A music critic found fault with her first public performance, which brought forth Harry's wrath in a hot-tempered letter. The critic gave the letter to the newspapers.

President Truman made several far-reaching decisions during his administration. One of the earliest was his order to drop atomic bombs on Hiroshima and Nagasaki, Japan, in August 1945. The bombings killed more than 100,000 Japanese and leveled the cities. But they helped to make a bloody invasion of Japan unnecessary. Japanese leaders realized they were helpless against such a weapon. World War II soon ended, and the possibility of nuclear war began.

Controversy swirled around Truman after the war as he battled Congress to retain wartime price controls. He lost. With controls removed and prices increasing, the nation hemorrhaged with strikes as labor sought increased wages. Truman threatened to draft railroad workers into the army if they did not end their walkout. He broke a coal strike by court injunction. None of this endeared him to labor. The question of Communist subversion in government became a hot issue, which Truman at first dismissed as a "red herring." Then, according to some critics, he swung too far the other way with antisubversion programs.

President Harry S. Truman observes U.S. Secretary of State Edward Stettinius signing the U.N. charter, June 25, 1945.

From his youth, Harry Truman was a better-than-fair pianist, and he occasionally played for guests in the White House.

The public generally supported Truman's foreign policy of "containing" Communism with the Truman Doctrine of aid to Greece and Turkey and with economic aid to Western Europe under the Marshall Plan. On the whole, though, Harry Truman had become a most unpopular President by 1948.

Political Upset of the Century

"To err is Truman" and "Had enough?" were only two derisive sayings making the rounds as confident Republicans chose Thomas E. Dewey to be their presidential candidate in 1948.

Taking his case to the people, Truman conducted a 31,000-mile (49,890-kilometer) "give 'em hell" whistle-stop campaign by train, making more than 350 speeches. He lambasted the "do-nothing," "antilabor," "antifarmer" 80th Congress, which Republicans controlled. Truman charged that the Republicans would dismantle the New Deal, destroying gains labor, farmers, and others had made. He promised to extend the New Deal with his own Fair Deal.

Much to the surprise of public opinion pollsters in particular, who had stopped asking questions in October, Truman's strategy paid off. Labor and farmers especially swung behind him, and he defeated Dewey by more than 2 million popular and 114 electoral votes. Harry S. Truman had pulled off the political upset of the century.

Truman had no easier time during his second term than before. He got few Fair Deal measures through Congress, usually being defeated by Republicans and conservative Democrats.

China became a Communist nation in 1949. The United States entered the Korean War in 1950, eventually facing Chinese as well as North Korean Communist armies there. Truman wanted to save South Korea's independence, but he was determined to keep the war from spreading. General Douglas MacArthur, then commanding UN forces in Korea, wanted to attack Chinese bases. He criticized Truman's policies. The President finally dismissed MacArthur in April 1951, setting off a fierce controversy in the United States.

Continued charges of Communist infiltration into the federal government were brought to the nation's attention. In 1950, Senator Joseph R. McCarthy of Wisconsin accused the Department of State of harboring Communists. President Truman and Secretary of State Dean Acheson denied McCarthy's charges.

Harry S. Truman refused to consider renomination in 1952. After he and Bess retired to Independence in March 1953, he wrote his memoirs, lectured at universities, oversaw the construction of the Truman Library that opened in 1957, and made speeches on behalf of Democratic candidates.

As President, Truman had never been concerned with "image." He always insisted that he said and did what he thought was right. A number of historians have concluded that he was right more often than not. Harry S. Truman died in Kansas City, Mo., on Dec. 26, 1972, at 88.

President Truman's Times
1945–1953

The U.S. Flag had 48 stars when Truman took office. No new states or territories were organized. The U.S. population was about 159,700,000 in 1953.

1945	On May 7, the German surrender ended World War II in Europe.
1945	On July 16, the atomic age opened when American forces tested the atomic bomb.
1945	Japan surrendered, ending World War II.
1946	The Cold War began.
1946	Congress created the Atomic Energy Commission.
1947	Congress passed the Taft-Hartley Act after the President had vetoed it.
1948–1949	An Allied airlift supplied blockaded West Berlin.
1948	The Marshall Plan began giving economic aid to war-torn countries.
1948	Israel became a republic.
1949	The United States and its allies set up the North Atlantic Treaty Organization (NATO).
1950	The Korean War began.
1951	Americans saw the first nationwide telecast.

DWIGHT D. EISENHOWER

34th President of the United States
1953–1961

For a nation that traditionally exalts the civilian over the soldier, the United States has had its share of soldier-Presidents, and Dwight D. Eisenhower was one. Eisenhower commanded the victorious Allied forces in Europe in World War II. A tall man with a broad grin and friendly manner, people everywhere admired him and called him "Ike." In 1952 and again in 1956, about 35 million Americans voted "I like Ike" to elect Eisenhower to two terms in office.

Eisenhower's first male ancestor in America reached Philadelphia from the Palatinate in Germany in 1741. The future President's grandfather Jacob, a pastor of the River Brethren Church, departed Pennsylvania for Kansas with his family in 1878 and settled on a farm in a River Brethren colony in Dickinson County. Dwight David, the third of seven sons of David Jacob and Ida Stover Eisenhower, was born in Denison, Tex., on Oct. 14, 1890. Before he was 2, the family moved back to Abilene, where Eisenhower grew up.

David Jacob Eisenhower worked as a mechanic in an Abilene creamery, and the Eisenhowers were among the poorer families in Abilene. Eisenhower himself worked part-time in the creamery as a youth.

Many persons who go on to fame as adults are hardly remarkable when young, and Eisenhower fit that pattern. Nor was Eisenhower outstanding at the U.S. Military Academy at West Point, where he injured his knee playing football. He graduated as a second lieutenant in 1915, 61st in a class of 164. Posted to Fort Sam Houston near San Antonio, Tex., that same year, he met Mamie Geneva Doud.

As first lady, Mamie Doud Eisenhower set a fashion by wearing her hair in bangs.

Full name: Dwight David Eisenhower

Born: Oct. 14, 1890

Birthplace: Denison, Tex.

Died: March 28, 1969

Burial site: Abilene, Kans.

Spouse: Mamie Geneva Doud

Occupation: Soldier

Political party: Republican

Terms: 1953–1961

Vice-President: Richard M. Nixon

Runner-up: Adlai E. Stevenson

Electoral votes: 442; 457

Runner-up: 89; 73

Popular votes: 33,936,137; 35,585,245

Runners-up: 27,314,649; 26,030,172

The Doud family of Denver had become fairly well-to-do in the meat-packing business, and they visited San Antonio on winter vacations. Mamie was 18 when Ike met her. "He was," Mamie said later, "the spiffiest-looking man I ever talked to in all my born life . . . big, blond, and masterful."

Mamie and Ike became engaged on Feb. 14, 1916, and were married on July 1 that year, the same day Eisenhower was promoted to first lieutenant. They had two sons, David, who died of scarlet fever at age 3, and John.

Eisenhower served at various army posts and then attended the Command and General Staff School at Fort Leavenworth, Kans. He graduated from there in 1926, first in a class of 275. Ike then spent time at the Army War College in Washington, D.C. He became a colonel in March 1941 and a brigadier general in September that year.

By then Eisenhower's army record had caught the attention of General George C. Marshall, army chief of staff. This led to his appointment as commanding general of American forces in Europe in 1942, shortly after America entered World War II. As commander of Allied invasion forces, Eisenhower then directed the Allied landings in North Africa, Sicily, and Italy. Named supreme commander of all Allied forces in 1943, Eisenhower directed the Normandy invasion of France in June 1944, which led to Allied victory there less than a year later. Ike's patience, tact, fairness, and persuasiveness were highly instrumental in welding the troops and leaders of the Allied countries into a unified, effective fighting force.

After the war, Eisenhower became army chief of staff, then served as president of Columbia University from 1948 to 1950. Returning to the army, he assumed command of the North Atlantic Treaty Organization forces in Europe in 1951.

Republican or Democrat?

Eisenhower's World War II record had made him a national hero, attractive to both Democrats and Republicans as a presidential candidate. He refused bids from both parties to consider running in 1948. In 1952, however, Eisenhower declared himself a Republican.

Most voters believed that someone who had commanded armies could run a country, and Ike's infectious grin made him seem fatherly and folksy. Eisenhower criticized retiring President Harry S. Truman's conduct of the Korean War and seemed to offer Americans a quiet, conservative future. Weary of depression, New Deal, war, Fair Deal, and conflicts with the Soviet Union, Americans were ready for that.

With Richard M. Nixon as his running mate in 1952, Ike easily won over Democrat Adlai E. Stevenson by 442 to 89 electoral votes. He increased his electoral total four years later, once more with Nixon against Stevenson, 457 to 73.

Mamie Eisenhower graced the White House as hostess, but a rheumatic heart condition limited her activity. She was also inclined to shun public attention. "Mrs. Ike," Eisenhower once said, "refused to get involved in public life herself—she was helpful in worthy causes, such as muscular dystrophy or the

General Dwight D. Eisenhower inspects an Army Group Head-quarters in Europe in May 1943.

heart fund; but she was very much against pushing forward into public view."

Eisenhower ran the presidency as he had an army command. He delegated authority and responsibility, freeing himself from details as much as possible. Sherman Adams, his principal aide, was referred to as "chief of staff." Overseeing rather than becoming directly involved enabled Eisenhower to maintain reasonable working hours, leaving him time for recreation such as fishing, bridge, and golfing.

The administration was conservative and more or less slanted toward business. Eisenhower appointed a Cabinet composed, it was said, of millionaires and one plumber. Secretary of Defense Charles E. Wilson, former president of General Motors, was one millionaire. Secretary of the Treasury George M. Humphrey of M. A. Hanna and Company, a Cleveland conglomerate, was another. The plumber was Secretary of Labor Martin Durkin, president of the United Association of Journeymen Plumbers and Steamfitters. In 1953 Congress created a 10th Cabinet-level agency, the Department of Health, Education, and Welfare. Eisenhower appointed Oveta Culp Hobby as the agency's first secretary. She had commanded the Women's Auxiliary Army Corps during the war.

The Eisenhower years, while prosperous for many Americans and for the most part free from war, were not entirely quiet. During his first election campaign, Eisenhower had pledged to go to Korea to observe the war there at first hand. He kept his promise shortly after the election. The trip brought no immediate results. China was warned that if it delayed peace talks, the United States would bomb the Chinese supply lines. The truce ending the Korean War was finally signed on July 27, 1953.

Senator Joseph R. McCarthy of Wisconsin kept the Communists-in-government issue stirred up. The chair of the Senate subcommittee that headed the search for Communists in government, McCarthy began attacking the Eisenhower Administration soon after the President took office. First, he accused Charles E. Bohlen of being a security risk. Eisenhower had nominated Bohlen to be U.S. ambassador to the Soviet Union. A special Senate committee cleared him. Later, McCarthy charged that the U.S. Information Agency had Communist books in its libraries in Europe.

In a speech at Dartmouth College, Eisenhower warned: "Don't join the book burners. . . . Don't be afraid to go in your library and read every book." But the President refused to make a public statement against McCarthy or to deal in "terms of personality." The Senate condemned McCarthy in 1954.

The U.S. Supreme Court that year declared racial segregation in schools unconstitutional, and there was violence over school desegregation in the South. In 1957, Eisenhower sent federal troops to Little Rock, Ark., to enforce the integration of the city's high school.

Many Americans worried about the Soviet Union's lead in the space race when the Soviets launched *Sputnik I,* the first human-made satellite, on Oct. 4, 1957. Eisenhower set up the office of Special Assistant to the President for Science and Technology to advise him. The *Explorer I,* the first U.S. satellite, went into orbit on Jan. 31, 1958. Six months later, Congress established the National Aeronautics and Space Administration (NASA) to coordinate American efforts to explore space.

Cold War and Cuba

The Cold War, the contest between the United States and the Soviet Union for worldwide influence, continued. Crises in the Middle East led the President to propose the Eisenhower Doctrine in 1957. This doctrine pledged U.S. military aid to any Middle East nation that asked for help against Communist aggression. In July 1958, Eisenhower used the doctrine to send troops to Lebanon to protect government from rebel forces.

When the Soviets shot down an American U-2 reconnaissance plane over Soviet territory in May 1960, Eisenhower admitted that U-2 flights had been going on for four years. Nikita Khrushchev, the Soviet premier, used the incident to break up a Paris summit conference planned for that month.

In 1959, Fidel Castro's revolution established a Communist government in Cuba. In 1960, he seized all property owned by American companies in Cuba. He later charged that the U.S. embassy in Havana was the center of "counter-revolutionary activi-

President Eisenhower was an avid golfer. Not surprisingly, his outings often attracted a large following.

ties" against Cuba. Eisenhower broke off diplomatic relations with Cuba on Jan. 3, 1961.

Ike was a popular President. It is possible that he could have won election to a third term. But the 22nd Amendment to the Constitution, proposed by a Republican Congress and ratified in 1951, prevented that. The amendment limits a person to two full elected terms as President.

In March 1961, Ike and Mamie retired to a farm they had purchased near Gettysburg, Pa. He died of heart failure on March 28, 1969, and was buried in Abilene, Kans.

President Eisenhower's Times
1953–1961

The U.S. Flag had 48 stars when Eisenhower took office. Two states joined the Union: Alaska in 1959 and Hawaii in 1959. No new territories were organized. The U.S. population was about 181,700,000 in 1961.

1953	On July 27, the Korean War ended.
1954	The Supreme Court ruled that racial segregation in public schools is unconstitutional.
1955	Jonas Salk's polio vaccine was declared safe.
1956–1961	Twenty-three African nations won independence.
1957	The Space Age began with the Soviet Union's *Sputnik I.*
1958–1959	U.S. airlines began jet passenger service.
1958	America launched its first satellite, *Explorer I.*
1959	The St. Lawrence Seaway was completed by the United States and Canada.

JOHN F. KENNEDY

35th President of the United States
1961–1963

At 43, John F. Kennedy became the youngest person ever elected President. At age 46, he was also the youngest to die in office, assassinated in Dallas, Tex., on Nov. 22, 1963.

Kennedy was Irish. Famine drove his great-grandfather Patrick Kennedy from Ireland in 1848, and he settled in Boston. Kennedy's grandfather, Patrick Joseph, ran a saloon there and was also Democratic boss of his ward. Patrick's son, Joseph Patrick, became wealthy trading stocks on Wall Street and dealing in real estate. He served under Franklin Delano Roosevelt on the Securities and Exchange Commission and as ambassador to Great Britain.

John Kennedy's mother, Rose, was the daughter of John "Honey Fitz" Fitzgerald, a two-term mayor of Boston, a state legislator, and a member of the U.S. House of Representatives. The future President was born to Rose and Joseph Kennedy on May 29, 1917, in Brookline, Mass., a Boston suburb. He was the second son of nine children, five girls and four boys.

John, also called "Jack," grew up in a family atmosphere that stressed competition. His father especially encouraged the children to participate in sports and in rough-and-tumble games, to play to win, and to excel in whatever they undertook.

After elementary school in Brookline and Riverdale, N.Y., Kennedy went to Canterbury School in New Milford, Conn., then to Choate Academy in Wallingford, Conn. Ralph Horton, Jr., a Choate classmate, remembered Kennedy in those years: "We were both skinny little guys and went out for the lowest class of football—C team. He was a boy of many interests but

Jacqueline Bouvier Kennedy was a very popular first lady who brought a sense of glamour to the White House.

Full name: John Fitzgerald Kennedy

Born: May 29, 1917

Birthplace: Brookline, Mass.

Died: Nov. 22, 1963

Burial site: Arlington, Va.

Spouse: Jacqueline Lee Bouvier

Occupation: Author

Political party: Democratic

Term: 1961-1963

Vice-President: Lyndon B. Johnson

Runner-up: Richard M. Nixon

Electoral vote: 303

Runner-up: 219

Popular vote: 34,221,344

Runner-up: 34,106,671

he would never stick to anything, give himself entirely to anything. He liked sports, he liked roughhousing, he liked to be sloppy, he liked to play golf, he liked girls, and he loved to come to New York to see me."

Graduating in 1935 from Choate at 18, Kennedy entered Harvard University the following year. He spent the spring and summer of 1939, on the eve of World War II, touring Europe. Out of that came his senior thesis, an analysis of factors behind the United Kingdom's lack of preparedness for the conflict that began in September 1939. It was published as *Why England Slept* and became a best seller.

War Hero

During World War II, Kennedy served as a naval officer in the Pacific fleet. He had a narrow escape from death in 1943 when a Japanese destroyer rammed and sank the PT boat he commanded. For keeping his crew together for five days until being rescued from a nearby island, and for wounds he suffered, Kennedy received the Navy and Marine Corps Medal and the Purple Heart.

Kennedy had a sharp wit and, like many self-confident people, he could joke at his own expense. In 1959 a high school boy asked him: "How did you become a war hero?"

"It was easy," Kennedy replied. "They sank my boat." Kennedy's political career began in 1946 with election to the U.S. House of Representatives from Massachusetts. After three terms there, he won a seat in the Senate in 1952. On Sept. 12, 1953, he married Jacqueline Bouvier, whom he had met at a dinner party in Washington, D.C., in 1951.

Like Kennedy, Jacqueline had grown up in wealth. Her father, John V. Bouvier III, was a prominent Wall Street broker. She attended Vassar College in Poughkeepsie, N.Y., the Sorbonne in Paris, and George Washington University in Washington, D.C. A beautiful and intelligent woman, she was well educated in the arts, and she spoke French and Spanish fluently.

As a senator, Kennedy is perhaps better remembered for a book he wrote than for any legislation he was connected with. He undertook the task while recovering from back operations in 1954 and 1955. An account of senators of the past who distinguished themselves with stands on principle, *Profiles in Courage* won the Pulitzer Prize for biography in 1957.

Kennedy sought but failed to win the Democratic vice-presidential nomination in 1956. After winning re-election to the Senate in 1958, he went after the presidential nomination, entering primary elections in a number of states in 1960.

With considerable personal and family wealth behind his political campaigns, Kennedy was able to pay for television and other advertising and to maintain a private jet in which he and his staff often traveled. Inevitably the Kennedy wealth stimulated talk that Joe Kennedy was using his money to buy his son the election.

Jack usually remained good humored about the matter. In a speech before newspeople in 1958 he noted that his father had cautioned him not to buy more votes than necessary, for Joe was

John Kennedy and Richard Nixon met in a series of four televised debates in 1960. These debates marked the first time in United States history that presidential candidates argued campaign issues face-to-face.

not going to pay for a landslide. Speaking at a dinner honoring the late Al Smith in New York in 1960, Kennedy observed that he had announced earlier that year that if he won the presidency he "would not consider campaign contributions as a substitute for experience in appointing ambassadors." Then he added: "Ever since I made that statement, I have not received one single cent from my father."

The fact that Kennedy was a Roman Catholic also figured in the 1960 campaign. Only one other Catholic had run for the presidency on a major party ticket—Democrat Alfred E. Smith in 1928. Smith's religion had been a factor in his defeat. Kennedy met the issue head-on, explaining his position on the question of the separation of church and state. His statements seemed to satisfy the majority of Americans.

After numerous primary victories, on the first ballot Kennedy won the Democratic nomination at Los Angeles in July 1960. Senator Lyndon B. Johnson of Texas, who had also tried for the nomination, became his running mate.

Richard M. Nixon, Vice-President under Dwight D. Eisenhower, headed the Republican ticket. Nixon was better known nationally than Kennedy, but that changed after four television "debates" between the two—the first ever held in a presidential campaign. Kennedy appeared younger than his 43 years, but he also seemed confident, well prepared, and knowledgeable on issues. Still, the election was close. Not until the next morning was it clear that Kennedy had won, and then by only about

119,000 popular votes. His margin in the Electoral College was 303 to 219.

The New Frontier

"We stand today on the edge of a new frontier—the frontier of the 1960's," Kennedy said in his acceptance speech in Los Angeles. "Ask not what your country can do for you," he urged in his inaugural address. "Ask what you can do for your country." The programs he proposed to "get the country moving again" after the allegedly stodgy Eisenhower years became known as the New Frontier.

Youth, action, and vigor characterized the Kennedy Administration, and the Kennedys, who had a 3-year-old daughter and an infant son, lent glamour to the presidential mansion. Jacqueline's major project became the restoration of White House furnishings to reflect its history. "I think the White House should show the wonderful heritage that this country has," she said. "It was such a surprise to come there and find so little that had association and memory. I'd feel terrible if I had lived there for four years and hadn't done anything about the house." Her restoration task nearly completed, she appeared on national television in February 1962 to conduct an hour-long tour of the mansion as cameras followed her.

Young, accomplished, and lovely, "Jackie" drew the interest not only of the women in her own country but of other nations as well. Her hairdo and clothing were copied. When she flew to Europe with her husband in 1961, huge crowds gathered wherever she went. At a Paris luncheon, President Kennedy presented himself by saying, "I am the man who accompanied Jacqueline Kennedy to Paris."

During the Kennedy Administration the White House became a center for the encouragement of the arts and artistic achievement. Among other greats, the famous cellist Pablo Casals performed there. In 1962, the Kennedys gave a reception for many winners of the Nobel Prize.

On the government side, Congress passed some New Frontier measures. It increased the minimum wage to $1.25. It granted authority for presidential agreements with other countries to reduce tariffs. Congress also enacted a law to aid economically depressed areas in the United States. Kennedy proposed a tax cut, but one was not passed before his death.

Demands for equal rights for blacks became the major domestic issue during the Kennedy Administration. A group of black and white "freedom riders" entered Montgomery, Ala., by bus to test local segregation laws. Rioting broke out, and Robert F. Kennedy, the President's brother and attorney general, sent U.S. marshals to the city to help restore order. The University of Mississippi matriculated its first black student in 1962. Rioting followed on the campus at Oxford. Racial protests and demonstrations climaxed on Aug. 28, 1963, when about 200,000 persons staged the Freedom March in Washington, D.C., to demonstrate their demands for equal rights for blacks.

Kennedy proposed civil rights legislation. He asked Congress to pass laws requiring hotels, motels, and restaurants to admit customers regardless of race. He also asked Congress to grant the attorney general authority to begin court suits to desegregate schools on behalf of private citizens who were unable to start legal action themselves. He said, "The time has come for the Congress of the United States to join with the executive and judicial branches in making it clear to all that race has no place in American life or law."

Foreign affairs proved troublesome. During Eisenhower's term, the United States had helped Cuban refugees plan an invasion of Cuba to overthrow the Communist regime there. Kennedy allowed the plan to proceed in April 1961, and the attempt, known as the Bay of Pigs invasion, was a complete failure. In June 1961, talks between Kennedy and Soviet Premier Nikita Khrushchev in Vienna, Austria, did little to ease the Cold War. In 1962, the administration discovered that the Soviet Union had installed missile bases in Cuba. The world seemed to hover on the brink of nuclear war that fall as Kennedy demanded that the bases be dismantled. The Soviet Union finally complied.

When the Communists threatened South Vietnam and Thailand, Kennedy ordered U.S. military advisers to the area in 1961 and 1962. He also sent advisers to Laos. Kennedy sent former Republican senator and vice-presidential candidate Henry Cabot Lodge, Jr., to South Vietnam as ambassador in 1963.

Kennedy did achieve a treaty with the Soviet Union and

President Kennedy greets Soviet Premier Nikita Khrushchev outside the U.S. embassy in Vienna, Austria, in June 1961. The two men discussed the status of the city of Berlin.

The presidential family—John, John-John, Jackie, and Caroline—caught here in a rare moment of relaxation together.

other nations banning nuclear testing in the atmosphere. And the Peace Corps, which his administration established in 1961, was highly successful. Under that program, thousands of enthusiastic Americans volunteered to work for little pay, helping people in developing countries raise their living standards. The volunteers demonstrated American generosity and a desire to help.

The Assassination

How the New Frontier might have turned out, no one will ever know. It came to an end in November 1963.

President and Mrs. Kennedy, along with Vice-President Johnson, went to Texas to try to mend political fences and quiet quarreling within the Texas Democratic Party. While riding in a motorcade through Dallas on November 22, Kennedy was shot and killed by bullets apparently fired from a window in a tall building near the route along which the procession traveled. Lyndon B. Johnson took the oath as President on the airplane that was to bear Kennedy's body back to Washington, D.C. Lee Harvey Oswald was arrested for the murder but was killed before he could be questioned at any length. A commission headed by Chief Justice Earl Warren investigated the assassination and reported in 1964 that Oswald had acted alone. However, many observers disputed this finding, convinced that Oswald was part of a group that planned the assassination. In 1978, a special committee of the House of Representatives concluded after reviewing the evidence that John F. Kennedy "was probably assassinated as a result of a conspiracy." This conclusion also was disputed. In 1982, the National Research Council disputed the House committee's finding that there had been a second gunman involved in the assassination. The Council studied the acoustical evidence and found that it did not support the committee's conclusion.

The sudden death of the young and vigorous American President shocked the world. The body was brought back to Washington, D.C., and placed in the East Room in the White House for 24 hours. Then, the Sunday after the assassination, the flag-draped coffin was carried to the Capitol Rotunda. Hundreds of thousands of persons filed past the guarded casket.

Representatives from over 90 countries attended the funeral on November 25. Millions of Americans witnessed it on television. Kennedy was buried with full military honors at Arlington National Cemetery across the Potomac from Washington, D.C.

Public buildings and geographical sites were named for President Kennedy. In one of his first acts, President Johnson named the NASA installation in Florida, The John F. Kennedy Space Center. Congress voted funds for the John F. Kennedy Center for the Performing Arts in the capital. The United Kingdom made 1 acre (0.4 hectare) of ground permanent U.S. territory as part of a Kennedy memorial at Runnymede.

President Kennedy's Times
1961-1963

The U.S. Flag had 50 stars when Kennedy took office. No new states or territories were organized. The U.S. population was about 190,417,800 in 1963.

1961	Yuri Gagarin became the first person in space.
1961	The Bay of Pigs invasion failed.
1961	The Berlin Wall cut off East from West Berlin.
1962-1963	The Supreme Court ruled official prayers and Bible reading in public schools unconstitutional.
1962	John H. Glenn, Jr., became the first American to orbit the earth.
1962	The United States launched *Telstar I*.
1962	The Cuban missile crisis threatened world peace.
1963	The Atomic Test-Ban Treaty was signed
1963	The Freedom March was staged to Washington, D.C.

LYNDON B. JOHNSON

36th President of the United States
1963–1969

Lyndon Baines Johnson, his wife Lady Bird once said, "behaves as if there were no tomorrow coming and he had to do everything today." His brother Sam Houston Johnson characterized Lyndon's loping walk as the "L.B.J. trot." Lyndon Johnson had always been in a hurry, and when he became President upon John F. Kennedy's assassination in November 1963, he seemed to double his pace.

The line that produced Lyndon can be traced to James Johnston, who was born in Virginia in the early 1600's. Jesse Johnson, Lyndon's great-grandfather, was the first of the family in Texas. He arrived in 1846 from Georgia. Lyndon was the eldest of five children of Samuel Ealy and Rebekah Baines Johnson. He was born on a farm near Stonewall, Tex., on Aug. 27, 1908. When Lyndon was 5 the family moved to Johnson City, which his grandfather Samuel Ealy Johnson, Sr., had founded. There he attended elementary school and graduated from high school in 1924 at 15.

Lyndon's father served five terms in the Texas legislature, and the boy got his first taste of government at 12 when he accompanied Sam Johnson to Austin, the capital. "Sam Johnson and I shared a desk in the chamber," Wright Patman, a fellow legislator, recalled later. "It was one of those desks that had leg space cut out for two men, and Lyndon liked to stand next to his father or sit with him and listen to the debate. He was around so much that some members thought he was a page and gave him little jobs to do."

After high school, Johnson refused to consider college. He went to California and worked at odd jobs there for over a year.

*Claudia Taylor Johnson, nick-
named Lady Bird, made the
beautification of the nation's
capital one of her main objec-
tives as first lady.*

Full name: Lyndon Baines
Johnson

Born: Aug. 27, 1908

Birthplace: Near
Stonewall, Tex.

Died: Jan. 22, 1973

Burial site: Near Johnson
City, Tex.

Spouse: Claudia Alta
(Lady Bird) Taylor

Occupation: Teacher

Political party:
Democratic

Terms: 1963–1969

Vice-President: Hubert H.
Humphrey

Runner-up: Barry M.
Goldwater

Electoral vote: 486

Runner-up: 52

Popular vote: 43,126,584

Runner-up: 27,177,838

Returning home, he worked on a highway construction crew.
Tired of laboring with his hands, he entered Southwest Texas
State Teachers College in San Marcos in February 1927, and
graduated in 1930. Johnson then spent a year teaching debate
and other subjects at Sam Houston High School in Houston.

Richard M. Kleberg, one of the owners of the huge King
Ranch near Kingsville, Tex., was elected to the U.S. House of
Representatives in 1931. He took young Lyndon to Washington,
D.C., with him as his secretary, and this marked the real begin-
ning of L.B.J.'s political education. In September 1934, while in
Austin on congressional business, Johnson met Claudia Alta
Taylor, known as "Lady Bird" since she was 2.

Lady Bird was the daughter of a wealthy Karnack, Tex.,
landowner and businessman. After graduating from high school,
she attended St. Mary's Episcopal School for Girls, a junior college in Dallas. She was shy and small, appearing much younger
than her years.

Lyndon found Lady Bird attractive, and wasted no time.
"My recollection is that he asked me to marry him on the first
or second date," she later said. "Let us say, the second date. I
just thought it was sheer lunacy. And I really didn't think he
meant it. But after a while I realized that he really did mean it."

"Some of the best deals are made in a hurry," her father
told her, and Lyndon and Lady Bird were married on Nov. 17,
1934. The Johnsons had two daughters—Lynda Bird and Luci
Baines.

Senator and President

At 26, Johnson became the Texas head of the National Youth
Administration, a federal agency that provided part-time jobs for
high school and college students during the depression of the
1930's. Then in 1937 he won a special election to the U.S. House
of Representatives. For several months after the United States
entered World War II, Johnson served as a lieutenant commander in the Pacific fleet until President Franklin D. Roosevelt
ordered all members of Congress in the armed forces home.
Then, in November 1948, Johnson easily won election as a U.S.
senator. "Mr. Johnson took to the Senate as if he'd been born
there," Walter Jenkins, one of his aides, remembered. "From the
first day on it was obvious that it was his place—just the right
size; he was at his best with small groups, and at that time he
was one of only 96 senators, while in the House he had been
one of 435, a group in which it was much more difficult to make
his influence felt, to be effective. But with only 95 others—he
knew he could manage that."

And manage he did. Johnson worked his way up to assistant Democratic leader in the Senate by 1951. He became minority leader two years later and majority leader in 1955 after Democrats won control of the Senate.

In this post, Johnson had the responsibility of keeping the
legislative process running smoothly. He decided when various
bills would be taken up and who would sponsor them. On controversial measures, he checked the views of each Democratic
senator. He delayed Senate voting until he had done everything

he could to persuade senators to vote his way. So skilled was Johnson in the techniques of give and take that Senator Hubert H. Humphrey of Minnesota described him as "a genius in the art of the legislative process."

Johnson was a strong supporter of the exploration of outer space and played a major role in establishing the Senate Aeronautical and Space Committee. He made himself the committee's first chairperson. He also sponsored the law that established the National Aeronautics and Space Administration (NASA). In 1957, Johnson put through the Senate the first civil rights bill in more than 80 years. Three years later, in 1960, he shepherded another civil rights measure through the Senate. Johnson's record made him legendary. His persuasive powers came to be known as the "L.B.J. treatment."

L.B.J.'s next goal was the presidency, and he sought the Democratic nomination in 1960. After it went to John F. Kennedy, Johnson accepted the number-two spot on the ticket. Kennedy's choice of Johnson as his running mate was intended to provide a balance that would attract Southern votes. In the November election, Kennedy and Johnson narrowly defeated the Republican ticket, Richard M. Nixon and Henry Cabot Lodge, Jr.

After Johnson was sworn in as Vice-President in January 1961, he took a more active role in the government than had any previous Vice-President. He served as chairperson of the National Aeronautics and Space Council, the Peace Corps National Advisory Council, and the President's Committee on Equal Employment Opportunity. Johnson also served on the National Security Council.

When Kennedy was assassinated, Johnson took the oath of office as President on an air force jet in Dallas, Tex., right before

Senators Clements, George, Johnson, and Hennings share congratulations as Democrats take control of the Senate in January 1955.

taking off for Washington, D.C. He was ready for the job. He had, in effect, trained for it for years.

Lady Bird Johnson had other feelings about becoming first lady. "I feel like I am suddenly on stage for a part I never rehearsed," Lady Bird said during her first hectic week in the White House. She adapted readily to duties as hostess, however, and Lady Bird made the beautification of interstate highways and the District of Columbia her main projects.

As to highways, this meant mainly a restriction on billboard advertising so that motorists could see and enjoy the countryside along which they drove. This was a tough bill to get through Congress, but L.B.J. managed it. In Washington, D.C., the program involved planting flower gardens and shrubbery, improving parks, and establishing playgrounds.

Lyndon Johnson was called domineering, changeable, hot-tempered, and impulsive, and he benefited from Lady Bird's gentle, never obtrusive companionship and advice. Said Wilbur J. Cohen, a Johnson aide: "Mrs. Johnson, I think, was the most valuable asset he had. She was the one person that could talk to him and he would listen, knowing that she had no ulterior purpose. He always looked at anything that anybody else said to him with this criteria—what is the self-interest, unspoken assumption on which that person is operating?" William S. White, a newspaper reporter, recalled: "Mrs. Johnson was extremely skillful at handling him, particularly when he was upset or angry or tired or depressed. She never frontally challenged him on anything, but she often had her way by a very soft manner of getting around him."

The Great Society

Johnson dominated the presidency just as he had the Senate, and his energy seldom flagged. He declared that his administration would create the Great Society and wage a "war on poverty" to open opportunity and a share of America's abundance to millions of persons to whom that had been denied. The amount of legislation Johnson got through Congress was astonishing.

Congress cut taxes and at the same time voted billions of dollars to raise standards of living and rehabilitate depressed areas such as the Appalachian Mountains region. It established the Office of Economic Opportunity to provide job training for unskilled people. Federal aid to education and libraries expanded tremendously. Special school programs such as Head Start projects got under way. Medicare, a national health insurance plan for those 65 and over, became law in 1965. Congress created two new Cabinet departments—Housing and Urban Development and Transportation. It passed a law providing more than $5 billion to help those in need to buy or rent housing. The Voting Rights Act of 1965 restricted the use of literacy tests and other means previously used to keep blacks from the polls. Another law forbade racial discrimination in hotels, restaurants, and other public places, and guaranteed equal job opportunities for all.

Johnson easily won election in his own right in 1964, defeating Senator Barry Goldwater of Arizona, the Republican can-

With members of Congress and Justices of the Supreme Court gathered around, President Lyndon B. Johnson signs the Civil Rights Act of 1968.

didate, 486 to 52 electoral votes. His popularity remained high for many months thereafter.

But the nation was distressed over racial issues and war in Vietnam. Although blacks had made political and economic gains, unrest remained. A riot in Watts, a black residential area in Los Angeles, occurred during the summer of 1965. Others in Detroit, Newark, N.Y., and elsewhere recurred in 1967 and 1968. Many people were killed and much property destroyed.

When L.B.J. became President, the United States had about 16,000 soldiers in Vietnam serving as military advisers. In 1965, the President ordered U.S. combat troops in to protect American bases and stop Communist advances. U.S. bombing increased. By 1968, the United States had more than 500,000 troops in Vietnam. American casualties and the cost of the war increased.

More and more Americans turned against the war. Two of the chief critics of the U.S. involvement were Democratic Senators Eugene McCarthy of Minnesota and Robert F. Kennedy of New York. In addition, Republicans in Congress opposed Great

*Lyndon B. Johnson announced that he would not run for another
term as President in a televised speech on March 31, 1968.*

Society programs. They disagreed with Johnson's position that
the United States could continue costly domestic programs and
also meet increasing costs of the war. Americans also began to
doubt the administration's statements on the progress of the
war. Johnson's popularity dropped as what was called a "credibility gap" grew.

L.B.J. in Trouble

Many Americans concluded that the United States should not
have entered the fighting. Others were convinced that the country was supporting a corrupt South Vietnamese government. An-
tiwar marches and demonstrations were staged in many American cities.

President Johnson refused to take the United States out of
the war, however. "Everything I knew about history told me
that if I got out of Vietnam . . . I'd be giving a big fat reward to
aggression," Johnson told Doris Kearns, a Harvard University
professor of government, after he had left the presidency. "And
I knew that if we let Communist aggression succeed in taking
over South Vietnam, there would follow in this country an end-

less national debate—a mean and destructive debate—that would shatter my presidency, kill my administration, and damage our democracy."

Opposition to Johnson continued to grow within the Democratic Party as well as in the country at large. By early 1968 his popularity had hit bottom. At last, speaking over national television on March 31, 1968, Johnson announced that he would not seek another term.

Nearly a year later, the Johnsons retired to their ranch along the Pedernales River in Texas. Johnson wrote his memoirs, and in 1971 he presided over the opening of the Lyndon B. Johnson Library at the University of Texas in Austin. On Jan. 22, 1973, he suffered a heart attack and died. He was buried on the ranch.

President Johnson's Times
1963–1969

The U.S. Flag had 50 stars when Johnson took office. No new states or territories were organized. The U.S. population was about 205,000,000 in 1969.

1960's	The Vietnam War grew into a full-scale war.
1966	Robert C. Weaver became the first black Cabinet member.
1966	Medicare went into effect.
1966	The UN General Assembly approved a treaty banning the use of nuclear and other mass-destruction weapons in outer space.
1967	Thurgood Marshall became the first black to serve on the U.S. Supreme Court.
1967	The first successful human heart transplant was performed.

RICHARD M. NIXON

37th President of the United States
1969–1974

In November 1962, a glum and disappointed Richard M. Nixon surveyed a bleak political future. He had just lost the race for the California governorship to Democrat Edmund G. Brown by about 300,000 votes. Two years earlier he had met defeat in his bid for the presidency against John F. Kennedy. After 14 years in the U.S. House of Representatives, the Senate, and the vice-presidency, it appeared that Nixon's public career had come to an end.

Events proved otherwise, however. Nixon came back to win election as President in 1968 and again in 1972. Then, in 1974, he became the first person to resign the nation's highest office.

Nixon's Scotch-Irish ancestors emigrated from Ireland in the 1700's to settle in Delaware. Descendants moved on to Pennsylvania and Ohio, and Nixon's father migrated from Ohio to California in 1907. Richard Nixon was born in Yorba Linda, southeast of Los Angeles, on Jan. 9, 1913, the second of five sons. In 1922, Frank and Hannah Nixon moved the family to Whittier, Calif. There Frank ran a gasoline service station and a grocery store.

When Richard was a boy, he began working in the grocery store. Later, as a college student, he was in charge of the store's fruit and vegetable section. Early each day he drove the family truck to the Los Angeles market to buy produce. That he liked; the task of sorting and cleaning the purchases, he did not. "I never drive by a vegetable stand without feeling sorry for the guy who picks out the rotten apples," he told a magazine writer years later.

Nixon starred in debate at Whittier High School and at Whittier College, which he entered at 17. After graduating in

Pat Ryan Nixon became the most traveled first lady ever, visiting many countries with her husband or on her own during his presidency.

Full name: Richard
 Milhous Nixon

Born: Jan. 9, 1913

Birthplace: Yorba Linda,
 Calif.

Died: April 22, 1994

Burial site: Yorba Linda,
 Calif.

Spouse: Thelma Catharine
 Ryan

Occupation: Lawyer

Political party:
 Republican

Terms: 1969–1974

Vice-Presidents: Spiro T.
 Agnew; Gerald R. Ford

Runners-up: Hubert H.
 Humphrey; George S.
 McGovern

Electoral votes: 301; 520

Runners-up: 191; 17

Popular votes: 31,785,148;
 47,170,179

Runners-up: 31,274,503;
 29,171,791

1934, he went to Duke University Law School in Durham, N.C., on a scholarship. He ranked third in his graduating class of 44 in 1937.

Returning to Whittier, Nixon joined a law firm. Shortly thereafter he met Thelma Catharine (Pat) Ryan. She grew up on a small farm near Whittier. Like the Nixons, the Ryans were far from well off and, like Richard, Pat went to work when very young. She later said, though, that "it was a good kind of life when you look back on it. It was a truck garden. All irrigation. There was a lot to do. And I loved to be out of doors, so I worked right along with my brothers in the field, really, which was lots of fun. . . . When I was real tiny I just tagged along. But when I got older I was able to do more. I drove the team of horses and things like that."

Earning income from odd jobs, Pat Nixon paid her way at Fullerton Junior College and at the University of Southern California, from which she graduated in 1937. She then took a job teaching commercial subjects at Whittier High School.

Richard and Pat met during tryouts for a community theater play in Whittier. Nixon asked Pat for a date on their first meeting. He repeated the request on the third meeting and when she laughed, according to a witness, he said, "Don't laugh. Someday I'm going to marry you." He pointed his finger at her and she laughed again.

"I thought he was nuts or something," Pat later told Nixon biographer Earl Mazo. "I guess I just looked at him. I couldn't imagine anyone ever saying anything like that so suddenly. Now that I know Dick much better I can't imagine that he would ever say that, because he is very much the opposite, he's more reserved." They dated, became engaged, and were married on June 21, 1940.

Having bought an automobile, the couple had $200 left, most of which went for a honeymoon in Mexico. "We just went," Pat later recalled. "We felt really splurgy." Nixon remembered: "Sometimes we drove all night to save the cost of a hotel, and I think we saw every temple, every church in old Mexico, and it all cost us only $178."

Success and Setbacks

Early in 1942, Nixon went to work for the Office of Price Administration in Washington, D.C. About a year later, he was on active duty with the navy in the Pacific Ocean, where he remained until World War II ended in 1945.

Richard Nixon first won political office as a Republican in 1946, elected to the House of Representatives from California. He was re-elected two years later. As a member of the House Committee on Un-American Activities, Nixon gained national attention by pursuing an investigation of Alger Hiss, a former Department of State employee accused of having been connected with a Soviet spy ring in the 1930's. Hiss was convicted of perjury, and publicity from the case helped elect Nixon to the Senate in 1950. In 1953, he became Vice-President, serving during Dwight D. Eisenhower's two terms as President.

Eisenhower supported Nixon for the presidency in 1960, but

he lost by 119,450 popular votes to John F. Kennedy. Then came his defeat in the California gubernatorial contest in 1962, and he retired to private life.

During the 1960's, Nixon practiced law in New York City, but he remained active in Republican Party affairs. He also traveled extensively both at home and abroad. Keeping his name before the public by speaking at meetings of civic groups and aiding Republican candidates, Nixon built political support. He won several presidential primaries in 1968 and gained the Republican nomination on the first ballot at the convention in Miami Beach that year. Governor Spiro Agnew of Maryland became his running mate.

In November 1968, Nixon won over Democrat Hubert H. Humphrey by about 812,000 popular votes, taking 301 electoral ballots to Humphrey's 191. Four years later, Nixon won a much greater victory over Democrat George S. McGovern, 520 to 17 electoral votes.

As White House hostess, Pat Nixon was among the busiest first ladies in American history. During her first three years she entertained more than 109,000 guests at state dinners, receptions, luncheons, and teas. Among the notables were President Tito of Yugoslavia, Prime Minister Indira Gandhi of India, Prime Minister William McMahon of Australia, Prime Minister Golda Meir of Israel, and Ethiopia's Emperor Haile Selassie. One of the spectacular Nixon events was a party for jazz composer, pianist, and

Flanked by Mamie and Pat, candidates Dwight D. Eisenhower and Richard M. Nixon at the Republican convention in 1952.

bandleader Duke Ellington on his 70th birthday. Mrs. Nixon also arranged "Evenings at the White House," featuring such entertainers as comedians Bob Hope and Red Skelton.

And there was a White House wedding. Patricia (Tricia), the Nixon's elder daughter, married Edward Finch Cox in the Rose Garden on June 12, 1971. Their younger daughter, Julie, had married David Eisenhower, the former President's grandson, three years earlier.

Nixon in Office

As President, Nixon gave particular attention to foreign affairs. His major goal was settlement of the Vietnam War. In his first inaugural address, Nixon said: "The greatest honor history can bestow is the title of peacemaker. This honor now beckons America."

In March 1969, Nixon ordered a stepped-up training program for South Vietnamese forces so that they could gradually take over the major burden of fighting the war. Responding to increasing popular and congressional opposition to U.S. involvement in Vietnam, he gradually withdrew U.S. combat troops beginning in July. This policy became known as Vietnamization.

The Vietnam peace talks, begun in 1968, continued in Paris, but the negotiators made little progress. Many Americans favored the gradual withdrawal Nixon had begun, but many others wanted the U.S. involvement to end immediately. Protests and demonstrations swept the nation.

On March 30, 1972, North Vietnam launched a major offensive in South Vietnam. In May, Nixon ordered a blockade of North Vietnam to cut off its war supplies from the Soviet Union and China. The blockade included the mining of North Vietnam's ports and the bombing of its rail and highway links to China. By the end of August 1972, the Communist offensive had been halted. U.S. troop withdrawals continued during 1972.

On January 27, 1973, a cease-fire agreement was signed in Paris by the United States, North Vietnam, South Vietnam, and the Viet Cong. On March 29, the exchange of war prisoners was completed, and the last American troops left South Vietnam. North Vietnam, South Vietnam, and the Viet Cong violated the cease-fire agreement and continued to fight. The end of the war came on April 30, 1975, when South Vietnam surrendered to the Communists.

Nixon worked to establish diplomatic relations with the Communist regime in China, which the United States had refused to recognize since it gained power in 1949. He approved the export of some U.S. goods to China in 1971, and in February 1972, he visited China for seven days. In 1973, the two nations opened diplomatic offices in each other's capital and exchanged visits by cultural groups.

Nixon's administration saw several far-reaching laws enacted. In 1969, Congress passed Nixon's proposal to establish a lottery system for the military draft. Also in 1969, Congress approved extensive reforms in federal tax laws. These reforms included increases in personal income tax deductions and cuts in tax benefits for foundations and oil companies. In 1970, Con-

President Richard M. Nixon is shown touring the Great Wall of China during his historic visit to China in February 1972.

gress established independent agencies to replace the Post Office Department and to operate the passenger trains that linked the nation's major cities. Also in 1970, Congress lowered the minimum voting age in federal elections to 18. The 26th Amendment to the U.S. Constitution, ratified in 1971, set the voting age at 18 for all elections. In 1972, Congress approved Nixon's revenue-sharing program. The federal government under this plan shared its tax revenues with state and local governments, providing them with billions of dollars.

The Nixon presidency began to unravel shortly after the 1972 election. The decline began with an attempted burglary and charges against Vice-President Agnew.

Early in the morning of June 17, 1972, Washington, D.C., police arrested five men who had broken into Democratic National Headquarters in the Watergate, an apartment and office complex. The men apparently sought to find documents and plant wiretaps to gather information on Democratic campaign plans for 1972. It soon came to light that they were employed by a Republican group, the Committee for the Re-election of the President. The White House denied any connection with what a Nixon staff member called a "third-rate burglary." Watergate

*At the height of the Watergate investigation, Richard M. Nixon
prepares to go on TV to discuss transcripts of his presidential tapes.*

did not become an issue in the 1972 election campaign.

Vice-President Agnew came under fire in 1973, accused of
evading income taxes and taking payoffs while he was an officeholder in Maryland. Agnew resigned on October 10. On December
6, Nixon appointed Gerald R. Ford, minority leader in the House of
Representatives to the vice-presidency.

Meanwhile, Watergate investigations picked up momentum.
Evidence was uncovered linking high White House aides with
either the break-in or attempts to hide information concerning it.
Nixon denied any part in the break-in or cover-up and promised a
full investigation. In May, Archibald Cox, a Harvard University law
professor, was named to head the investigation.

A Senate committee learned that Nixon had routinely made
tape recordings of conversations with his staff and others in his
office. Cox and the Senate committee asked for tapes that they
thought could aid the investigations. Nixon refused to give up the
tapes, and Cox and the committee filed court petitions. U.S. District
Judge John Sirica reviewed the tapes and ordered Nixon to give
them to him. Nixon lost an appeal of that order, then offered to
give Cox and the committee summaries of the tapes. Cox refused,
insisting that summaries did not constitute proper evidence. Nixon
then had Cox fired.

Cox's firing triggered a move for Nixon's impeachment, and
hearings began in October 1973. The President finally released edited transcripts of 31 taped conversations in April 1974, and these
weakened his case.

The House Judiciary Committee recommended in July 1974
that Nixon be impeached on three counts: obstructing justice, abus-
ing presidential authority, and withholding evidence.

Resignation

Then on August 2, a conversation was discovered between Nixon and his chief of staff, H. R. Haldeman, that took place on June 23, 1972, six days after the Watergate break-in. The tape was among 64 being turned over to special prosecutor Leon Jaworski, Cox's successor. It showed that the President was both aware of the case and involved in the cover-up at that time.

Faced with almost certain impeachment by the House of Representatives, Nixon resigned the presidency on Aug. 9, 1974. Vice-President Gerald R. Ford took the oath of office as President at noon that day.

About 40 persons were tried for crimes related to Watergate. Most were convicted. The charges included conspiracy, violating campaign financing laws, and using government agencies to harm political opponents.

Nixon escaped any legal consequences. On Sept. 8, 1974, President Ford pardoned him for any crimes he might have committed while in office. Ford did so, he said, to "reconcile divisions in our country and heal the wounds that had festered too long."

For the next 20 years, Nixon sought to reestablish himself as a national figure by writing numerous books and offering his views on a variety of political issues. He died on April 22, 1994, at the age of 81.

President Nixon's Times
1969–1974

The U.S. Flag had 50 stars when Nixon took office. No new states or territories were organized. The U.S. population was 203,235,298 in 1970.

1969	On July 20, two U.S. astronauts, Neil A. Armstrong and Edwin E. Aldrin, Jr., became the first people to set foot on the moon.
1969	Congress approved a lottery system for the military draft.
Early 1970's	Women's Liberation, a movement aimed at winning equal opportunities for women, intensified.
1970	Congress authorized the creation of the National Railroad Passenger Corporation (Amtrak).
1971	The Supreme Court approved busing as a way to integrate public schools in areas where state laws had resulted in segregation.
1971	China became a member of the United Nations.
1973	The United States completed its withdrawal of combat forces from South Vietnam.

GERALD R. FORD

38th President of the United States
1974–1977

Gerald R. Ford holds two distinctions in American history. He was the first person to serve as Vice-President without being elected to the office. Then on Aug. 9, 1974, he became President of the United States without having been elected to the presidency or vice-presidency.

Ford's roots in America have been traced to a grandfather, Charles Henry King, who lived in California and Wyoming. The future President was born in Omaha, Neb., on July 14, 1913, the son of Leslie Lynch King and Dorothy Gardner King. He was christened Leslie Lynch King, Jr. His parents divorced when Ford was about 2, and he and his mother moved to Grand Rapids, Mich. There Dorothy King married Gerald Rudolph Ford, owner of a paint company. He adopted the boy, giving him his name.

After completing elementary school, Ford attended Grand Rapids South High School. He was a big, husky youth, and he excelled in football, playing center. Ford was also a good student, achieving high marks. He usually wore a suit and tie while other male classmates dressed in more casual attire. Ford was not stuffy, though. On the contrary, he was popular and well liked.

Ford went to the University of Michigan, where he played football and also made good marks. He could have played professional football after graduating from Michigan, but he chose instead to go to Yale University as assistant football coach and boxing coach. Coaching was not his life ambition, however. In 1941, he graduated from the Yale Law School.

With a partner, Ford opened an office in Grand Rapids in 1941, but America's entry into World War II interrupted his law practice. He joined the navy in 1942 as an ensign. Ford spent

Gerald R. Ford

Elizabeth Bloomer Ford was a popular and often controversial first lady, speaking out on political and social issues.

much of the war in the Pacific Ocean on the aircraft carrier U.S.S. *Monterey,* and he was discharged as a lieutenant commander in 1946.

Resuming his Grand Rapids law business, Ford also became active in local Republican politics. This led to his election to the U.S. House of Representatives in 1948 for the first of 13 terms. Ford also got married that year, in the midst of campaigning for Congress, to Elizabeth (Betty) Bloomer.

Elizabeth Bloomer was born in Chicago in 1918, and her family moved to Grand Rapids when she was 3. Betty began dancing lessons as a child, and in the 1930's she joined the Martha Graham dance group in New York City. Returning to Grand Rapids in 1942, she married William C. Warren, a furniture salesman.

Betty had just been divorced when she and Ford had their first date in August 1947. She had a job as a fashion coordinator at a Grand Rapids department store. Betty recalled that the first evening Ford asked her out she was working on an assignment for the store that was due the next day, and she at first begged off. "It was my livelihood," she remembered, "but Jerry persisted. . . . And I don't know about Jerry, but that first date was it as far as I was concerned."

The wedding took place on Oct. 15, 1948. Ford was obviously nervous—about the coming congressional election as well as about the wedding. Some people attending noticed that he wore one black and one brown shoe. The marriage turned out well, however, and the Fords had three sons and a daughter.

As a conservative Republican, Ford served his Michigan district well in the House. In 1963, he was appointed a member of the Warren Commission investigating the assassination of President John F. Kennedy. Two years later, he became House minority leader.

Gerald Ford and Richard M. Nixon had been friends in Congress, and Ford had supported Nixon's policies in the presidency. When Vice-President Spiro Agnew resigned under fire in October 1973, Ford seemed a wise choice to succeed him by presidential appointment. He was respected in Congress, had been the center of no controversy, and had a solid, conservative Republican record. Furthermore, as Ford himself noted, he had "lots of adversaries, but no enemies that I can remember."

As Vice-President, Ford went on a nationwide speaking tour and expressed his faith in Nixon, who was nonetheless becoming deeply implicated in the Watergate scandal. Ford addressed business, civic, and youth groups in cities throughout the country. Ford also took part in many Republican fund-raising activities and campaigned for Republican candidates. By mid-1974, the Vice-President had visited about 40 states and made several hundred public appearances.

Full name: Gerald
Rudolph Ford

Born: July 14, 1913

Birthplace: Omaha, Nebr.

Spouse: Elizabeth (Betty)
Bloomer

Occupation: Lawyer

Political party:
Republican

Term: 1974–1977

Vice-President: Nelson A.
Rockefeller

Presidential Successor

In 1974, upon Nixon's resignation, Ford became President, and he appreciated his peculiar position. In a brief speech to the nation, he said:

*Representative Gerald R. Ford and Senator Everett M. Dirksen at
a press conference following a meeting with President Nixon in 1969.*

> I am acutely aware that you have not elected me
> as your President by your ballots. So I ask you to
> confirm me as your President with your prayers.
> . . . If you have not chosen me by secret ballot,
> neither have I gained office by any secret prom-
> ises. I have not campaigned either for the presi-
> dency or the vice-presidency. I have not sub-
> scribed to any partisan platform. I am indebted to
> no man, and only to one woman—my dear
> wife—as I begin this very difficult job.

Ford kept all of Nixon's Cabinet officers at the start of his administration. He nominated Nelson A. Rockefeller, former governor of New York, as Vice-President. Rockefeller took office in
December 1974.

Public faith in government had plunged to its lowest level
in years, largely because of the Watergate scandal. In addition,
the Nixon impeachment crisis had slowed the work of many
federal agencies and created confusion about various government
policies. Ford hoped to heal the wounds the nation had suffered
from the Watergate affair and Nixon's resignation and to restore
Americans' faith in government. He got involved in controversy
almost immediately, though, when he granted a presidential pardon to Nixon on Sept. 8, 1974, for whatever crimes Nixon might
have committed while in office. Many Americans thought that
Nixon's involvement in Watergate deserved thorough investigation and that he should be charged with crimes and prosecuted
if evidence pointed to that.

Eight days after he pardoned Nixon, the Amnesty Program
was announced by Ford. He offered amnesty to draft dodgers
and deserters of the Vietnam War period. The program required

most of the participants to work in a public service job for up to
two years. About 22,000 people applied for amnesty under the
program. Many others refused to apply.

A high inflation rate and an economic recession that began
in 1974 plagued Ford's administration. The unemployment rate
went to 9 per cent by May 1975 and dropped slowly during the
recovery. In October 1976, it stood at about 8 per cent.

Fighting on the Mediterranean island of Cyprus provided
the first foreign crisis for the new President. In August 1974,
Turkish troops invaded Cyprus and took control of a large part
of the island. The take-over occurred after Turkish Cypriots
strongly protested the formation of a new government by Greek
Cypriots. Angry Greeks, Greek Cypriots, and Americans of
Greek ancestry charged that the United States should have used
its influence to stop the Turks.

Foreign Negotiations

Ford worked to continue Nixon's program to improve U.S. relations with China and Russia. On foreign policy, he relied heavily on the guidance of Secretary of State Henry A. Kissinger,
who had also been Nixon's chief adviser. In November 1974,
Ford went to Vladivostok in the Soviet Union, where he and Soviet Communist Party Leader Leonid I. Brezhnev reached a ten-
tative agreement on limiting offensive nuclear arms.

In the final days of the Vietnam War, Ford asked Congress
to give South Vietnam more military aid, but Congress did not.
He then arranged for the evacuation of Vietnamese refugees, and
about 100,000 came to the United States. Ford also sent 200 Ma-

*With Betty at his side, Gerald R. Ford takes the oath of office as
President before Chief Justice Warren Burger.*

rines to the Gulf of Siam in May 1975 after Cambodian Communist troops seized the *Mayagüez*, a U.S. merchant ship. The Marines found the ship abandoned. The 39-member crew, who had been taken to Cambodia, eventually were released in a Thai fishing boat to return to the ship. Also in 1975, Ford and Kissinger helped Egypt and Israel settle a territorial dispute that had resulted from a war between the two nations in 1973.

Ronald Reagan, former governor of California, challenged Ford in several presidential primaries in 1976 and made a strong showing at the Republican convention in Kansas City that year. Ford won the nomination on the first ballot, however, and lost to Democrat Jimmy Carter, former governor of Georgia, in November. Carter took 51 per cent of the popular vote and 297 electoral votes to Ford's 240.

On Jan. 20, 1977, Gerald Ford left office. While in retirement in Palm Springs, Calif., he remained active in Republican Party affairs and his opinion and comment on national and international affairs were often sought.

President Ford's Times
1974–1977

The U.S. Flag had 50 stars when Ford took office. No new states or territories were organized. The U.S. population was about 220,000,000 in 1977.

1974	Ford pardoned Nixon for all federal crimes that Nixon may have committed while President.
1975	The Vietnam War ended.
1975	The *Mayagüez,* a U.S. merchant ship, was seized by Cambodian troops and recaptured.
1975	Manned U.S. *Apollo* and Soviet *Soyuz* space vehicles linked up in space in the *Apollo Soyuz* Test Project.
1976	Americans celebrated the bicentennial, or 200-year, anniversary of their nation's founding.
1976	In July, the unmanned *Viking I* became the first U.S. spacecraft to land on Mars.

JIMMY CARTER

39th President of the United States
1977–1981

Two Jameses who ran for the presidency—James K. Polk in 1844 and James Earl Carter, Jr., in 1976—had name recognition problems. In both cases, the public's first response was "Who?" But both Polk and Carter won election.

Kindred Carter, the future President's great-great-great-great-grandfather, was the first of the family line to reach Georgia, in about 1787. He and his descendants were successful farmers. Great-great-grandfather Wiley Carter left not only land, but also $22,000 to each of his 12 heirs. The son of James Earl Carter, Sr., and Lillian Gordy Carter was born in Plains, Ga., on Oct. 1, 1924. His father was a farmer who also owned timberland, bought and sold peanuts, and ran a general store.

Known from infancy as Jimmy, the younger James Earl grew up in an atmosphere of hard work and high expectations for good performance. A small youth, he played on the Plains High School basketball team, although he probably felt more comfortable as a member of the Book Lovers Club. Jimmy liked to read, and he made good grades in school.

Upon graduation in 1941, Carter enrolled in Georgia Southwestern College, a junior college in Americus. The following year he won appointment to the U.S. Naval Academy at Annapolis, Md. Carter then attended the Georgia Institute of Technology for a year to pick up mathematics courses he lacked. He graduated from the academy in 1946, and on July 7 he married Rosalynn Smith.

Rosalynn was also a native of Plains and a good friend of Carter's sister Ruth. After high school Rosalynn, too, went to Georgia Southwestern College. She and Jimmy had their first

Jimmy Carter

*Rosalynn Smith Carter
helped run the peanut business and greatly assisted
Jimmy in his campaigns for
the Georgia governorship
and the presidency.*

Full name: James Earl
Carter, Jr.

Born: Oct. 1, 1924

Birthplace: Plains, Ga.

Spouse: Rosalynn Smith

Occupation:
Businessperson

Political party:
Democratic

Term: 1977–1981

Vice-President: Walter F.
Mondale

Runner-up: Gerald R.
Ford

Electoral vote: 297

Runner-up: 240

Popular vote: 40,830,763

Runner-up: 39,147,793

date in 1945, when he was home from Annapolis on vacation. As Rosalynn recalled, she and Ruth Carter had spent the day helping clean a neighbor's house: "We just slaved all day and then I went to the Methodist Youth Fellowship at the church. . . . After supper Ruth and her date came by and Jimmy was sitting in the rumble seat. He got out of the car and asked me if I'd go to a movie with them. I was so excited. It was wonderful." Carter remembered: "I returned home later that night and told my mother that Rosalynn had gone to the movies with me. Mother asked if I liked her, and I was already sure of my answer when I replied, 'She's the girl I want to marry.' Rosalynn has never had any competition for my love."

During his first two years as a naval officer, Carter was an instructor in electronics. He then took submarine training and became one of a group of officers involved in the development of nuclear submarines.

The Businessman

His father died in 1953, and Carter left the navy, returned to Plains, and took over the family farm and peanut business. He quickly became a successful farmer and businessman. He was also a civic leader.

Jimmy relied heavily on Rosalynn in the business, seeking and taking her advice. After mastering an accounting course by correspondence, she said: "I was sure I could have even passed the test for CPA." Jimmy, she remembered, "came to me on all the decisions about the business, and I could advise him, because I kept all the books, I studied the tax laws, I knew everything that was going on—and it was always exciting."

Carter entered politics in 1962, winning election as a Democrat to the Georgia state senate. He was re-elected two years later. At that point, he set his sights on the governorship but lost his first attempt in 1966. He then campaigned almost steadily for the office during the next four years. As he described his routine:

I would go to the warehouse or farm early, and perform my extracurricular duties, along with my regular business work until late in the afternoon. Then I would drive somewhere in Georgia to make a speech, and return home late at night. Names, information about the community, and speech notes for later use were all dictated into a small tape recorder in the automobile. The next day Rosalynn wrote thank-you notes on an automatic typewriter which also recorded names and addresses and code descriptions of the persons I had met.

Carter was elected governor of Georgia in 1970.

The 1950's saw the beginning of change in race relations in the South. Aided by Supreme Court decisions and federal laws, blacks gradually gained educational, economic, and political rights and opportunities hitherto denied them in the region. There was considerable white resistance to change. While Jimmy Carter did not join that at the time, neither did he strongly oppose it. However, upon becoming governor in January 1971, he declared, "I say to you quite frankly that the time for racial discrimination is over. No poor, rural, weak, or black person should ever have to bear the additional burden of being deprived of the opportunity of an education, a job, or simple justice." During the Carter Administration in Georgia the number of blacks on major state boards and agencies rose from 3 to 53. The number of black state employees nearly doubled.

While governor, Carter began to move toward national Democratic politics, but he was almost completely unknown when he announced late in 1974 that he would be a candidate for the Democratic presidential nomination. Leaving the governorship in January 1975, he spent many months campaigning outside Georgia. Even so, a public opinion poll in October 1975 ranking possible candidates did not mention him.

The effects of the Watergate scandal lingered among Americans in 1976. Washington, D.C., "insiders" were still suspect, and confidence in professional politicians remained low. Carter stressed that he was an "outsider." He knew nothing about Washington but he would, if elected, become a breath of fresh and honest air in that city. And the name recognition problem faded as Jimmy Carter won numerous primaries in 1976. At the Democratic convention in New York City that summer he received the nomination on the first ballot.

Carter went on to win in November. He defeated President Gerald R. Ford by about 1.6 million popular votes, gaining 297 to Ford's 240 votes in the electoral college.

Once in the White House, Carter ended much of the ceremony and pageantry that had marked official receptions there. For example, he eliminated the practice of having trumpeters announce the presidential family and of having a color guard precede it. Most state dinners ended about 11 P.M., far earlier than those of most previous Presidents. Carter conducted official business during some state functions in the White House and worked after others.

President Jimmy Carter and Republican candidate Ronald Reagan at a television debate in the fall of 1980.

*Carter meets with Egypt's Anwar al-Sadat (left) and Israel's
Menachem Begin (right) during 1978 peace talks at Camp David.*

Rosalynn Carter, became an active representative of Carter's
administration. In 1977, she led a U.S. delegation on a tour of Latin
America. She also worked to help women gain equal rights and to
improve care for the elderly and the mentally ill.

A Challenged Presidency

Inflation and energy proved to be Carter's chief problems in the
presidency. He spent much time trying to develop an energy policy
that would reduce American dependence on imported oil. Congress created a Department of Energy in 1977 to coordinate federal
efforts. No Carter program had much effect on inflation, though.
The rate hit 15 per cent in 1980.

President Carter made other nations' adherence to human
rights an important foreign affairs issue. In 1978, he strengthened
ties between the United States and the Communist regime in
China. He also won Senate ratification of two treaties that eventually turn over control of the Panama Canal to Panama. He reached
a second Strategic Arms Limitation Treaty with the Soviet Union
(SALT II), then asked the U.S. Senate to postpone considering it for
ratification after Soviet troops invaded Afghanistan in 1979. Perhaps President Carter's greatest achievement was in getting Israel
and Egypt to sign a peace treaty in March 1979, ending a 30-year
state of war between the two nations.

One of his most troublesome problems came when militants in Iran seized the U.S. embassy in Teheran, the capital, in November 1979, and held more than 50 Americans seized there as hostages for more than a year. Carter imposed an embargo on U.S. exports to Iran and asked Western European nations to sever relations with the country. But nothing he tried succeeded. On April 25, 1980, he assumed full responsibility for the failure of a secret rescue mission. After the attempt had been called off, a helicopter collided with a transport plane at a desert rendezvous point in Iran, killing eight members of the rescue team.

In the eyes of many people, Carter's policies in general lacked firmness, consistency, and effectiveness. By 1980, Jimmy Carter had become an unpopular President.

He gained popularity during late 1979 and early 1980, partly for his handling of the Iranian crisis. He won enough delegates in primary elections to win renomination on the first ballot at the Democratic National Convention in New York City. But he failed to gain public support during his campaign. As a result, Republican Ronald Reagan won a landslide victory in November 1980. Reagan's popular vote was 43,899,248 to Carter's 35,481,435. The electoral count was 489 to 49.

Carter returned to Plains, Georgia, after leaving the White House. Since the mid-1980's, Carter has worked as a volunteer for Habitat for Humanity, a nonprofit organization that builds houses for the poor. He has also conducted peace negotiations and helped to monitor elections in many troubled places around the world.

President Carter's Times
1977–1981

The U.S. Flag had 50 stars when Carter took office. No new states or territories were organized. The U.S. population was about 224,226,000 in 1981.

1978	World's first two "test-tube" babies were born
1978	During the Camp David accords, Egypt and Israel agreed to a framework for peace.
1979	The United States and China established full diplomatic relations.
1979	The worst nuclear accident in U.S. history occurred at Three Mile Island, Pa.
1979	Gas shortages led to sharp price increases.
1979	The United States returned sovereignty over the Panama Canal Zone to Panama.
1980	Thousands of Cuban refugees landed in Florida.

RONALD REAGAN

40th President of the United States
1981–1989

At 69, Ronald Reagan became the oldest person ever elected President, surpassing William Henry Harrison, who turned 68 shortly before his inauguration in March 1841, and who died 30 days later. But age was hardly a barrier to Reagan, who looked far younger than his years. He was a vigorous leader who led a conservative "revolution" that brought an end to the era of government spending for expensive domestic social programs.

Before entering politics, Reagan spent nearly 30 years as a movie actor in Hollywood. His experience before the camera turned out to be a valuable asset in an era when television dominated the world of politics and public opinion.

Reagan's great-grandparents, Michael and Catherine Reagan, were both originally from Ireland. The couple emigrated from England to Canada before settling in Fairhaven, Ill., in 1858. Their great-grandson Ronald was born in Tampico, Ill., on Feb. 6, 1911, the younger of John Edward and Nelle Wilson Reagan's two sons.

The Reagan family lived in several small towns in Illinois during Ronald's boyhood, while his father worked as a shoe salesman and at various other jobs. They moved to the town of Dixon when Ronald was 9. Poverty never seemed to cast a shadow over the boy's sunny disposition. Reagan later looked back on his childhood as "one of those rare Huck Finn-Tom Sawyer idylls," of fishing, hunting, swimming in the river, and other simple pleasures. In his words, "We were poor, but we didn't know we were poor."

Sports and drama were two of Reagan's major interests in high school in Dixon and at Eureka College in Eureka, Ill. Rea-

Ronald Reagan

As first lady, Nancy Davis Reagan became active in a nationwide campaign to help stop drug abuse.

Full name: Ronald Wilson Reagan

Born: Feb. 6, 1911

Birthplace: Tampico, Ill.

Spouses: Jane Wyman; Nancy Davis

Occupation: Actor

Political party: Republican

Term: 1981–1989

Vice-President: George Bush

Runner-up: Jimmy Carter; Walter F. Mondale

Electoral vote: 489; 525

Runner-up: 49; 13

Popular vote: 43,904,153; 54,455,075

Runner-up: 35,483,883; 37,577,185

gan entered college in 1928. He starred in various school productions and was on the football, track, and swim teams. Baseball was the one sport he didn't enjoy playing, because nearsightedness made it hard for him to see the ball. Reagan's classmates elected him student council president in high school and president of the student body at Eureka.

After graduating from Eureka in 1932, Reagan landed a job as a sports announcer for radio station WOC in Davenport, Iowa. He soon moved to station WHO in Des Moines, where he broadcast play-by-play accounts of major league baseball games, college football games, and other sports events.

In 1937, Reagan went to California to report on the spring training season of the Chicago Cubs baseball team. While there, he made a screen test for the Warner Brothers motion picture studio. The studio offered him a contract, and Reagan began his career as a movie actor.

Reagan made more than 50 movies between 1937 and 1964. His roles included portrayals of Western heroes, American servicemen, and sports figures. Two of his most noteworthy pictures were *Knute Rockne—All American,* in which he played college football star George (the Gipper) Gipp, and *King's Row,* in which he played a young man whose legs were amputated.

Reagan married actress Jane Wyman in 1940. They had a daughter, Maureen Elizabeth, and they adopted a son, Michael Edward. The marriage ended in divorce in 1948.

During World War II, Reagan served in the Army Air Forces. His poor eyesight disqualified him from combat duty, and he spent most of the war years in Hollywood, making training films.

After the war, Reagan served as president of the Screen Actors Guild (SAG), a union of film performers. The post-war years were a time of strong anti-Communist feeling in the United States, and Reagan worked to remove suspected Communists from the movie industry. As SAG president he also led a long and successful strike against the movie studios to win payment for actors and actresses whose films were sold to television.

In 1951, Reagan met actress Nancy Davis, the adopted daughter of a Chicago surgeon. Davis had complained to SAG about receiving unwanted Communist mailings. Reagan met her for a dinner date to discuss her concerns—a date that turned out to be the first of many. The two were married on March 4, 1952. Nancy Reagan often said, "My life really began with Ronnie," and Reagan returned the obvious adoration of his devoted wife. The Reagans had two children—Patricia Ann and Ronald Prescott.

Early Political Career

Reagan's longtime interest in politics at first included support for Democratic programs and candidates. He admired Franklin Roosevelt and worked actively on behalf of Harry Truman and Democratic congressional candidates in the 1948 campaign. But Reagan's political views gradually began to get more conservative. He campaigned as a Democratic supporter of Dwight D. Eisenhower in 1952 and 1956, and of Richard Nixon in 1960. In

Aided by a chart concerning taxes, President Reagan discusses his proposed economic program on television in February 1981.

1962, Reagan formally changed his political party registration to Republican.

Reagan's political evolution coincided with his career as a television star. From 1954 through 1962, he hosted and occasionally starred in "The General Electric Theater," a weekly series sponsored by the General Electric Company. Between appearances, Reagan toured the country as a spokesman for General Electric. He visited company factories and made speeches before chambers of commerce and other civic groups. His talks stressed the value of the free enterprise system and the dangers of "big" government encroaching on individual freedoms. From 1964 through 1965, Reagan hosted and performed in "Death Valley Days," and made commercials for its sponsor, the United States Borax & Chemical Corporation.

In 1964, Reagan made a rousing television speech on behalf of Republican presidential candidate Barry Goldwater. In his speech, Reagan attacked high taxes, wasteful government spending, soaring welfare costs, the rising crime rate, and the growth of government agencies. The speech brought in a record number of contributions for Goldwater, and it propelled Reagan into the national spotlight as a leading spokesman for conservatives.

Reagan's Goldwater speech and his earlier oratory for General Electric won him the backing of wealthy Republicans in California, who urged him to run for governor in 1966. Reagan defeated the incumbent Democratic governor, Edmund G. (Pat) Brown, by a landslide, and was reelected in 1970.

Election as governor aroused Reagan's interest in running for the presidency. He campaigned briefly for the Republican nomination in 1968, but the bid went to Richard Nixon. He tried again in 1976, challenging President Gerald Ford for the nomination. Although Reagan won considerable support among conservatives in the South and West, he narrowly lost to Ford.

Reagan's Presidential Terms

Reagan planned ahead for the next presidential election, and by November 1979, when he announced his candidacy, he held a huge lead over other Republicans in the public opinion polls. By the end of May 1980, he had won 20 out of 24 primary elections. In July he won the nomination on the first ballot at the Republican convention in Detroit. George Bush was nominated for Vice-President.

With President Jimmy Carter at a low point in popularity, due mainly to high inflation, unemployment, energy problems, and the hostage crisis in Iran, Reagan won the 1980 election by a wide margin. He carried 44 states, with 489 electoral votes, while Carter took 6 states and the District of Columbia, with a total of 49 electoral votes.

As President, Reagan enjoyed great personal popularity, which helped him gain broad Congressional support during his first term and an easy reelection in 1984. Reagan and Bush won a second term by defeating Democratic nominees Walter F. Mondale and Geraldine A. Ferraro, 525 electoral votes to 13.

Reagan projected an image of indomitable optimism, even in the face of two life-threatening crises. An assassination attempt in 1981 left him seriously wounded, but he made a quick recovery. The assailant, John W. Hinckley, Jr., was judged insane and placed in a mental institution. In 1985, Reagan underwent surgery for cancer of the colon and again recovered rapidly.

Unlike many of his predecessors, Reagan shunned the idea of putting in long hours at his desk in the Oval Office. He delegated many responsibilities and relied on aides to provide him with information and options for decision-making. Critics questioned whether Reagan had the ability to understand complex issues. But Reagan generally came across as a forceful leader with a mastery of communication skills used in televised speeches and weekly radio addresses to the nation.

In the White House, the Reagans restored much of the traditional pageantry that President Carter had ended.

Domestic Policies

The Reagan presidency brought about a sharp turnaround in government policies that had begun with the New Deal of the 1930's. Reagan succeeded in winning congressional approval in 1981 for a number of legislative proposals, including the largest income tax cut in U.S. history. Spending for welfare, unemployment, and a wide variety of other social programs was slashed, while the allotment for defense expenditures was increased.

The loss of tax revenues and the increased spending for defense contributed to the largest budget deficit in U.S. history. To reduce the deficit, Congress passed tax increases in 1982 and 1984. Huge deficits continued to be a problem, however. Reagan

President Reagan with the Supreme Court of the United States after appointment of Sandra Day O'Connor, first woman justice.

nevertheless refused to heed calls for additional taxes, insisting that Congress would simply use the revenues for more government programs, rather than to reduce the deficits. In 1986, Reagan signed landmark legislation that simplified the income tax system and lowered tax rates for most individuals.

Reagan's policies had mixed effects on the U.S. economy. The nation's high inflation rate slowed, but a recession in 1981 and 1982 led to widespread business bankruptcies and an unemployment rate of about 11 per cent—the worst rate in 40 years. The economy began a recovery in 1983. Inflation continued to subside, and unemployment eventually dipped to below 7 per cent. Some critics contended, however, that unemployment was decreasing because many people had given up looking for work.

Reagan left a conservative imprint on the Supreme Court through his power of appointment. In 1981, he appointed Sandra Day O'Connor, who became the first woman justice to the Supreme Court. In 1986, he appointed Antonin Scalia to the court and elevated William Rehnquist to the position of chief justice.

Foreign Policies

International terrorism became a recurring problem during Reagan's years in office. In 1983, a terrorist explosion killed 241 U.S. Marines in Beirut, Lebanon. Palestinian terrorists hijacked an Italian cruise ship, the *Achille Lauro,* in 1985 and killed an American passenger. Reagan took bold action against terrorism in 1986, when he ordered U.S. air strikes against military and suspected terrorist centers in Libya. But terrorism struck again in December 1988 when a bomb exploded on board a U.S. airliner over Lockerbie, Scotland, killing all 258 persons aboard.

In other foreign affairs matters, Reagan took a tough stand

*President Reagan and Mikhail Gorbachev sign the historical INF
Treaty in Moscow. Provisions of the March, 1988 treaty included a freeze
on nuclear weapons and agreement on the destruction of existing nuclear missiles.*

against perceived Communist threats. He justified his build-up
of the nation's defense arsenals as being necessary to counter a
Soviet military advantage. Reagan met with Soviet leader Mikhail
Gorbachev in Geneva, Switzerland, in 1985 and in Reykjavík, Ice-
land, in 1986. The two men discussed arms reduction, but failed
to reach agreements. The Soviets expressed strong opposition to
Reagan's plans for a Strategic Defense Initiative, a controversial
research program.

Reagan's concerns over Communist expansion influenced
his policies in the Caribbean and Central America. In 1983, he
ordered U.S. forces to invade the Caribbean island of Grenada to
help defeat rebels who had overthrown the government there.
Reagan said the invasion was necessary to protect Americans in
Grenada and to prevent Cuba from using Grenada as a military
base. Reagan also attempted to counter Soviet and Cuban support
for rebels in El Salvador as well as for the leftist government of
Nicaragua. At Reagan's urging, the United States sent advisers
and military equipment to the government of El Salvador and to
the Nicaraguan rebels, known as *contras*. Opponents of Reagan's
policies toward Nicaragua contended that the contras were linked
to the right-wing dictatorship that had formerly ruled Nicaragua
and were guilty of widespread human-rights violations. But Reagan called the contras "freedom fighters," and he also claimed that
Nicaragua's leftist government wanted to "subvert and topple its
democratic neighbors."

Reagan's support for the contras became part of a compli-
cated scandal that threatened to seriously taint the Reagan presidency. In 1986, it was revealed that the United States had secretly
approved shipments of arms to Iran in an attempt to gain the
release of American hostages being held by Iranian-backed terrorists in Lebanon. Iran was at war with Iraq at the time, and the
arms sales were contrary to stated U.S. policy. Profits from the
arms sales were then diverted to the Nicaraguan contras, in

spite of a congressional ban on such aid. Reagan admitted that he had approved the arms shipments to Iran, but denied any knowledge of the diversion of funds to the contras.

A congressional committee found in 1987 that the Iran-contra scheme had been largely directed by Lt. Oliver L. North, a National Security Council aide, and had involved other government officials, as well as private arms dealers and donors. The Reagan Administration was harshly criticized for making foreign policy decisions without informing Congress.

Many consider Reagan's September 1987 summit meeting in the USSR with Soviet leader Mikhail Gorbachev the highlight of his presidency. The meetings resulted in the two superpowers signing the INF Treaty in March 1988, which included a freeze on the production of nuclear weapons and an agreement by both powers to destroy a number of existing intercontinental ballistic missiles.

Reagan's economic legacy as he left office included the longest economic expansion in U.S. history, yet a federal-budget deficit of $2.6 trillion.

Reagan retired to his ranch in Santa Barbara, California. He also traveled on a goodwill tour to Europe in June 1989 and to Japan in October 1989.

In 1994, Reagan revealed that he was suffering from the early stages of Alzheimer's disease. This brain disease causes an increasing loss of memory and other mental abilities.

President Reagan's Times
1981–1989

The U.S. Flag had 50 stars when Reagan took office. No new states or territories were organized. The U.S. population was about 247,498,000 in 1989.

1981	Iran freed 52 hostages held 444 days.
1981	The U.S. space shuttle *Columbia,* the first reusable spacecraft, was launched for the first time.
1983	French scientists discovered a virus linked to the disease AIDS (Acquired Immune Deficiency Syndrome).
1986	The explosion of the space shuttle *Challenger* brought the U.S. manned space program to a standstill.
1987	The U.S. stock market withstood the largest single-day plunge in its history.
1988	The U.S.S. *Vincennes* shot down an Iranian civilian airliner, mistaking it for a fighter plane.
1988	Much of North America was hit by its worst drought in 50 years.
1988	Mikhail Gorbachev meets with Reagan and Bush after addressing the U.N. General Assembly in New York City.

GEORGE BUSH

41st President of the United States
1989-1993

After serving two terms as Vice-President under Ronald Reagan, George Bush won the Republican nomination for President in 1988. He defeated Massachusetts Governor Michael Dukakis to become the nation's 41st President.

George Herbert Walker Bush was born on June 12, 1924, in Milton, Mass., to Dorothy and Prescott Bush. Bush's father, a successful businessman and investment banker, developed an interest in politics and represented Connecticut in the U.S. Senate from 1952 to 1962.

Bush attended school at Phillips Academy in Andover, Mass., where he earned good grades and was well liked by other students. With the U.S. entrance into World War II in 1941, Bush postponed his plan to enter Yale and chose instead to enlist in the Navy Reserve as a seaman second class. Receiving his wings and commission while still 18, Bush became the youngest pilot in the U.S. Navy. On active duty from 1943 to 1945, he flew torpedo bombers from aircraft carriers in the Pacific.

George Bush and Barbara Pierce were married on Jan. 6, 1945. The couple eventually had six children—George, Robin (who died of leukemia), John, Neil, Marvin, and Dorothy.

When the war ended, Bush entered Yale, majored in economics, and graduated Phi Beta Kappa in 1948. After graduation, Bush and his family moved to Texas, where he took a job with Dresser Industries. With friends in Texas in the 1950's, Bush formed two oil companies, the Bush-Overbey Oil Development Company and the Zapata Off-Shore Company. Through his career as an oilman, Bush became wealthy.

First lady Barbara Bush made a strong commitment to the family literacy movement.

Early Political Career

After an unsuccessful run for the U.S. Senate in 1964, Bush was elected to the U.S. House of Representatives in 1966 as a Republican from Texas' Seventh District. In 1970, Bush gave up his seat in the House to run for the Senate. He was defeated, however, by Democrat Lloyd Bentsen.

George Bush then served as United States ambassador to the United Nations from 1971 to 1973, and as chairman of the Republican National Committee from 1973 to 1974. In September 1974, Bush was appointed chief of the U.S. liaison office in Beijing. Upon his return from China, Bush served as director of the Central Intelligence Agency.

In May 1979, George Bush launched his first campaign for the presidency. His chief rival was Ronald Reagan, against whom he could not maintain an advantage. He withdrew his candidacy in May 1980. Reagan invited Bush to be his vice-presidential running mate. Bush was sworn in as the 43rd Vice-President of the nation on Jan. 20, 1981, and was reelected as Vice-President in 1984.

The Presidency

Bush entered the 1988 presidential campaign with the advantage of having served under an enormously popular President. His name was well known and his campaign was well organized. He easily won his party's nomination for President in New Orleans in August of 1988 and named Senator J. Danforth (Dan) Quayle of Indiana as his vice-presidential choice. The Democrats nominated Governor Michael Dukakis of Massachusetts for President and Senator Lloyd Bentsen of Texas for Vice-President. In the general election on Nov. 8, 1988, Bush and Quayle defeated Dukakis and Bentsen.

When Bush took office in January 1989, his major concerns were illegal drug traffic and keeping his campaign promise of "no new taxes." He also was determined to be known as "the education President" and "the environment President." During his campaign, he had convinced voters that he was the candidate who could best solve the nation's economic problems and provide direction in foreign affairs. Throughout the first year of his presidency, Bush faced challenges in both arenas that would give him the opportunity to turn his policies into action.

Soon after entering office, Bush had to deal with the worst crisis in the savings and loan industry since the Great Depression of the 1930's. More than 1,000 savings and loan institutions had failed and hundreds more neared bankruptcy—largely as a result of customers' nonpayment of loans, poor regulation, and fraud and mismanagement within the industry. Bush proposed legislation to rescue and restructure the savings and loan industry, and by mid-1989, the U.S. government had committed about $50 billion to fund the bailout. Government experts later estimated that the bailout would eventually cost taxpayers between $130 billion and $500 billion.

Meanwhile, a devasting oil spill increased the public's environmental concerns. In March 1989, the U.S. tanker *Exxon Valdez*

Full name: George Herbert Walker Bush

Born: June 12, 1924

Birthplace: Milton, Mass.

Spouse: Barbara Pierce

Occupation: Businessperson

Political party: Republican

Term: 1989-1993

Vice-President: J. Danforth (Dan) Quayle

Runners-up: Michael S. Dukakis; Lloyd Bentsen

Electoral vote: 426

Runners-up: 111 (Dukakis); 1 (Bentsen)

Popular vote: 48,886,097

Runner-up: 41,809,074

George Bush, who made "family values" a key part of his campaign for reelection, visits here with a group of elementary-school children.

struck a reef near the port of Valdez, Alaska, spilling nearly 11 million gallons (42 million liters) of crude oil into Prince William Sound in the largest oil spill ever to take place in North American waters. After many people became dissatisfied with Exxon's handling of the cleanup, Bush ordered the U.S. military and other federal authorities to take over the efforts.

During the year, Bush continued his fight against drugs. In September 1989, he presented a federal strategy for reducing the use of illegal drugs in the United States. The strategy included a recommendation for stronger law enforcement efforts against drug abusers, and outlined ways to reduce the production and trafficking of illegal drugs.

Dramatic political changes taking place around the world also demanded Bush's attention. Democratic reform swept through Eastern Europe during 1989, foreshadowing the end of the Cold War just two years later. In December 1989, Bush and Soviet leader Mikhail Gorbachev met aboard Soviet ships off the coast of Malta to discuss arms control and the future of Eastern Europe. Bush was praised for his diplomatic approach in these discussions.

Later in December, Bush took bold military action in Central America by ordering U.S. troops into Panama to overthrow the dictatorship of General Manuel Antonio Noriega. The military operation was successful, and Noriega was removed from power.

Bush faced another military challenge in August 1990, when Iraq invaded and took over the tiny, oil-rich country of Kuwait. He sent hundreds of thousands of troops to the Middle East to prevent a possible Iraqi attack on Saudi Arabia and, along with several other world leaders, demanded that Iraq withdraw from Kuwait. Bush also ordered U.S. Navy ships to help enforce a UN embargo on the shipment of goods to and from Iraq.

When Iraq did not withdraw from Kuwait by Jan. 15, 1991—the deadline imposed by the United Nations—U.S. forces, on Bush's orders, joined a coalition of nations in bombing Iraqi targets in Iraq and Kuwait. This military effort, which began on January 17 in Iraq (January 16, U.S. time), became known as Operation Desert Storm. Bush also ordered U.S. participation in a massive ground attack that began on February 24 (February 23, U.S. time) and defeated Iraq's military after about 100 hours of fighting.

In August 1991, Bush's diplomatic skills were again put to the test when hard-line Communist officials in the Soviet Union attempted to overthrow Gorbachev's government. Although the coup failed after three days, it seriously weakened the Soviet central government. By the end of 1991, the Soviet Union had been dissolved. Eleven of the former Soviet republics then formed a loose confederation called the Commonwealth of Independent States (CIS). Bush responded to the changing political situation by seeking assurances that Soviet nuclear weapons were safely under control. He also quickly established diplomatic relations with each of the former Soviet republics.

The Reelection Campaign

By 1992, as Bush sought a second term as President, the nation's attention had turned from foreign affairs to domestic issues. The country had been in an economic recession since July 1990, and the unemployment rate had climbed to the highest level since 1984. The American people were becoming increasingly concerned about growing racial conflict, crime, poverty, and what they saw as a decline in U.S. productivity compared with that of other nations. Of particular concern was the federal government's policy of *deficit spending,* or borrowing money to finance expenditures.

In the midst of these growing fears for the nation's economic and social health, Bush ran for a second term as President against Governor Bill Clinton of Arkansas, his Democratic opponent. Bush again selected Vice-President Dan Quayle as his running mate, while Clinton chose Al Gore, a Democratic senator from Tennessee.

During the campaign, Bush focused on his foreign policy successes and declared his commitment to "family values." His platform also emphasized cutting the growth of government spending, decreasing the size of government, and reducing the national debt.

On the campaign trail, Bush often characterized Clinton as a draft evader and "tax-and-spender" who could not be trusted. He also warned voters that Clinton lacked experience in international affairs. However, for many voters, Bush's efforts to bring Clinton's character into question were countered by their doubts about Bush's credibility. After promising "no new taxes" during his 1988 presidential campaign, he had broken his pledge in November 1990

President Bush's Times
1989-1993

The U.S. Flag had 50 stars when Bush took office. No new states or territories were organized. The U.S. population was about 256,300,000 in 1993.

June 1989	In Beijing's Tiananmen Square, hundreds of protesting students were massacred by government troops.
Nov. 1989	The Berlin Wall was opened.
Aug. 1990	Iraq invaded and took control of Kuwait.
Jan. 1991	The Persian Gulf War began.
April 1991	The Persian Gulf War ended.
Aug. 1991	In the Soviet Union, an attempted coup led by conservative Communist leaders against Mikhail Gorbachev's government failed, and Gorbachev returned to power.
Dec. 1991	The Soviet Union was dissolved, and 11 of the 12 remaining Soviet republics agreed to join a new, loose confederation known as the Commonwealth of Independent States.
April-May 1992	Riots erupted in Los Angeles, Calif., after a jury acquitted four police officers in the beating of a black motorist.

by signing legislation that increased federal taxes. In addition, his "family values" theme was weakened in September 1992 when he vetoed the Family Leave Act. The legislation would have allowed workers in companies employing at least 50 people up to 12 weeks of unpaid leave to take care of a new baby or for family medical emergencies.

The presidential campaign took a surprising turn in October 1992 when Texas billionaire H. Ross Perot reentered the race as an independent candidate. Perot had declared his candidacy for President earlier in the year, but had withdrawn from the race shortly thereafter.

From the start, Bush's campaign was unable to generate enthusiasm, and he trailed Clinton significantly in preelection polls throughout the summer and most of the fall. On November 3, Bush lost his bid for a second term to Bill Clinton and thus became the third one-term President in 20 years.

In April 1993, the former President visited Kuwait as "Citizen Bush." Three weeks later, U.S. government officials learned of an Iraqi plot to assassinate Bush during his visit. All but one of the suspects were taken into custody.

BILL
CLINTON

42nd President of the United States
1993-2001

At the age of 17, after meeting President John F. Kennedy on a 1963 trip to Washington, D.C., young Bill Clinton decided that he would pursue a political career. At the time, Clinton was a delegate to the American Legion Boys Nation, a citizenship training program in which young people form a model of national government. Thirty years later, 46-year-old Clinton would return to Washington, D.C., to be inaugurated as the 42nd President of the United States—the third youngest person, after John F. Kennedy and Theodore Roosevelt, to hold that office.

A skillful public speaker known for his ability to capture the attention of a wide variety of audiences, Clinton overcame a difficult childhood to excel in high school and college before embarking on what was to be a distinguished political career. At the age of 32, he became one of the youngest people ever elected state governor when he won that office in Arkansas. Clinton was serving his fifth term as governor when he was elected President.

Growing Up in Arkansas

Bill Clinton was named William Jefferson Blythe IV when he was born on Aug. 19, 1946, in Hope, Ark., to Virginia Cassidy Blythe and the late William Jefferson Blythe III. Three months before Bill was born, his father died as a result of a car accident. When Bill was 4, his mother married Roger Clinton. In 1953, the family moved to Hot Springs, Ark.

Bill enjoyed his schoolwork and earned good grades. But life at home was far from easy. His stepfather was an alcoholic who sometimes verbally or even physically abused Bill's mother. At least once, Bill stood up to his stepfather to protect his mother. Later, on the rare occasions when Clinton spoke of his troubled

First Lady Hillary Rodham Clinton played an active role in her husband's administration, focusing her efforts on health care reform.

family life, he would say that it helped him become skilled at solving disagreements and avoiding conflicts. However, during his campaign for the presidency, he steadfastly refused to use his past as a way to gain favor with voters. When his staff tried to include some lines about his childhood in his speeches, he often crossed them out, saying that it "...sounds too self-pitying." After graduating from high school in 1964, Clinton attended Georgetown University in Washington, D.C. The social turbulence of the 1960's, particularly the civil rights movement, deeply affected Clinton. He memorized every word of Martin Luther King, Jr.'s famous "I Have a Dream" speech. In April 1968, when widespread rioting erupted in Washington after King's assassination, Clinton worked as a Red Cross volunteer, bringing food and clothing to people whose homes had burned.

Following his graduation from Georgetown, Clinton entered Oxford University in England as a Rhodes scholar. He studied at Oxford for two years before entering Yale Law School in 1970. While at Yale, Clinton met Hillary Rodham, whom he married on Oct. 11, 1975. In 1980, the couple had a daughter, Chelsea.

Early Political Career

After receiving his law degree in 1973, Clinton returned to Arkansas. In 1976, he ran unopposed for attorney general of Arkansas and took office in 1977. In early 1978, midway through his two-year term as attorney general, Clinton became a candidate for governor of Arkansas. He easily defeated his Republican opponent, and took office in January 1979.

As governor, Clinton tried—but failed—to gather support for a wide range of programs and policies. To pay for the road improvement he had promised voters during his campaign, Clinton pushed a controversial measure through the legislature raising various fees and taxes, including gasoline taxes and motor vehicle license fees. These increases were extremely unpopular and were a factor in his unsuccessful bid for a second term.

In 1982, Clinton ran for governor again—this time successfully. During his second term in office, he worked hard to build a broad base of support for his policies. He also concentrated on two main problems—education and the economy—rather than a wide range of issues.

Beginning in 1983, Clinton set about improving the quality of education in Arkansas by pushing several major reforms through the legislature. At Clinton's urging, Arkansas passed a law—the first of its kind in the nation—requiring teachers to pass a basic skills test to keep their jobs. Under Clinton's leadership, Arkansas became one of the first states to establish a policy of open enrollment that allowed children to attend any of the state's public schools, providing racial balance was maintained.

Clinton also made important strides in Arkansas' economic development. He worked to broaden the state's industrial base, urging the legislature to pass an economic package designed to attract businesses to Arkansas—particularly high-technology com-

Full name: William Jefferson Clinton

Born: Aug. 19, 1946

Birthplace: Hope, Ark.

Spouse: Hillary Rodham

Occupation: Lawyer

Political party: Democrat

Term: 1993-2001

Vice-President: Al Gore

Runners-up: George Bush, H. Ross Perot; Robert Dole, H. Ross Perot

Electoral vote: 370; 379

Runners-up: 168 (Bush), 0 (Perot); 159 (Dole), 0 (Perot)

Popular vote: 43,860,888; 47,198,755

Runners-up: 38,220,427 (Bush), 19,266,862 (Perot); 39,198,755 (Dole), 8,085,402 (Perot)

panies such as computer and electronics firms. His actions helped Arkansas reduce unemployment and increase production in the late 1980's and early 1990's.

Clinton was reelected as governor in 1984 and again in 1986, each time by a wide margin. He was elected to a fifth term in 1990.

Road to the Presidency

In October 1991, Clinton formally announced his candidacy for the Democratic nomination for President. His chief challengers for the nomination were former Senator Paul E. Tsongas of Massachusetts and former Governor Jerry Brown of California. Tsongas, an early front-runner, suspended his campaign in March 1992. Clinton soon had enough delegates to ensure the nomination. However, Clinton still faced opposition from H. Ross Perot, a Texas billionaire running for President as an independent.

In July 1992, Clinton was named the Democratic presidential nominee at the Democratic National Convention in New York City. At his request, Al Gore, a Democratic senator from Tennessee, was nominated for Vice-President. During the convention, Perot dropped out of the race. Clinton's Republican opponent was incumbent President George Bush.

Clinton's campaign sparked enthusiasm from the start, as he and Gore embarked on a well-publicized bus trip across nine Middle Atlantic and Midwestern states immediately after the convention. Charging that Bush was unconcerned about domestic issues, Clinton promised to stimulate economic growth by increasing government spending, rebuilding the nation's transportation and communication networks, and encouraging business expansion. He also called for changes in education to improve America's competitive position in the world marketplace. Clinton indicated that he would raise taxes on wealthy Americans to help reduce the federal budget deficit.

In October 1992, the campaign took an unexpected turn as Perot reentered the race. In the general election held on November 3, Clinton defeated Bush by a decisive margin. Although Perot was unable to muster a single electoral vote, he made an impressive showing in the popular vote in what was perhaps the best third-party race since Theodore Roosevelt's in 1912.

As he took office in January 1993, President Clinton faced several challenges. During his first 100 days, Clinton began the difficult task of stimulating the dragging economy while putting an end to Congressional gridlock. However, his proposal to raise taxes in order to reduce the federal deficit was met with mixed reactions. In April, his $16.3 billion short-term economic stimulus plan—the so-called "jobs bill"—was defeated in the Senate.

At the same time, Clinton's proposal to lift the ban on homosexuals in the military sparked a major controversy. Nevertheless, Clinton continued to push through his program of change by signing the emergency Family Leave Act and forming a task force to reform the U.S. health care system. He also managed to salvage the part of the jobs bill that would extend unemployment compensation benefits to about 1.9 million people without jobs.

Struggles with Congress

In August 1994, President Clinton won a victory when Congress passed an anticrime law he supported. The law called for spending billions of dollars on crime prevention, law enforcement, and prison construction. It also outlawed the sale of certain types of assault weapons, guns that many people believe are designed specifically for killing or injuring people. Clinton also strongly backed the Brady bill, which requires people to wait five working days between the time they buy a handgun and the time they take possession of it. Congress approved the law in November 1994.

In the elections that same month, however, the Democrats lost control of both houses of Congress to the Republicans. This set the stage for a lengthy partisan struggle between the Republicans in Congress and the President. Although Clinton's budgets of 1993 and 1994 include cuts in government spending that helped reduce the federal budget deficit, the Republicans called for even larger cuts. Their goal was to erase the deficit and achieving a balanced budget by the year 2002. Clinton criticized some of those cuts as too sharp and proposed his own plan for ending the deficit.

By the start of the government's new fiscal year on October 1, 1995, Congress had failed to pass some of the appropriations bills that fund the government's operations. Congress tried to exert its control by passing a series of bills that allowed spending to continue, but which contained other provisions that Clinton opposed. Clinton vetoed those bills, and Congress refused to remove the provisions. The resulting lack of funding forced many federal government operations to shut down for 6 days in November 1995 and for 21 days from December 1995 to January 1996.

In 1996, Congress created legislation to revise the welfare system. Clinton vetoed two bills, claiming they included changes that would harm the poor too much. But he approved a third welfare bill in August 1996, upsetting many in his own party. The bill placed limits on how long people can receive welfare benefits, and it shifted much responsibility for administering welfare from the federal government to the states. Clinton also called for an increase in the legal minimum wage, which Congress approved in August 1996.

Clinton and Foreign Policy

International affairs presented Clinton with many problems. A U.S. military mission in Somalia ran into disaster in 1993. Congress called for the withdrawal of U.S. troops from the UN command after 18 U.S. soldiers were killed in a battle with supporters of a clan leader. The troops returned home in March 1994.

In September 1994, Clinton threatened to use armed force against Haiti's military dictators if they did not allow democratically elected Jean-Bertrand Aristide to return to power. Haiti's top military leader, Lieutenant General Raoul Cedras, agreed to step down. United States troops were sent to help ensure the transfer of power to Aristide.

Clinton achieved one of his major foreign policy goals in November 1993, when Congress approved the North American Free Trade Agreement (NAFTA). Clinton strongly supported the pact, which will gradually eliminate tariffs and other trade barriers between the United States, Mexico, and Canada. In December 1994, Clinton won Congress's approval of an expansion of the General Agreement on Tariffs and Trade (GATT). This expanded GATT plan called for large reductions in trade barriers among many nations.

In late 1995, Clinton helped bring about a meeting of representatives of the sides in the Bosnian civil war that began in 1992. The representatives began meeting in Dayton, Ohio, in November. In December in Paris, they signed a peace plan that included a cease-fire. Under the plan, the cease-fire was to be policed by a force of about 60,000 troops from the North Atlantic Treaty Organization (NATO). Clinton agreed to send about 20,000 United States troops to Bosnia to serve in the force.

Bill Clinton and Al Gore celebrate their 1996 election in Little Rock, Arkansas.

The 1996 Election

At the Democratic National Convention in Chicago in August 1996, Clinton and Gore were renominated without opposition. The Republicans nominated Robert Dole of Kansas for President and Jack Kemp of New York for vice president. Ross Perot ran for President on the Reform Party ticket. In the campaign, Clinton pointed to his first-term record, emphasizing improvements in the economy and such laws as gun control measures and the minimum-wage increase. He also said he had kept Congress from cutting important government programs too deeply. In the November presidential election, the voters reelected Clinton and Gore.

Clinton Under Fire

During his presidency, Clinton struggled to clear himself of charges of financial and sexual misconduct. The financial charges centered on the Whitewater Development Corporation, a small company that bought land in Arkansas for a vacation home development. The sexual misconduct charges centered on accusations of sexual harassment made by Paula Jones and suspicions that Clinton may have lied about an affair with White House intern Monica Lewinsky.

The Clintons had invested in the Whitewater Development Corporation in 1978, shortly before Bill Clinton was elected governor of Arkansas, and sold their interest in the company in 1992. They denied any wrongdoing and pointed out that they had lost a large sum of money on their investment. In January 1994, Attorney General Janet Reno appointed a Republican lawyer, Robert B. Fiske, to investigate the Whitewater affair. In August 1994, a panel of federal judges appointed another Republican lawyer, Kenneth W. Starr to take Fiske's place.

A historic agreement between Israel and the Palestine Liberation Organization (PLO) was signed in Washington, D.C., in September 1993. Bill Clinton looks on as Israeli Prime Minister Yitzhak Rabin (left) and PLO leader Yasir Arafat (right) shook hands following the signing.

In 1994, a case of sexual harassment was brought against the President by Paula Jones. Jones claimed that Clinton acted improperly with her when he was Governor of Arkansas. While Clinton was defending himself under oath in the Jones case, he was questioned about his more recent relationship with a White House intern, Monica S. Lewinsky. He denied allegations that he had a sexual affair with her and also that he had tried to cover it up.

Later, Jones's case was dismissed, but Starr pressed for further investigation of the President's dealings with Lewinsky. In August 1998, Clinton admitted on national television that he had an "inappropriate" relationship with her. Following the broadcast, the President was the subject of much criticism, and some members of the media even speculated that he might resign or be impeached. The prospect of impeachment grew more serious in October when, for the third time in U.S. history, the House launched impeachment proceedings against a President when Representatives authorized an open-ended inquiry against Clinton.

In December 1998, the House impeached Clinton for perjury and obstruction of justice. He was charged with lying to a grand jury about his extramarital affair with Lewinsky. Other charges included hindering the investigation by lying to his aides and by encouraging others to lie and conceal evidence on his behalf. The Senate, however, acquitted Clinton in February 1999.

President Clinton's Times

1993-2001

The U.S. Flag had 50 stars when Clinton took office. The U.S. population was about 275,119,000 in 2000.

Feb. 1993	A powerful car bomb explodes in the World Trade Center in New York City, killing six people and injuring more than 1,000.
April 1994	South Africans participate in the first all-racial elections in the nation's history, ending white-minority rule of the country.
Nov. 1994	The Channel Tunnel, a 31-mile (50-kilometer) tunnel under the English Channel that links England to France, opens to passenger traffic.
Nov. 1995	The presidents of Bosnia-Herzegovina, Croatia, and Serbia meet to sign an agreement aimed at bringing peace to the war-torn Balkan region.
April 1996	Theodore J. Kaczynski, believed to be the Unabomber responsible for a 17-year-long string of package bombs, is arrested.
July 1996	The first clone of an adult mammal, sheep named Dolly, is born in Scotland.
March 1997	The Hale-Bopp Comet, last visible 4,000 years ago, becomes visible in the night sky.
June 1997	Sovereignty and control of Hong Kong pass back to China, after the territory's 156 years under control of the United Kingdom.
July 1997	NASA's Pathfinder spacecraft lands on Mars and begins transmitting television pictures of the surface.
August 1997	Diana, Princess of Wales, and former wife of Prince Charles, is killed in a car crash.
Jan. 1998	Iraq blocks UN weapons inspectors, a violation of terms set at the end of the Gulf War.
Oct. 1998	John Glenn returns to space aboard the space shuttle *Discovery.*
April 1999	Canada created a third territory, Nunavut, to give the Inuit an opportunity for self-government.
July 1999	John F. Kennedy, Jr., son of President John F. Kennedy, died in a plane crash.
August 1999	A powerful earthquake struck Turkey, killing more than 15,000. Three months later, another devastating earthquake struck nearby.
Jan. 2000	The Thomas Jefferson Memorial Foundation announced that Jefferson was most likely the father of his slave Sally Hemings' six children.

GEORGE W. BUSH

43rd President of the United States
2001-

When Bush was elected President in 2000, it marked only the second time in U.S. history that the son of a former president was elected to the office. Bush's father, George Herbert Walker Bush, served as president from 1989 to 1993. The only other father and son to be elected president were John Adams and John Quincy Adams.

Ironically, both John Quincy Adams and George W. Bush entered the White House in unusual circumstances. Adams' election was decided by the House of Representatives because none of the candidates had a majority of the electoral votes. A Supreme Court ruling helped determine the outcome of Bush's election. Another coincidence, both Bush and Adams lost the popular vote.

Politics and business have permeated Bush's life. His grandfather, Prescott Sheldon Bush, was a U.S. senator from Connecticut. His father was a member of the U.S. House of Representatives from 1967 to 1971, and during the 1970's, served as U.S. ambassador to the United Nations, U.S. envoy to China, and head of the Central Intelligence Agency. He was U.S. vice president under President Ronald Reagan from 1981 to 1989 and U.S. president from 1989 to 1993. In addition, Bush's father made millions of dollars in the oil business. His mother, Barbara Pierce Bush grew up in New York. Her father was the publisher of Redbook and McCall's magazines. So, it should come as no surprise that Bush and his siblings also live the life of business and politics.

Growing Up in Texas

George Walker Bush was born on July 6, 1946, in New Haven, Connecticut, to George and Barbara Bush. He was the first of the

First Lady Laura Bush has made early childhood development and education her priority during her husband's presidency.

Full name:
  George Walker Bush

Born: July 6, 1946

Birthplace: New Haven, Connecticut

Spouse: Laura Welch

Occupation:
  Businessperson

Political party: Republican

Term: 2001-

Vice-President:
  Richard B. Cheney

Runners-up: Al Gore; Ralph Nader

Electoral vote: 271

Runners-up: 266 (Gore); 0 (Nader); 1 (abstention)

Popular vote: 49,820,518*

Runners-up:
  50,158,094* (Gore); 2,783,728* (Nader)

Unofficial vote totals as of December 13, 2000.

couple's six children. His father was studying at Yale University at the time. When Bush was two, the family moved to Midland, Texas, so his father could enter the oil business, a path Bush would follow. When Bush was seven, his younger sister, Robin, died of leukemia. The family was grief-stricken. His parents later told friends that young George helped them deal with their sorrow.

Bush attended Sam Houston Elementary School in Midland, then went on to San Jacinto Junior High, where he spent just one year. In 1959, the family moved to Houston, and Bush entered a private school, Kinkaid School. There, he joined the football team. Bush then spent his final years of high school at his father's alma mater, Phillips Academy in Andover, Massachusetts. He pursued basketball, baseball, and cheerleading.

In 1964, Bush again followed in his father's footsteps, beginning his studies at Yale University. He majored in history, served as president of his fraternity, and belonged to Yale's elite secret society, Skull & Bones.

In 1968, as Bush was finishing up at Yale, the United States was deeply involved in the Vietnam War. Just before graduation, Bush was accepted as an airman in the Texas Air National Guard. He trained for a year to become a pilot. He graduated in December 1969 and then trained on the F-102 jet fighter. He tried to enter a program to fly in Vietnam but was not accepted, as he had not logged enough flight hours.

Bush finished his active duty in the Texas Air National Guard in 1970 and began three years of what he later called his "nomadic" days. During that time, he continued to fulfill his commitment to the National Guard but did not find lasting, full-time employment. He applied to law school but was not accepted. In 1973, he entered Harvard Business School, and he graduated in 1975 with an M.B.A.

Early Political and Business Ventures

After graduating from Harvard, Bush returned to Midland and went to work in the oil business. In 1977, the congressional representative for the district that included Midland announced his retirement. Bush filed as a candidate to fill the seat. He won the nomination but lost the election. But his run for the seat was not all bad. While campaigning, he met Laura Welch, and the two began dating. They were married just three months later, on November 5, 1977. Laura was working as a librarian when she met Bush. She had also been a schoolteacher. They later went on to have twin daughters in 1981, Barbara and Jenna.

After losing the election, Bush decided to focus on business. In the late 1970's, he set up Arbusto Energy Incorporated, an oil exploration company, later called Bush Exploration Company. When oil prices fell in the early 1980's, Bush merged his company with another small oil firm, Spectrum 7 Energy Corporation, and became the company's chief executive officer. Still, the oil business was not kind to Bush, and Spectrum 7 did not do well. The company was taken over by Harken Oil and Gas, Incorporated, later named Harken Energy Corporation. Bush received stock for his Spectrum shares and became a member of Harken's board of directors. Bush sold most of his shares shortly before the company claimed huge losses. Later, critics charged that Bush knew that the company was in trouble and had sold most of his shares before the information became public. The Securities and Exchange Commission investigated Bush, but no charges were filed against him.

In the late 1980's, Bush returned to politics. His father, then the U.S. vice president, was running for president in the 1988 election. The younger Bush moved his family to Washington, D.C., to help manage his father's political campaign. After his father won the election, Bush moved to Dallas.

In 1989, Bush and a group of investors put together a successful bid to buy the Texas Rangers baseball team. After their purchase, the new owners successfully convinced the city of Arlington to build a baseball stadium for the team. Bush worked hard to increase attendance at the games. However, as much as he enjoyed working in baseball, politics was calling his name.

Governor of Texas

In 1993, President Bush lost his run for reelection. In the same year, the younger Bush announced his candidacy for governor of Texas, and his brother, Jeb, decided to run for governor of Florida. George Bush's opponent was Democrat Ann W. Richards, seeking a second term. Richards accused Bush of running on his family name. Bush criticized her record and focused on presenting his views. He supported welfare reform, stronger criminal laws, and reform of the justice system that was burdened with unimportant lawsuits. Bush won the election by a wide margin; his brother lost in Florida.

As governor, Bush worked on legislation to give schools more authority, crack down on juvenile offenders, and place limits on civil lawsuits. In 1997, he presented a plan to restructure the Texas tax system and increase funding for schools. His proposal to raise taxes received criticism and was not accepted.

In 1998, Bush ran for reelection and won, defeating Texas Land Commissioner Garry Mauro. And during this election, his brother won in Florida as well. During Bush's second term, Texas increased school funding and continued to adopt education reforms. But Bush was criticized for not having done enough to protect the environment, combat racism, or eradicate poverty.

The Run for the Presidency

In June 1999, Bush announced he would run for president of the United States. As soon as he entered the race, his critics brought up his past. He was accused of receiving preferential treatment to enter the Texas Air National Guard, and reporters asked Bush if he had used cocaine in his youth. Bush stated that neither he nor his father had sought to influence his selection in the National Guard. He did not respond to the question of cocaine use. At the Republican National Convention in August 2000, Bush was named the Republican presidential nominee. At Bush's request, Richard B. Cheney, former congressman and U.S. secretary of defense, was nominated as his running mate. The Democrats nominated Vice President Al Gore for president and Senator Joseph I. Lieberman of Connecticut for vice president.

During the campaign, Bush called Gore "the candidate of the status quo." He emphasized what he called "compassionate conservatism." He pledged to cut taxes, strengthen the Social Security system, and rebuild the military. Gore argued that Bush lacked the experience to be president.

Too Close to Call

The American people were used to having the results of a presidential election the same day as the election. But November 7, 2000, proved to be no ordinary Election Day.

The first indication of the election not following an ordinary course happened when in the evening of Election Day, major television networks projected that Gore would win the popular and, therefore, the electoral votes for Florida. The networks retracted that projection a few hours later when vote counts put Bush in the lead. Oddly enough, the networks made this same error hours later in the morning of November 8, only this time it was a projection for Bush that was made and then retracted.

As the counts came in for more and more states, Florida's electoral votes took on an extreme significance. Neither Bush nor Gore had the majority needed to win the election, but Florida's votes would give either of them enough to win. Nervously, the nation waited to hear the outcome.

The morning after Election Day, newspapers couldn't run headlines declaring the winner because there still was no clear

Before the manual recounts were stopped, election workers from Miami-Dade County, Florida, and representatives of each party carefully reviewed and counted their county's ballots by hand.

winner. Bush had a slight majority of Florida's popular vote—only 1,784 out of more than 6 million votes cast—but it was so slight a majority that an automatic recount was required by Florida law. The recount again showed Bush in the lead, but this time by an even smaller amount, 930 votes including overseas ballots.

Over the next days, controversies surfaced in Florida over election issues. Some claimed that the ballot used in one county was so confusing that many people accidentally voted for the wrong candidate. And with Bush's lead cut nearly in half after the automatic recount, Gore asked for hand recounts of ballots in several counties hoping to pick up enough popular votes to win Florida's electoral votes.

Legal maneuverings began with Bush suing to stop the hand recounts. Lawsuits surfaced from many sources, some to get more time to finish hand recounts, some to stop the recount, some even asking for a new vote. The most heated court battles were over the hand recount, and appeals to rulings quickly advanced that matter all the way to the Supreme Court.

For the first time since 1876, it looked like a state legislature was going to select a state's electors. The Florida Legislature called a special session and announced that they would pick a slate of electors if the legal matters weren't settled in time to meet the constitutional deadline for selecting electors.

On December 12, the day the Florida Legislature was going to announce their electors, the Supreme Court ruled that the hand recounts should not continue. The following evening Gore conceded the election to Bush, stating he would stand behind Bush, and Bush became the nation's 43rd president.

On December 13, 2000, George W. Bush addressed the nation,
accepting the presidency and pledging to unify the country.

Treasured Words from the Presidents

John Adams   Adams was a scholarly political philosopher and activist who was one of the framers of the Declaration of Independence. He also wrote most of the Massachusetts state constitution. In 1821, Adams wrote to Thomas Jefferson:

> *I think a free government is necessarily a complicated piece of machinery, the nice and exact adjustment of whose springs wheels and weights are not yet well comprehended by the artists of the age and still less by the people.*

John Quincy Adams   John Quincy Adams often repeated his strong views concerning the role of government in supporting national growth and improvements. He echoed the sentiments of many before him in calling for the construction of, among other things, a national university. He delivered this classic statement in his first annual message to Congress on Dec. 6, 1825.

> *The great object of the institution of civil government is the improvement of the condition of those who are parties to the social compact, and no government, in whatever form constituted, can accomplish the lawful ends of its institution but in proportion as it improves the condition of those over whom it is established. . . . For the fulfillment of those duties governments are invested with power, and to the attainment of the end—the progressive improvement of the condition of the governed—the exercise of delegated powers is a duty as sacred and indispensable as the usurpation of powers not granted is criminal and odious.*

Chester Alan Arthur   The rights of native Americans are still at issue today, as they were a century ago. Chester Arthur, in his first annual message to Congress on Dec. 6, 1881, admitted:

> *We have to deal with the appalling fact that though thousands of lives have been sacrificed and hundreds of millions of dollars expended in the attempt to solve the Indian problem, it has until within the past few years seemed scarcely nearer a solution than it was half a century ago.*

The last months of Buchanan's term found the nation in the throes of secession. His feelings concerning the division of the Union are evident from these words in his message to Congress on Jan. 8, 1861.

James Buchanan

> *Time is a great conservative power. Let us pause at this momentous point and afford the people, both North and South, an opportunity for reflection. . . . I therefore appeal through you to the people of the country to declare in their might that the Union must and shall be preserved by all constitutional means. I most earnestly recommend that you devote yourselves exclusively to the question how this can be accomplished in peace. All other questions, when compared to this, sink into insignificance. . . . A delay in Congress to prescribe or to recommend a distinct and practical proposition for conciliation may drive us to a point from which it will be almost impossible to recede.*

In his inaugural address on Jan. 20, 1989, Bush called for "a new activism, hands-on and involved."

George H. W. Bush

> *I've spoken of a thousand points of light—of all the community organizations that are spread like stars throughout the nation doing good. We will work hand in hand, encouraging, sometimes leading, sometimes being led, rewarding. We will work on this in the White House, in the Cabinet agencies. I will go to the people and the programs that are the brighter points of light, and I'll ask every member of my Government to become involved. The old ideas are new again because they're not old, they are timeless: duty, sacrifice, commitment, and a patriotism that finds its expression in taking part and pitching in.*

When Bush was running for the Presidency, an office vacated by President Bill Clinton (who had been plagued by scandal), many Americans were concerned about what they saw as a decline in moral values, particularly among the country's leaders. Bush recognized their concern and addressed it at the Republican National Convention in Philadelphia in August 2000.

George W. Bush

> *. . . to lead this nation to a responsibility era, a president himself must be responsible. And so when I put my hand on the Bible, I will swear to not only uphold the laws of our land, I will swear to uphold the honor and dignity of the office to which I have been elected, so help me God. I believe the presidency—the final point of decision in the American government— was made for great purposes. It is the office of Lincoln's conscience and Teddy Roosevelt's energy and Harry Truman's integrity and Ronald Reagan's optimism. For me, gaining this office is not the ambition of a lifetime, but it IS the opportunity of a lifetime.*

James Earl Carter, Jr.   Jimmy Carter felt strongly about human rights. He explained his position with the following remarks made on Dec. 6, 1978, at a White House meeting commemorating the 30th anniversary of the signing of the Universal Declaration of Human Rights.

> . . . human rights are not peripheral to the foreign policy of the United States. Our human rights policy is not a decoration. It is not something we've adopted to polish up our image abroad or to put a fresh coat of moral paint on the discredited policies of the past. Our pursuit of human rights is part of a broad effort to use our great power and our tremendous influence in the service of creating a better world, a world in which human beings can live in peace, in freedom, and with their basic needs adequately met.
>
> Human rights is the soul of our foreign policy. And I say this with assurance, because human rights is the soul of our sense of nationhood.

Grover Cleveland   Cleveland's first inaugural address on March 4, 1885, called for close scrutiny of government officials.

> Your every voter, as surely as your Chief Magistrate, under the same high sanction, though in a different sphere, exercises a public trust. . . . Every citizen owes to the country a vigilant watch and close scrutiny of its public servants and a fair and reasonable estimate of their fidelity and usefulness. Thus is the people's will impressed upon the whole framework of our civil polity.

Bill Clinton   In his inaugural address on Jan. 20, 1993, Clinton urged every American to take responsibility for the renewal of America.

> I challenge a new generation of young Americans to a season of service; to act on your idealism by helping troubled children, keeping company with those in need, reconnecting our torn communities. There is so much to be done. Enough, indeed, for millions of others who are still young in spirit to give of themselves in service, too.

Calvin Coolidge   Coolidge's conservatism was reflected in the opening remarks of his inaugural address on March 4, 1925.

> If we wish to erect new structures, we must have a definite knowledge of the old foundations. We must realize that human nature is about the most constant thing in the universe and that the essentials of human relationship do not change. . . . If we examine carefully what we have done, we can determine the more accurately what we can do.

Dwight David Eisenhower   Eisenhower, the World War II military hero who spent his presidency fighting for peace, is perhaps best remembered for his warning in his farewell address on Jan. 17, 1961.

> In the councils of government, we must guard against the acquisition of unwarranted influence, whether sought or unsought, by the military-industrial complex. The potential for the disastrous rise of misplaced power exists and will persist. . . . We should take nothing for granted. Only an alert and knowledgeable citizenry can compel the proper meshing of the huge industrial and military machinery of defense with our peaceful methods and goals, so that security and liberty may prosper together.

Fillmore made this unpretentious reply to biographer L. J. Cist in a letter dated Jan. 4, 1855.

Millard Fillmore

In compliance with your request I have frankly stated these facts connected with my early history, and as no man is responsible for the circumstances of his birth, they furnish nothing of which he should be ashamed or proud, and therefore while they require no apology they can justify no boasting.

In an attempt to restore the confidence of Americans following the crushing blows of Watergate, Ford spoke these words after taking the oath of office on Aug. 9, 1974.

Gerald Rudolph Ford

. . . our long national nightmare is over.
Our Constitution works; our great Republic is a government of laws and not of men. Here the people rule. . . .
As we bind up the internal wounds of Watergate, more painful and more poisonous than those of foreign wars, let us restore the golden rule to our political process, and let brotherly love purge our hearts of suspicion and hate.

In a speech in New York City on Aug. 6, 1880, Garfield spoke on behalf of blacks who fought for the Union in the Civil War.

James Abram Garfield

We have seen white men betray the flag and fight to kill the Union, but in all that long, dreary war we never saw a traitor in a black skin. . . . and now that we have made them free, so long as we live we will stand by these black citizens. We will stand by them until the sun of liberty, fixed in the firmament of our Constitution, shall shine with equal rays upon every man, black or white, throughout the Union.

Grant, in his second annual message to Congress on Dec. 5, 1870, urged Congress to remedy what he felt was a long-standing problem.

Ulysses Simpson Grant

It is a reform in the civil service of the country. . . . I would have it govern, not the tenure, but the manner of making all appointments. There is no duty which so much embarrasses the Executive and heads of departments as that of appointments, nor is there any such arduous and thankless labor imposed on senators and representatives as that of finding places for constituents. The present system does not secure the best men, and often not even fit men, for public place. The elevation and purification of the civil service of the government will be hailed with approval by the whole people of the United States.

Harding, the first businessperson in the presidency, called Congress into extraordinary session on April 12, 1921, to consider "national problems far too pressing to be long neglected." He urged the enactment of an emergency tariff:

Warren Gamaliel Harding

I believe in the protection of American industry, and it is our purpose to prosper America first.

In the same message, Harding rejected American membership in the League of Nations.

In the existing League of Nations, world-governing with its superpowers, this republic will have no part. There can be no misinterpretation, and there will be no betrayal of the deliberate expression of the American people in the recent election. . . . we can recognize no super-authority.

Benjamin Harrison   Harrison's inaugural address on March 4, 1889, contains at least one hint of the notion of corporate responsibility, which gained currency in the 1990's.

> *If our great corporations would more scrupulously observe their legal limitations and duties, they would have less cause to complain of the unlawful limitations of their rights or of violent interference with their operations.*

William Henry Harrison   Here is an excerpt from Harrison's inaugural address, the longest on record, delivered on March 4, 1841.

> *The spirit of liberty is the sovereign balm for every injury which our institutions may receive. On the contrary, no care that can be used in the construction of our government, no division of its powers, no distribution of checks in its several departments, will prove effectual to keep us a free people if this spirit is suffered to decay; and decay it will without constant nurture.*

Rutherford Birchard Hayes   In calling for civil service reform, Hayes threw a punch at the patronage system. These words are from his letter of acceptance of the Republican nomination in Columbus, Ohio, on July 8, 1876.

> *This [patronage] system destroys the independence of the separate departments of the government; it tends directly to extravagance and official incapacity; it is a temptation to dishonesty; it hinders and impairs that careful supervision and strict accountability by which alone faithful and efficient public service can be secured; it obstructs the prompt removal and sure punishment of the unworthy. In every way it degrades the civil service and the character of the government.*

Herbert Clark Hoover   Hoover's inaugural address on March 4, 1929, reflected the optimism that preceded the Great Depression.

> *The questions before our country are problems of progress to higher standards; they are not the problems of degeneration. . . . Ours is a land rich in resources; stimulating in its glorious beauty; filled with millions of happy homes. . . . In no nation are the fruits of accomplishment more secure. . . . I have no fears for the future of our country. It is bright with hope.*

Andrew Jackson   Jackson issued the Proclamation to the People of South Carolina [Against Nullification] on Dec. 10, 1832, after South Carolina attempted to nullify a disagreeable tariff measure.

> *We have hitherto relied on [the Constitution] as the perpetual bond of our Union; we have received it as the work of the assembled wisdom of the nation; we have trusted to it as to the sheet anchor of our safety in the stormy times of conflict with a foreign or domestic foe. . . . Were we mistaken, my countrymen, in attaching this importance to the Constitution of our country? . . . Did we pledge ourselves to the support of an airy nothing—a bubble that must be blown away by the first breath of disaffection? . . . No; we did not err. Our Constitution does not contain the absurdity of giving power to make laws and another to resist them.*

Jefferson wrote his own epitaph. It says nothing about the presidency, but simply reads as follows:

Thomas Jefferson

> *There was buried Thomas Jefferson, author of the Declaration of American Independence, of the statute of Virginia for religious freedom, and father of the University of Virginia.*

This excerpt is from the Virginia Statute for Religious Freedom, Jan. 16, 1786.

> *Whereas Almighty God hath created the mind free; that all attempts to influence it by temporal punishments or burdens. . . . tend only to beget habits of hypocrisy and meanness, . . . that the impious presumption of legislators and rulers, civil as well as ecclesiastical, . . . setting up their own opinions and modes of thinking as the only true and infallible, and as such endeavoring to impose them on others, hath established and maintained false religions over the greatest part of the world, and through all time; . . . that our civil rights have no dependence on our religious opinions, any more than our opinions in physics or geometry; . . . Be it enacted by the general assembly, that no man shall be compelled to frequent or support any religious worship, place or ministry whatsoever . . . but that all men shall be free to profess, and by argument to maintain, their opinion in matters of religion.*

In a speech to the First Colored Regiment of the District of Columbia on Oct. 10, 1865, Andrew Johnson insisted:

Andrew Johnson

> *Henceforth each and all of you must be measured according to your merit. If one man is more meritorious than the other, they cannot be equals; and he is the most exalted that is the most meritorious, without regard to color. And the idea of having a law passed in the morning that would make a white man a black man before night, and a black man a white man before day, is absurd. That is not the standard. It is your own conduct; it is your own merit; it is the development of your own talents and of your own intellectuality and moral qualities.*

In his first State of the Union message to Congress on Jan. 8, 1964, Johnson issued a call to action:

Lyndon Baines Johnson

> *Let this session of Congress be known as the session which did more for civil rights than the last hundred sessions combined . . . which enacted the most far-reaching tax cut . . . which declared all-out war on human poverty and unemployment . . . which finally recognized the health needs of all our older citizens . . . and as the session which helped to build more homes, more schools, more libraries, and more hospitals than any single session of Congress in the history of our Republic.*

John Fitzgerald Kennedy   Kennedy is perhaps best known for his eloquent inaugural address on Jan. 20, 1961.

Let the word go forth from this time and place, to friend and foe alike, that the torch has been passed to a new generation of Americans . . . unwilling to witness or permit the slow undoing of those human rights to which this nation has always been committed. . . .

Let every nation know, whether it wishes us well or ill, that we shall pay any price, bear any burden, meet any hardship, support any friend, oppose any foe to assure the survival and success of liberty. . . .

And so, my fellow Americans: ask not what your country can do for you—ask what you can do for your country.

My fellow citizens of the world: ask not what America will do for you, but what together we can do for the freedom of man.

Abraham Lincoln   This extract is from Lincoln's famous Gettysburg Address, delivered on Nov. 19, 1863.

Fourscore and seven years ago our fathers brought forth on this continent a new nation, conceived in liberty, and dedicated to the proposition that all men are created equal.

Now we are engaged in a great civil war, testing whether that nation, or any nation so conceived and so dedicated, can long endure. . . . from these honored dead we take increased devotion to that cause for which they gave the last full measure of devotion; that we here highly resolve that these dead shall not have died in vain; that this nation, under God, shall have a new birth of freedom; and that government of the people, by the people, for the people, shall not perish from the earth.

James Madison   The War of 1812 was often called "Mr. Madison's War." In his second inaugural address on March 4, 1813, James Madison spoke these words in defense of the war.

As the war was just in its origin and necessary and noble in its objects, we can reflect with a proud satisfaction that in carrying it on no principle of justice or honor, no usage of civilized nations, no precept of courtesy or humanity, have been infringed. The war has been waged on our part with scrupulous regard to all these obligations, and in a spirit of liberality which was never surpassed.

William McKinley   McKinley was staunch when tariffs were at issue. In a speech in Boston on Feb. 9, 1888, he insisted:

Every yard of cloth imported here makes a demand for one yard less of American fabrication. Let England take care of herself, let France look after her own interests, let Germany take care of her own people but in God's name let Americans look after America!

The Monroe Doctrine has been a cherished national principle since James Monroe announced it in his seventh annual address to Congress on Dec. 2, 1823. Here is an extract:

James Monroe

> . . . the occasion has been judged proper for asserting, as a principle in which the rights and interests of the United States are involved, that the American continents, by the free and independent condition which they have assumed and maintain, are henceforth not to be considered as subjects for future colonization by any European powers. . . . We . . . declare that we should consider any attempt on their part to extend their system to any portion of this hemisphere as dangerous to our peace and safety.

Nixon attempted to restore a positive attitude in the United States in his first inaugural address on Jan. 20, 1969.

Richard Milhous Nixon

> Our greatest need now is to reach beyond government, to enlist the legions of the concerned and the committed.
> What has to be done, has to be done by government and people together or it will not be done at all. The lesson of past agony is that without the people we can do nothing—with the people we can do everything.

In his inaugural address on March 4, 1853, Pierce referred to the Compromise of 1850, which carved the map of America into slave and free states.

Franklin Pierce

> I believe that involuntary servitude, as it exists in different states of this Confederacy, is recognized by the Constitution. I believe that it stands like any other admitted right, and that the states where it exists are entitled to efficient remedies to enforce the Constitutional provisions.

Polk was one of many Presidents who found the office a heavier burden than he had anticipated. On Feb. 13, 1849, he made this note in his diary:

James Knox Polk

> I am heartily rejoiced that my term is so near its close. I will soon cease to be a servant and become a sovereign. As a private citizen I will have no one but myself to serve, and will exercise a part of the sovereign power of the country. I am sure I will be happier in this condition than in the exalted station I now hold.

This excerpt is from Reagan's State of the Union Address of January 26, 1987. It was delivered before the 100th Congress of the United States of America in the 200th anniversary year of the Constitution.

Ronald Wilson Reagan

> I've read the constitutions of a number of countries, including the Soviet Union's. Now, some people are surprised to hear that they have a constitution, and it even supposedly grants a number of freedoms to its people. . . . Well, if this is true, why is the Constitution of the United States so exceptional?
> Well, the difference is so small that it almost escapes you, but it's so great it tells you the whole story in just three words: We the people. In those other constitutions, the Government tells the people of those countries what they're allowed to do. In our Constitution, we the people tell the Government what it can do, and it can do only those things listed in the document and no others.

Franklin Delano Roosevelt

F.D.R.'s first inaugural address on March 4, 1933, is among his most famous speeches.

> *. . . the only thing we have to fear is fear itself—nameless, unreasoning, unjustified terror which paralyzes needed efforts to convert retreat into advance. In every dark hour of our national life a leadership of frankness and vigor has met with that understanding and support of the people themselves which is essential to victory. I am convinced that you will again give that support to leadership in these critical days.*

F.D.R. outlined his hopes for a "world founded on four essential human freedoms" in a message to Congress on Jan. 6, 1941. The first was freedom of speech; the second, freedom of religion.

> *The third is freedom from want—which, translated into world terms, means economic understandings which will secure to every nation a healthy peace-time life for its inhabitants—everywhere in the world. The fourth is freedom from fear—which . . . means a worldwide reduction of armaments to such a point and in such a thorough fashion that no nation will be in a position to commit an act of physical aggression against any neighbor—anywhere in the world. That is no vision of a distant millennium. It is a definite basis for a kind of world attainable in our own time and generation.*

Theodore Roosevelt

Roosevelt was known to oppose the misuse of economic power. In his second annual message to Congress on Dec. 2, 1902, he clarified his position.

> *Our aim is not to do away with corporations; on the contrary, these big aggregations are an inevitable development of modern industrialism, and the effort to destroy them would be futile unless accomplished in ways that would work the utmost mischief to the entire body politic. . . . We draw the line against misconduct, not against wealth.*

William Howard Taft

Taft discussed his Dollar Diplomacy on Dec. 3, 1912.

> *The diplomacy of the present administration has sought to respond to modern ideas of commercial intercourse. This policy has been characterized as substituting dollars for bullets. It is one that appeals alike to idealistic humanitarian sentiments, to the dictates of sound policy and strategy, and to legitimate commercial aims. . . . Because modern diplomacy is commercial, there has been a disposition in some quarters to attribute to it none but materialistic aims. How strikingly erroneous is such an impression.*

Zachary Taylor

Zachary Taylor had high standards for presidential appointments. From Taylor's inaugural address on March 5, 1849:

> *The appointing power vested in the President imposes delicate and onerous duties. So far as it is possible to be informed, I shall make honesty, capacity, and fidelity indispensable prerequisites to the bestowal of office, and the absence of either [sic] of these qualities shall be deemed sufficient cause for removal.*

Truman announced the Atomic Age on Aug. 6, 1945.   **Harry S. Truman**

Sixteen hours ago an American airplane dropped one bomb on Hiroshima, an important Japanese Army base. That bomb had more power than 20,000 tons of TNT. . . . It is an atomic bomb. It is a harnessing of the basic power of the universe. The force from which the sun draws its power has been loosed against those who brought war to the Far East. . . . The fact that we can release atomic energy ushers in a new era in man's understanding of nature's forces.

Tyler's message to Congress on Dec. 7, 1841, contained these   **John Tyler**
thoughts on the nation's hard-pressed economy:

Nothing can be more ill judged than to look to facilities in borrowing or to a redundant circulation, for the power of discharging pecuniary obligations. The country is full of resources and the people full of energy, and the great and permanent remedy for present embarrassments must be sought in industry, economy, the observance of good faith, and the favorable influence of time.

Van Buren made the following observation in a message to Congress   **Martin Van Buren**
on Sept. 4, 1837.

All communities are apt to look to government for too much. . . . But this ought not to be. The framers of our excellent Constitution . . . wisely judged that the less government interferes with private pursuits the better for the general prosperity. It is not its legitimate object to make men rich. . . . But its real duty . . . is to enact and enforce a system of general laws commensurate with, but not exceeding, the objects of its establishment, and to leave every citizen and every interest to reap under its benign protection the rewards of virtue, industry, and prudence.

This admonition is from Washington's farewell address in Philadel-   **George Washington**
phia on Sept. 17, 1796.

Observe good faith and justice toward all nations. Cultivate peace and harmony with all. . . . It will be worthy of a free, enlightened, and at no distant period a great nation to give to mankind the magnanimous and too novel example of a people always guided by an exalted justice and benevolence. . . . Can it be that Providence has not connected the permanent felicity of a nation with its virtue? The experiment, at least, is recommended by every sentiment which ennobles human nature.

On April 2, 1917, Woodrow Wilson announced, "We have seen the   **Woodrow Wilson**
last of neutrality. . . . " His war message is perhaps his most
famous address.

. . . right is more precious than peace, and we shall fight for the things which we have always carried nearest our hearts,—for democracy, for the right of those who submit to authority to have a voice in their own governments. . . . To such a task we can dedicate our lives and our fortunes, everything that we are and everything that we have, with the pride of those who know that the day has come when America is privileged to spend her blood and her might for the principles that gave her birth and happiness and the peace which she has treasured. God helping her, she can do no other.

Appendixes

Facts About the President

Election, Term, and Retirement

Qualifications The U.S. Constitution provides that a candidate for the presidency must be a "natural-born" U.S. citizen. The candidate must also be at least 35 years old and must have lived in the United States for at least 14 years. No law or court decision has yet defined the exact meaning of natural-born. Authorities assume the term applies to citizens born in the United States and its territories. But they are not sure if it also includes children born to U.S. citizens elsewhere.

How nominated National political party convention.

How elected By a majority vote of the Electoral College, held in December following the general election held on the first Tuesday after the first Monday in November of every fourth year.

Inauguration Held at noon on January 20 after election. If January 20 is a Sunday, the ceremony may be held privately that day and publicly on January 21.

Term The President is elected to a four-year term. A President may not be elected more than twice.

Income $400,000 a year salary, a $50,000 annual allowance for expenses, and up to $100,000 for travel expenses and $12,000 for official entertainment for allocation within the Executive Office of the President. After leaving office, the President is eligible for a yearly pension, clerical assistants, office space, and free mailing privileges. Widowed spouses of former Presidents get a yearly pension.

Removal from office Impeachment by a majority vote of the House of Representatives and trial and conviction by a two-thirds vote of those present in the Senate.

Powers

As chief executive Enforces acts of Congress, judgments of federal courts, and treaties. Grants reprieves and pardons for offenses against the United States (except in cases of impeachment). May use emergency powers (for example, in a labor-management crisis). Nominates members of the Cabinet, justices of the Supreme Court, ambassadors, and other high officials. Shapes policy, delegates functions and authority, coordinates and reorganizes agencies, issues executive orders.

As foreign policy director Makes treaties and appoints ambassadors and ministers, subject to approval of Senate. Makes executive agreements with other nations.

As commander in chief Decides disputes among branches of the armed forces. May send the armed forces into situations that are equal to war. (Only Congress has the power to declare war.) Controls the nation's nuclear weapons.

As legislative leader Recommends laws to Congress. Can veto bills.

Modes of Selection

Electoral Votes

The chief road to the White House is the presidential election, which is held every four years.

Political parties nominate their candidates for President and Vice-President at national conventions.

The nation's voters select a President and Vice-President by casting ballots for presidential electors.

The Electoral College, made up of electors chosen by all the states and the District of Columbia, elects the President and Vice-President.

Selection by Congress

If the Electoral College fails to give any candidate a majority, these steps can follow:

The House of Representatives chooses the President from among the top three candidates. Each state's House delegation has only one vote, and the winner must receive a majority of the votes that are cast.

If the House fails to choose a President, the Vice-President, chosen by the Electoral College or the Senate, becomes President.

If both houses fail to choose a President or Vice-President, Congress shall by law deal with the situation. Congress would probably make the terms of the Presidential Succession Act applicable in this case. The Speaker of the House would then become President.

Presidential Succession

If the President dies, resigns, or is removed from office, the Vice-President becomes President. If the President becomes unable to perform the duties of office, the Vice-President serves as acting President during the President's disability.

The Vice-President, upon succeeding to the presidency, may then nominate a new Vice-President who takes office after being approved by Congress.

Next in line to the presidency after the Vice-President are the following government officials:

1. Speaker of the House
2. President *Pro Tempore* of the Senate
3. Secretary of State
4. Secretary of the Treasury
5. Secretary of Defense
6. Attorney General
7. Secretary of the Interior
8. Secretary of Agriculture
9. Secretary of Commerce
10. Secretary of Labor
11. Secretary of Health and Human Services
12. Secretary of Housing and Urban Development
13. Secretary of Transportation
14. Secretary of Energy
15. Secretary of Education
16. Secretary of Veterans Affairs

Presidential Oath of Office

I do solemnly swear (or affirm) that I will faithfully execute the Office of President of the United States, and will to the best of my Ability, preserve, protect and defend the Constitution of the United States.

Constitution of the United States, Article II

The Executive Branch

Section 1   (1) The executive power shall be vested in a President of the United States of America. He shall hold the office during the term of four years, and, together with the Vice-President, chosen for the same term, be elected, as follows:

(2) Each state shall appoint, in such manner as the legislature thereof may direct, a number of electors, equal to the whole number of senators and representatives to which the state may be entitled in the Congress: but no senator or representative, or person holding an office of trust or profit under the United States, shall be appointed an elector.

> This section established the Electoral College, a group of people chosen by the voters of each state to elect the President and Vice-President. See "Facts about the President" in this appendix for more information about the Electoral College.

(3) The electors shall meet in their respective states, and vote by ballot for two persons, of whom one at least shall not be an inhabitant of the same state with themselves. And they shall make a list of all the persons voted for, and of the number of votes for each; which list they shall sign and certify, and transmit sealed to the seat of the government of the United States, directed to the president of the Senate. The president of the Senate shall, in the presence of the Senate and House of Representatives, open all the certificates, and the votes shall then be counted. The person having the greatest number of votes shall be the President, if such number be a majority of the whole number of electors appointed; and if there be more than one who have such majority, and have an equal number of votes, then the House of Representatives shall immediately choose by ballot one of them for President; and if no person have a majority, then from the five highest on the list the said House shall in like manner choose the President. But in choosing the President, the votes shall be taken by states, the representation from each state having one vote; a quorum for this purpose shall consist of a member or members from two-thirds of the

states, and a majority of all the states shall be necessary to a choice. In every case, after the choice of the President, the person having the greatest number of votes of the electors shall be the Vice-President. But if there should remain two or more who have equal votes, the Senate shall choose from them by ballot the Vice-President.

> The 12th Amendment changed this procedure for electing the President and Vice-President. See "Facts About the President" in this appendix for more information about presidential election.

(4) The Congress may determine the time of choosing the electors, and the day on which they shall give their votes; which day shall be the same throughout the United States.

(5) No person except a natural-born citizen, or a citizen of the United States at the time of the adoption of this Constitution, shall be eligible to the office of President; neither shall any person be eligible to that office who shall not have attained to the age of thirty-five years, and been fourteen years a resident within the United States.

(6) In case of the removal of the President from office, or of his death, resignation, or inability to discharge the powers and duties of the said office, the same shall devolve on the Vice-President, and the Congress may by law provide for the case of removal, death, resignation or inability, both of the President and Vice-President, declaring what officer shall then act as President, and such office shall act accordingly, until the disability be removed, or a President shall be elected.

> On Aug. 9, 1974, President Richard M. Nixon resigned as Chief Executive and was succeeded by Vice-President Gerald R. Ford. Until then, only death had ever cut short the term of a President of the United States. See "Facts About the President" in this appendix for more information about presidential succession.

(7) The President shall, at stated times, receive for his services, a compensation, which shall neither

be increased nor diminished during the period for which he shall have been elected, and he shall not receive within that period any other emolument from the United States, or any of them.

> The Constitution provides a salary for the President that cannot be raised or lowered during the term of office. The chief executive may not receive any other pay from the federal government or the states.

(8) Before he enters on the execution of his office, he shall take the following oath or affirmation: "I do solemnly swear (or affirm) that I will faithfully execute the Office of President of the United States, and will to the best of my Ability, preserve, protect and defend the Constitution of the United States."

> The Constitution does not say who shall administer the oath to the newly elected President. George Washington was sworn in by Robert R. Livingston, then a state official in New York. After that, it became customary for the Chief Justice of the United States to administer the oath.

Section (2) (1) The President shall be commander in chief of the Army and Navy of the United States and of the militia of the several states, when called into the actual service of the United States; he may require the opinion, in writing, of the principal officer in each of the executive departments, upon any subject relating to the duties of their respective offices, and he shall have power to grant reprieves and pardons for offenses against the United States, except in cases of impeachment.

> The President's powers as commander in chief are far-reaching. But even in wartime, the President must obey the law of the land.

(2) He shall have power, by and with the advice and consent of the Senate, to make treaties, provided two-thirds of the senators present concur; and he shall nominate, and by and with the advice and consent of the Senate, shall appoint ambassadors, other public ministers and consuls, judges of the Supreme Court, and all other officers of the United States, whose appointments are not herein otherwise provided for, and which shall be established by law; but the Congress may be law vest the appointment of such inferior officers, as they think proper, in the President alone, in the courts of law, or in the heads of departments.

> The framers of the Constitution intended that in some matters the Senate should

serve as an advisory body for the President. The President has the power to make treaties and to appoint various government officials, but two-thirds of the senators must approve before a treaty or appointment is confirmed.

(3) The President shall have power to fill up all vacancies that may happen during the recess of the Senate, by granting commissions which shall expire at the end of their next session.

> This means that when the Senate is not in session, the President can make temporary appointments to offices which require Senate confirmation.

Section 3 He shall from time to time give the Congress information of the state of the Union, and recommend to their consideration such measures as he shall judge necessary and expedient; he may, on extraordinary occasions, convene both houses, or either of them, and in case of disagreement between them, with respect to the time of adjournment, he may adjourn them to such time as he shall think proper; he shall receive ambassadors and other public ministers; he shall take care that the laws be faithfully executed, and shall commission all the officers of the United States.

> The President gives his State of the Union message to Congress each year. Presidents George Washington and John Adams delivered their messages in person. For more than 100 years after that, most Presidents sent a written message, which was read in Congress. President Woodrow Wilson delivered his messages in person, as did President Franklin D. Roosevelt and all Presidents after Roosevelt. Famous messages to Congress include the Monroe Doctrine and Wilson's "Fourteen Points."
>
> During the 1800's, Presidents often used their power to call Congress into session. Today, Congress is in session most of the time. The President has never had to adjourn Congress.
>
> The responsibility to "take care that the laws be faithfully executed" puts the President at the head of law enforcement for the national government. Every federal official, civilian or military, gets authority from the President.

Section 4 The President, Vice-President and all civil officers of the United States, shall be removed from office on impeachment for, and conviction of, treason, bribery, or other high crimes and misdemeanors.

Vice-Presidents of the United States

Adams, John (1735-1826)

Served as Vice-President under George Washington from 1789 to 1797. Served as President from 1797 to 1801. See biography in this volume.

Agnew, Spiro Theodore (1918-1996)

Served as Vice-President under Richard M. Nixon from 1969 to 1973. Agnew became the only Vice-President of the United States to resign his office while under criminal investigation. He resigned in 1973 after a federal grand jury began hearing charges that he had participated in widespread graft as an officeholder in Maryland.

Agnew became the second Vice-President to resign. In 1832, Vice-President John C. Calhoun gave up his office after being chosen to fill a U.S. Senate seat from South Carolina.

Arthur, Chester A. (1829-1886)

Served as Vice-President under James A. Garfield in 1881. Served as President from 1881 to 1885. See biography in this volume.

Barkley, Alben William (1877-1956)

Served as Vice-President under Harry S. Truman from 1949 to 1953. As Vice-President, Barkley showed great skill in presiding over the U.S. Senate. He enjoyed the personal confidence of Truman and was known throughout the nation as *The Veep*. Barkley was the first Vice-President to sit on the National Security Council and to assist officially in formulating important policy for the President's consideration.

Barkley began his national political service in 1913 when he was elected as a Democrat from Kentucky to the U.S. House of Representatives. From 1927 to 1949, he served in the Senate. After his vice-presidency, he was again elected senator from Kentucky in 1954.

Breckinridge, John Cabell (1821-1875)

Served as Vice-President under James Buchanan from 1857 to 1861. In 1869, the Southern Democrats nominated him for President. Breckinridge received 72 electoral votes, but was defeated.

Breckinridge entered the Confederate Army in 1861. He fought in the battles of Shiloh, Murfreesboro (Stone River), and Chickamauga. He defeated Union forces at New Market, Va., on May 15, 1864. He became a major general and was Confederate secretary of war from February 1865 until the war ended.

Burr, Aaron (1756-1836)

Served as Vice-President under Thomas Jefferson from 1801 to 1805. Burr ran with Jefferson for the presidency of the United States both in 1796 and 1800. In 1800, he tied with Jefferson and the U.S. House of Representatives had to take 36 ballots to choose Jefferson over Burr.

His brilliant career and promising future ended disastrously when he killed Alexander Hamilton in a gun duel in 1804. Afterward, he became one of the most controversial figures in U.S. history.

Bush, George Herbert Walker (1924-)

Served as Vice-President under Ronald Reagan from 1981 to 1989. He served as President from 1989 to 1993. See biography in this volume.

Calhoun, John Caldwell (1782-1850)

Served as Vice-President under John Quincy Adams and Andrew Jackson from 1821 to 1832. Only one other Vice-President, George Clinton, served as Vice-President under two Presidents.

Calhoun played an important part in national affairs for 40 years. He served as a member of the U.S. House of Representatives and the Senate, and he also served as secretary of war and secretary of state. But Calhoun never became President, and this was a bitter disappointment to him during his later years. He is best remembered as the theorist of the doctrines of states' rights and nullification. His leadership in these doctrines helped inspire the South's effort to achieve national independence in the Civil War.

Cheney, Richard Bruce (1941-)

Served as Vice-President under George W. Bush starting in 2001. They defeated Vice-President Al Gore and Senator Joseph I. Lieberman to take office.

Cheney won election to the U.S. House of Representatives as a Republican from Wyoming in 1978 and was reelected five times. He served as U.S. secretary of defense under George H. W. Bush from 1989 to 1993. As secretary of defense, Cheney advised the president on military strategy against Iraq during the Persian Gulf War (1991).

Clinton, George (1739-1812)

Served as Vice-President under Thomas Jefferson and James Madison from 1805 until his death. Only one other Vice-President, John C. Calhoun, served as Vice-President under two Presidents.

Clinton also was the first governor of New York. He was elected in 1777 after New York's constitutional convention, and served seven terms, a record that still stands. Clinton strongly believed in states' rights, and at first opposed New York's ratification of the Constitution.

Colfax, Schuyler (1823-1885)

Served as Vice-President under Ulysses S. Grant from 1869 to 1873. He also was an active leader of the Whig and Republican parties and a prominent member of Congress.

Colfax was elected to the U.S. House of Representatives in 1855 and remained there for 14 years. He joined the new Republican Party and became Speaker of the House in 1863. Colfax held the post until he was inaugurated Vice-President.

Coolidge, Calvin (1872-1933)

Served as Vice-President under Warren G. Harding from 1921 to 1923. Served as President from 1923 to 1929. See biography in this volume.

Curtis, Charles (1860-1936)

Served as Vice-President under Herbert Hoover from 1929 to 1933. He had served in the U.S. House of Representatives from 1893 to 1907, and in the U.S. Senate from 1907 to 1913 and 1915 to 1929.

Curtis was an experienced parliamentarian as a member of the Senate Rules Committee. He became majority leader of the Senate during the administration of President Calvin Coolidge.

Dallas, George Mifflin (1792-1864)

Served as Vice-President under James K. Polk from 1845 to 1849. He was a loyal supporter of Polk's policies. His tie-breaking vote in favor of a low tariff bill Polk favored in 1846 destroyed him politically in Pennsylvania, his home state.

He served as a Democratic U.S. senator from Pennsylvania from 1831 to 1833, as minister to Russia from 1837 to 1839, and as a minister to England from 1856 to 1861. While in England, he helped settle disputes over the Clayton-Bulwer Treaty.

Dawes, Charles Gates (1865-1951)

Served as Vice-President under Calvin Coolidge from 1925 to 1929. He shared the 1925 Nobel Peace Prize for arranging a plan for German reparations after World War I. Dawes entered national politics when he handled Republican Party finances in the 1896 campaign.

He served on the Allied General Purchasing Board during World War I and became the first director of the federal budget in 1921. He served as ambassador to Great Britain from 1929 to 1932 and as the first chair of the Reconstruction Finance Corporation in 1932.

Fairbanks, Charles Warren (1852-1918)

Served as Vice-President under Theodore Roosevelt from 1905 to 1909. He hoped to be the Republican presidential candidate in 1908. But he did not get along well with Roosevelt, and the President helped William Howard Taft win the nomination.

Fairbanks again was Republican vice-presidential candidate in 1916. But he and presidential candidate Charles Evans Hughes lost the election to Woodrow Wilson and Thomas R. Marshall.

Fillmore, Millard (1800-1874)

Served as Vice-President under Zachary Taylor from 1849 to 1850. Served as President from 1850 to 1853. See biography in this volume.

Ford, Gerald R. (1913-   )

Served as Vice-President under Richard Nixon from 1973 to 1974. Served as President from 1974 to 1977. See biography in this volume.

Garner, John Nance (1868-1967)

Served as Vice-President under Franklin D. Roosevelt from 1933 to 1941. Garner helped put through the early New Deal program, but later broke with Roosevelt and opposed the President. He actively opposed a third term for Roosevelt and ran against him unsuccessfully at the Democratic National Convention in 1940.

Garner served in the U.S. House of Representatives as a Democrat from Texas from 1903 to 1933. He was elected Speaker of the House in 1931.

Gerry, Elbridge (1744-1814)

Served as Vice-President under James Madison in 1813 and 1814. He also was a signer of the Declaration of Independence, a member of the Continental Congress, and a delegate to the Federal Convention of 1787. He represented Massachusetts in the House of Representatives for four years. In 1797, he went to France to establish diplomatic relations with that country. Gerry served as governor of Massachusetts from 1810 to 1812.

Gore, Al (1948-   )

Served as Vice-President under Bill Clinton from 1993 to 2001. They defeated incumbent President George H. W. Bush and Vice-President Dan Quayle in 1992 and were reelected in 1996. Gore was elected to the U.S. House of Representatives in 1976 and was reelected in 1978, 1980, and 1982. He won election to the U.S. Senate in 1984 and was reelected in 1990.

Gore played a leading role in foreign affairs, trade policy, protection of the environment, and communications technology and policy. Gore unsuccessfully tried to succeed Clinton as president; George W. Bush, governor of Texas and son of former President George H. W. Bush, defeated him.

Hamlin, Hannibal (1809-1891)

Served as Vice-President under Abraham Lincoln from 1861 to 1865. He also served as governor of Maine in 1857 and in the U.S. House of Representatives and the U.S. Senate.

Hamlin strongly opposed slavery. He left the Democratic Party in 1856 and helped organize the Republican Party as an antislavery group. He was not considered for a second vice-presidential term. Instead, Andrew Johnson, a War Democrat of the Union Party, was chosen for the 1864 Republican ticket. It was a fateful choice, because Andrew Johnson became President shortly after Lincoln's second term began.

Hendricks, Thomas Andrews (1819-1885)

Served as Vice-President under Grover Cleveland for eight months in 1885. He had sought the Democratic presidential nomination in 1868, 1876, 1880, and 1884. Although he was not a nominee in 1872, he received 42 of the 66 Democratic electoral votes won in the election. This happened because Horace Greeley, the Democratic presidential nominee, died before the Electoral College met.

Hendricks was the unsuccessful Democratic nominee for Vice-President in 1876 before winning with Cleveland in 1884.

Hobart, Garret Augustus (1844-1899)

Served as Vice-President under William McKinley from 1897 until he died. He was a close friend of McKinley and was often called "The Assistant President." He influenced the U.S. Senate to promote administration policy.

Hobart's death made it necessary for the Republicans to find another running mate for McKinley in 1900. Their choice of Theodore Roosevelt was fateful, because McKinley was assassinated in 1901 and Roosevelt became President.

Humphrey, Hubert Horatio (1911-1978)

Served as Vice-President of the United States under Lyndon B. Johnson from 1965 to 1969. He was the Democratic presidential nominee in 1968. Humphrey lost to former Vice-President Richard M. Nixon.

Before his election as Vice-President in 1964, Humphrey has been elected to the U.S. Senate three times. He was the first Democrat ever elected to the Senate from Minnesota. In 1970, he was again elected to the Senate, and he was re-elected in 1976. In 1977, the Senate made Humphrey the deputy president pro tempore of the Senate, and he was re-elected in 1976. In 1977, the Senate made Humphrey the deputy president pro tempore of the Senate, a new post created to honor him. The title will be given to all former Presidents and Vice-Presidents who later serve in the Senate.

Jefferson, Thomas (1743-1826)

Served as Vice-President under John Adams from 1797 to 1801. Served as president from 1801 to 1809. See biography in this volume.

Johnson, Andrew (1808-1875)

Served as Vice-President under Abraham Lincoln in 1865. Served as President from 1865 to 1869. See biography in this volume.

Johnson, Lyndon B. (1908-1973)

Served as Vice-President under John F. Kennedy from 1961 to 1963. Served as President from 1963 to 1969. See biography in this volume.

Johnson, Richard Mentor (1780-1850)

Served as Vice-President under Martin Van Buren from 1837 to 1841. He was the only Vice-President ever elected by the Senate. In the election of 1836, no vice-presidential candidate received the majority of electoral votes required by the 12th Amendment. The Senate then chose Johnson, a Democrat, on one ballot.

Congress presented him with a sword for his bravery during the War of 1812. Johnson served in the U.S. House of Representatives at various times, and in the Senate from 1819 to 1829.

King, William Rufus Devane (1786-1853)

Served as Vice-President under Franklin Pierce for six weeks in 1853. King was seriously ill at the time, and by special act of Congress he was permitted to take his oath of inauguration before an American consul in Havana, Cuba, where he was convalescing. He died six weeks later, without ever performing the duties of Vice-President.

King served in the U.S. House of Representatives from 1811 to 1816 as a Democrat from North Carolina, and in the U.S. Senate as a Democrat from Alabama from 1819 to 1844 and from 1848 to 1852.

Marshall, Thomas Riley (1854-1925)

Served as Vice-President under Woodrow Wilson from 1913 to 1921. He made the famous remark: "What this country needs is a good five-cent cigar."

He was the first Vice-President in nearly 100 years to serve two terms with the same President. Marshall refused to listen to those who urged him to declare himself President after President Wilson became seriously ill in 1919.

Mondale, Walter Frederick (1928-   )

Served as Vice-President under Jimmy Carter from 1977 to 1981. Ran for President in the 1984 election, but lost to incumbent Ronald Reagan. Before Mondale's election as Vice-President, he was a U.S. senator from Minnesota. He had a reputation as a liberal who supported government action in many fields.

Morton, Levi Parsons (1824-1920)

Served as Vice-President under Benjamin Harrison from 1889 to 1893. He also was minister to France from 1881 and 1885 and governor of New York in 1895 and 1896. His political success started in 1879 when he was elected to a term in the New York House of Representatives.

Nixon, Richard M. (1913-1994)

Served as Vice-President under Dwight D. Eisenhower from 1953 to 1961. Served as President from 1969 to 1974. See biography in this volume.

Quayle, J. Danforth (1947-)

Served as Vice-President under George H. W. Bush from 1989 to 1993. They defeated their Democratic opponents, Massachusetts Governor Michael S. Dukakis and U.S. Senator Lloyd Bentsen. In 1976, Quayle won election to the U.S. House of Representatives, where he served two terms. From 1980 to 1988, he served as the junior senator from Indiana in the U.S. Senate.

Rockefeller, Nelson Aldrich (1908-1979)

Served as Vice-President under Gerald R. Ford from 1974 to 1977. He filled a vacancy that was created when Vice-President Ford succeeded Richard M. Nixon, who have resigned as President. Ford nominated Rockefeller for the vice-presidency.

Rockefeller's nomination required the approval of both houses of Congress under procedures established in 1967 by the 25th Amendment to the Constitution. He was the second person to become Vice-President under terms of the 25th Amendment. Ford became the first to do so in 1973. Rockefeller, a Republican, had served as governor of New York from 1959 to 1973. Before he took office as governor, he had held a number of posts in the federal government.

Roosevelt, Theodore (1858-1919)

Served as Vice-President under William McKinley in 1901. Served as President from 1901 to 1909. See biography in this volume.

Sherman, James Schoolcraft (1855-1912)

Served as Vice-President under William Howard Taft from 1909 to 1912. He became the first Vice-President to be renominated in the history of the Republican Party, but he died during the election campaign.

His death created a unique situation in American politics. It was too late to replace him on the ballot, and over 3 million people voted for Taft and Sherman. Sherman's eight electoral votes were cast for Columbia University president Nicholas Murray Butler.

Stevenson, Adlai Ewing (1835-1914)

Served as Vice-President under Grover Cleveland from 1893 to 1897. He was the grandfather of Adlai E. Stevenson, the Democratic presidential nominee in 1952 and 1956.

Stevenson was an inflationist in a sound-money administration. Largely for this reason, the public was never informed when Cleveland underwent an emergency operation during the business panic of 1893. His advisers feared the panic might increase if there seemed to be any possibility of Stevenson succeeding to the presidency.

Tompkins, Daniel D. (1774-1825)

Served as Vice-President under James Monroe from 1817 to 1825. He was governor of New York from 1807 to 1817, favoring the War of 1812 and defending New York from the British as commander of the state militia.

He was handicapped by inadequate accounting methods during this trying period. During most of the rest of his life, Tompkins fought rumors that he had misappropriated funds entrusted to him as wartime governor. These false charges affected him as Vice-President.

Truman, Harry S. (1884-1972)

Served as Vice-President under Franklin D. Roosevelt in 1945. Served as President from 1945 to 1953. See biography in this volume.

Tyler, John (1790-1862)

Served as Vice-President under William Henry Harrison in 1841. Served as President from 1841 to 1845. See biography in this volume.

Van Buren, Martin (1782-1862)

Served as Vice-President under Andrew Jackson from 1833 to 1837. Served as President from 1837 to 1841. See biography in this volume.

Wallace, Henry Agard (1888-1965)

Served as Vice-President under Franklin D. Roosevelt from 1941 to 1945. He was also secretary of agriculture from 1933 to 1940 and secretary of commerce in 1945 and 1946. In 1948, he was the presidential nominee of the Progressive Party, a third political party.

Wallace was one of the most controversial figures of the New Deal and Fair Deal periods. He urged adoption of the Agricultural Adjustment Act, the first of many New Deal plans to regulate the farm problem by government planning.

Wheeler, William Almon (1819-1887)

Served as Vice-President under Rutherford B. Hayes from 1877 to 1881. He also served in the U.S. House of Representatives from 1861 to 1863 and from 1869 to 1877. As a member of Congress, he devised the Wheeler adjustment in 1874 to settle a disputed election in Louisiana.

Wheeler showed that he had strict principles by opposing the Salary Grab Act of 1873. Congress, however, voted itself the disputed pay increase. Wheeler refused to profit from the additional income. He bought government bonds and then had the bonds canceled.

Wilson, Henry (1812-1875)

Served as Vice-President under Ulysses S. Grant from 1873 to 1875. He was a Republican U.S. senator from Massachusetts from 1855 to 1873.

Wilson helped found the Republican Party. He served in both houses of the Massachusetts legislature but was defeated when he ran for governor in 1853. Wilson was chair of the Senate Military Affairs Committee during the Civil War, and a "Radical Republican" during Reconstruction.

Vice-Presidents of the United States

	Birthplace	Occupation or Profession	Political Party	Age at Inauguration	Served	President
1. Adams, John*	Braintree (now Qunicy) Mass.	Lawyer	Federalist	53	1789-1797	Washington
2. Jefferson, Thomas*	Goochland (now Albermarle) County, Va.	Planter, lawyer	Democratic-Republican	53	1797-1801	J. Adams
3. Burr, Aaron	Newark, N.J.	Lawyer	Democratic-Republican	45	1801-1805	Jefferson
4. Clinton, George**	Little Britain, N.Y.	Soldier, lawyer	Democratic-Republican	65 / 69	1805-1809 / 1809-1812	Jefferson / Madison
5. Gerry, Elbridge**	Marblehead, Mass.	Businessperson	Democratic-Republican	68	1813-1814	Madison
6. Tompkins, Daniel D.	Fox Meadows, N.Y.	Lawyer	Democratic-Republican	42	1817-1825	Monroe
7. Calhoun, John C.†	Abbeville District, S.C.	Lawyer	Democratic-Republican / Democratic	42 / 46	1825-1829 / 1829-1832	J. Q. Adams / Jackson
8. Van Buren, Martin*	Kinderhook, N.Y.	Lawyer	Democratic	50	1833-1837	Jackson
9. Johnson, Richard M.	Beargrass, Ky.	Lawyer	Democratic	56	1837-1841	Van Buren
10. Tyler, John††	Charles City County, Va.	Lawyer	Whig	50	1841	W. H. Harrison
11. Dallas, George M.	Philadelphia, Pa.	Lawyer	Democratic	52	1845-1849	Polk
12. Fillmore, Millard††	Locke, N.Y.	Lawyer	Whig	49	1849-1850	Taylor
13. King, William R. D.**	Sampson County, N.C.	Lawyer	Democratic	66	1853	Pierce
14. Breckinridge, John C.	Near Lexington, Ky.	Lawyer	Democratic	36	1857-1861	Buchanan
15. Hamlin, Hannibal	Paris, Me.	Lawyer	Republican	51	1861-1865	Lincoln
16. Johnson, Andrew††	Raleigh, N.C.	Tailor	National Union‡	56	1865	Lincoln
17. Colfax, Schuyler	New York, N.Y.	Editor	Republican	45	1869-1873	Grant
18. Wilson, Henry**	Farmington, N.H.	Businessperson	Republican	61	1873-1875	Grant
19. Wheeler, William A.	Malone, N.Y.	Lawyer	Republican	57	1877-1881	Hayes
20. Arthur, Chester A.††	Fairfield, Vt.	Lawyer	Republican	51	1881	Garfield
21. Hendricks, Thomas A.**	Near Zanesville, O.	Lawyer	Democratic	65	1885	Cleveland
22. Morton, Levi P.	Shoreham, Vt.	Banker	Republican	64	1889-1893	B. Harrison
23. Stevenson, Adlai E.	Christian County, Ky.	Lawyer	Democratic	57	1893-1897	Cleveland
24. Hobart, Garret A.**	Long Branch, N.J.	Lawyer	Republican	52	1897-1899	McKinley
25 Roosevelt, Theodore*††	New York City, N.Y.	Author, rancher	Republican	42	1901	McKinley
26. Fairbanks, Charles W.	Near Unionville Center, O.	Lawyer	Republican	52	1905-1909	T. Roosevelt
27. Sherman, James S.**	Utica, N.Y.	Lawyer	Republican	53	1909-1912	Taft
28. Marshall, Thomas R.	North Manchester, Ind.	Lawyer	Democratic	58	1913-1921	Wilson
29. Coolidge, Calvin*††	Plymouth Notch, Vt.	Lawyer	Republican	48	1921-1923	Harding
30. Dawes, Charles G.	Marietta, O.	Lawyer	Republican	59	1925-1929	Coolidge
31. Curtis Charles	Topeka, Kans.	Lawyer	Republican	69	1929-1933	Hoover
32. Garner, John N.	Red River County, Tex.	Lawyer	Democratic	64	1933-1941	F. Roosevelt
33. Wallace, Henry A.	Adair County, Ia.	Farmer, editor	Democratic	52	1941-1945	F. Roosevelt
34. Truman, Harry S.*††	Lamar, Mo.	Businessperson	Democratic	60	1945	F. Roosevelt
35. Barkley, Alben W.*	Graves County, Ky.	Lawyer	Democratic	71	1949-1953	Truman
36. Nixon, Richard M.*	Yorba Linda, Calif.	Lawyer	Republican	40	1953-1961	Eisenhower
37. Johnson, Lyndon B.*††	Near Stonewall, Tex.	Teacher	Democratic	52	1961-1963	Kennedy
38. Humphrey, Hubert H.	Wallace, S. Dak.	Pharmacist	Democratic	53	1965-1969	L. Johnson
39. Agnew, Spiro T.†	Towson, Md.	Lawyer	Republican	50	1969-1973	Nixon
40. Ford, Gerald R.‡‡§	Omaha, Nebr.	Lawyer	Republican	60	1973-1974	Nixon
41. Rockefeller, Nelson A.‡‡	Bar Harbor, Me.	Businessperson	Republican	66	1974-1977	Ford
42. Mondale, Walter F.	Ceylon, Minn.	Lawyer	Democratic	49	1977-1981	Carter
43. Bush, George H. W.*	Milton, Mass.	Businessperson	Republican	56	1981-1989	Reagan
44. Quayle, J. Danforth	Indianapolis, Ind.	Publisher	Republican	41	1989-1993	G. H. W. Bush
45. Gore, Al	Washington, D.C.	Journalist	Democratic	45	1993-2001	Clinton
46. Cheney, Richard B.	Lincoln, Nebr.	Businessperson	Republican	59	2001-	G. W. Bush

Note: Each Vice-President has a capsule biography in this appendix.   *Elected to the presidency.   **Died in office.   †Resigned.   ††Succeeded to the presidency upon death of the President.   ‡The National Union Party consisted of Republicans and War Democrats. Johnson was a Democrat.
‡‡Became Vice-President by filling a vacancy.   §Succeeded to the presidency upon resignation of the President.

Index

Note: Page numbers in italic type are references to illustrations.

Acknowledgments

Credits read from top to bottom, left to right, on their respective pages.

Cover: Granger Collection; Oil painting on canvas (1796) by Gilbert Stuart (Granger Collection)

3 Corbis/Bettmann

15-16 Jointly owned by the National Portrait Gallery, Smithsonian Institution, and the Museum of Fine Arts, Boston (detail)

17-19 Library of Congress

21-22 Granger Collection

25 Harvard University Portrait Collection, gift of Andrew Craigie, 1794

26 The New York Historical Society, New York City (detail)

27 Library of Congress

28 Henry Francis du Pont Winterthur Museum (detail)

31 © White House Historical Association, photography by National Geographic Society

32 Thomas Jefferson Memorial Foundation (detail)

33 Granger Collection

35 Louisiana Historical Society

37 Franklin D. Roosevelt Library

38 Thomas Jefferson Papers, University of Virginia Library

41 National Gallery of Art, Washington, D.C., Alisa Mellon Bruce Fund (detail)

42 The New York Historical Society, New York City (detail)

43 Scott Kingsley, Virginia Division of Tourism

44 Granger Collection

47 Pennsylvania Academy of the Fine Arts (detail)

48 Mrs. Gouverneur Hoes from White House Historical Society, photography by National Geographic Society (detail)

49 Granger Collection

50 Library of Congress

53 National Gallery of Art, Washington, D.C., Andrew W. Mellon Collection (detail)

54 © White House Historical Association, photography by National Geographic Society (detail)

57 Daughters of the American Revolution, Washington, D.C.

58 Ladies Hermitage Association, Hermitage, Tenn. (detail)

59 © White House Historical Association, photography by National Geographic Society; Chicago Historical Society (detail)

61 Granger Collection

62 © White House Historical Association, photography by National Geographic Society

65 Metropolitan Museum of Art, gift of Mrs. Jacob H. Lazarus, 1893 (detail)

66 © White House Historical Association, photography by National Geographic Society; (detail)

67 Martin Van Buren National Historic Site/White House Historical Association, photography by National Geographic Society

69 National Portrait Gallery, Smithsonian Institution, Washington, D.C. (detail)

70 President Benjamin Harrison Home, Indianapolis, Ind. (detail)

71 Francis Vigo Chapter, Daughters of the American Revolution, Vincennes, Ind. from the White House Historical Association, photography by National Geographic Society (detail)

73 Corcoran Gallery of Art (detail)

74-75 © White House Historical Association, photography by National Geographic Society (details)

77 Corcoran Gallery of Art (detail)

78 James K. Polk Memorial Association (detail)

79 Granger Collection

81 Corcoran Gallery of Art (detail)

82 Granger Collection (detail); Courtesy of Ruth C. Tate from *Seventy-Five Years of White House Gossip* by Edna M. Colman. Doubleday & Company, Inc.

83 © White House Historical Association, photography by National Geographic Society (detail)

85 National Portrait Gallery, Smithsonian Institution, Washington, D.C. (detail)

86 Buffalo & Erie County Historical Society (detail); Granger Collection

87 Buffalo & Erie County Historical Society (detail)

89 National Portrait Gallery, Smithsonian Institution, Washington, D.C. (detail)

90 The Pierce Brigade, Concord, N.H.

93 Corcoran Gallery of Art (detail)

94 © White House Historical Association, photography by National Geographic Society (detail)

95 Library of Congress

97 Huntington Library and Art Gallery, San Marino, Calif.

98 Granger Collection (detail)

99 University of Michigan Museum of Art, bequest of Henry C. Lewis

100 Illinois State Historical Library

103 Library of Congress

104 J. Doyle DeWitt Collection, University of Hartford

107 Tennessee Historical Society

108 © White House Historical Association, photography by National Geographic Society (detail)

109 Culver (detail); Library of Congress

111 Library of Congress

113 National Portrait Gallery, Smithsonian Institution, Washington, D.C. (detail)

114 The Smithsonian Institution (detail)

115 Granger Collection

116 Library of Congress

119-120 © White House Historical Association, photography by National Geographic Society (details)

121 Rutherford B. Hayes Presidential Center

123 Corcoran Gallery of Art (detail)

124 © White House Historical Association, photography by National Geographic Society (detail)

127 Corcoran Gallery of Art, gift of William Wilson Corcoran (detail)

128 © White House Historical Association, photography by National Geographic Society (detail); Corbis/Bettmann

129 Courtesy of Ruth C. Tate from *White House Gossip from Andrew Jackson to Calvin Coolidge* by Edna M. Colman. Doubleday & Company, Inc. (detail)

131 National Portrait Gallery, Smithsonian Institution, Washington, D.C. (detail)

132 © White House Historical Association, photography by National Geographic Society (detail)

134 Corbis/Bettmann (detail)

135 Library of Congress

137-138 © White House Historical Association, photography by National Geographic Society (details)

141 Corcoran Gallery of Art (detail)

142 © White House Historical Association, photography by National Geographic Society (detail)

143 Library of Congress

144 Brown Bros.

147 © White House Historical Association, photography by National Geographic Society (detail)

148 Theodore Roosevelt Collection, Harvard College Library (detail)

149 © White House Historical Association, photography by National Geographic Society (detail)

150 Theodore Roosevelt Collection, Harvard College Library

151 Corbis/Bettmann

152 Culver

155-156 © White House Historical Association, photography by National Geographic Society (detail)

157 Library of Congress

159 Brown Bros.

161 National Portrait Gallery, Smithsonian Institution, Washington, D.C. (detail)

162 Woodrow Wilson House from White House Historical Association, photography by National Geographic Society (detail)

163 © White House Historical Association, photography by National Geographic Society (detail)

164 Culver

165 Imperial War Museum, London (detail)

166 Corbis/Bettmann

169 National Portrait Gallery, Smithsonian Institution, Washington, D.C. (detail)

170 © White House Historical Association, photography by National Geographic Society (detail)

173 Union League Club, New York City

174 © White House Historical Association, photography by National Geographic Society (detail)

175-177 Corbis/Bettmann

179 National Portrait Gallery, Smithsonian Institution, Washington, D.C. (detail)

180 © White House Historical Association, photography by National Geographic Society (detail)

181 Herbert Hoover Library

183 Corbis/Bettmann

185-186 © White House Historical Association, photography by National Geographic Society (details)

187 *The New York Daily News*

189-191 Corbis/Bettmann

192 Franklin D. Roosevelt Library

195-196 © White House Historical Association, photography by National Geographic Society (details)

197 Harry S. Truman Library

198 © Alfred Wagg, FPG

201-202 © White House Historical Association, photography by National Geographic Society (details)

203 Dwight D. Eisenhower Library

205 AP/Wide World

207-208 © White House Historical Association, photography by National Geographic Society (details)

209-211 AP/Wide World

212 John F. Kennedy Library

215-216 © White House Historical Association, photography by National Geographic Society (details)

217 AP/Wide World

219-220 Lyndon Baines Johnson Library

223-224 © White House Historical Association, photography by National Geographic Society (details)

225 AP/Wide World

227-228 National Archives

231-232 © White House Historical Association, photography by National Geographic Society (details)

233-234 Corbis/Bettmann

237-238 © White House Historical Association, photography by National Geographic Society (details)

239 Jimmy Carter Library

240 Karl Schumacher, The White House

243-244 © White House Historical Association, photography by National Geographic Society (details)

245 © O. Franken, Sygma

247 Bill Fitz-Patrick, The White House

248 © Boccon-Gibod, Sipa

251 The White House

252 © Chris Gulker

253 Susan Biddle, The White House

257 Democratic National Committee

258 Cynthia Johnson, © *Time* magazine

261 © Wally McNamee, Corbis/Sygma

262 AP/Wide World

265 © Bob Daemmrich, Corbis/Sygma

266 © John Edwards, Liaison Agency

268-269 AP/Wide World